I0516964

SPES NOSTRA

✝

Spes Nostra

*Profound Words of Encouragement & Consolation
for Weary Members of the Mystical Body*

COMPILED BY THE SLAVES OF
THE IMMACULATE HEART OF MARY
Richmond, New Hampshire

MMXXV

First edition published by Arouca
Press in co-operation with the Slaves
of the Immaculate Heart of Mary.

ISBN: 978-1-998492-53-4 (pbk)
ISBN: 978-1-998492-54-1 (special edition)

Arouca Press
PO Box 55003
Bridgeport PO
Waterloo, ON N2J 3G0

www.aroucapress.com
Send inquiries to info@aroucapress.com

NOTA BENE

For the sake of clarity and simplicity, we opted not to
make use of the ellipses, brackets, or italics that would
otherwise have been indicative of the minor editing
employed while remaining scrupulously faithful to
the original texts.

In place of a bibliography—which would have been
both cumbersome and incomplete, considering the
wide range of sources from which these passages
were culled—we have included a list of recommended
reading.

To Jesus through Mary...

Mother of Mercy,
Our Life, Our Sweetness,
Our & Hope.

All those who are likely to read this book love God, and lament that they do not love Him more; all desire something for His glory — the spread of some good work, the success of some devotion, the coming of some good time. One man has been striving for years to overcome a particular fault, and has not succeeded. Another mourns, and almost wonders while he mourns, that so few of his relations and friends have been converted to the Faith. One grieves that he has not devotion enough; another that he has a cross to carry which is a peculiarly impossible cross to him; while a third has domestic troubles and family unhappinesses which feel almost incompatible with his salvation; and for all these things, prayer appears to bring so little remedy. But what is the remedy that is wanted? What is the remedy indicated by God Himself? If we may rely on the disclosures of the saints, it is an immense increase of devotion to our Blessed Lady; but, remember, nothing short of an immense one.

FR. FREDERICK FABER

❧ FROM HIS INTRODUCTION TO *TRUE DEVOTION TO MARY* ❧

TABLE OF CONTENTS

PART TWO
The Perfecting of Hope

PART THREE
Saved by Hope

INTRODUCTION

They that hope in the Lord shall renew their strength,
they shall take wings as eagles, they shall run and
not be weary, they shall walk and not faint.

(ISAIAS THE PROPHET)

CALLED TO FIGHT

There are many beautiful symbols by which we Catholics are encouraged to picture ourselves in relation to God and His Church. We are as fish happily caught and enclosed in the net of the Gospel; we are as sheep of the One Fold, safe under the benevolent eyes of our Good Shepherd; we are children asleep in the arms of Divine Providence; citizens who *have not here a lasting city*; we are hunters, harvesters, and wayfarers. But of all these mystical images, none is held so sacrosanct by Holy Mother Church, none brought so often and forcefully to our minds by her constant repetition of it, as this one — *we are warriors.*

Armed with *the sword of the spirit and the shield of faith,* protected by the *helmet of salvation, and the breastplate of justice,* we have been enlisted in the ranks of the Lord of Hosts *to fight the good fight* in the cause of the Prince of Peace, under the banner of the Queen of the Universe; to win for ourselves and as many other souls as possible that *coveted crown* that has been *prepared for us from all eternity.* Such is the spiritual life as all the saints would have us envision it. A battle. A glorious battle to cooperate with grace despite the obstacles facing us from without and within, and become ourselves so imbued with the divine nature that the charity of Christ can flow through us to help, even heal, those suffering around us. What violence should we not be willing to do to ourselves in order that His eyes may console others through ours, His hands support others through ours, and His words inspire others through ours. Unspeakable vocation! To be living, breathing images of Divine Love Incarnate! To "vanquish the enemy," as St. Maximilian says, "and extend the kingdom of God not by brutal carnage but by deeds of love and mercy"!

Our enemy will stop at nothing to deter us from such a life.

He will distract us, if he can. Yet it is not always easy to distract a devout soul determined to abide by the Commandments of God and of the Church, who thirsts for her own spiritual advancement and is willing to make sacrifices for that of others. No. For us who glory in the office of *warrior*, the devil's strategy is much more subtle.

He shows us our weakness. He reminds us of our many, many past failings, and hisses into our hearts the humiliating question, "Who do you think you are — trying to play the hero when you are no better than a coward and a traitor?" Or he presents to us how little all our efforts over the years have accomplished: "If God is not blessing your work, clearly it is because your self-love has spoiled it all." Finally, he throws constantly before our mind's eye the incredible odds that we are up against, the evils rampant everywhere in society and even in the Church, and he jeers, "Go ahead. Try and fix them." And while we are loath to admit it, his words hit painfully close to home. *Because they are true.*

EXPOSING THE DEVIL'S STRATEGY

Yes, we are weak. Yes, our attempts at winning others over to the Faith have borne very but pitiful fruit. And, yes, the clearing up of the diabolical disorientation in the world is, to all appearances, a lost cause. *Especially nowadays.* We often feel, do we not, as St. John Henry Newman did when he said,

> I know that all times are perilous, and that in every time serious and anxious minds, alive to the honor of God and the needs of man, are apt to consider no times so perilous as their own. At all times the enemy of souls assaults with fury the Church which is their true Mother, and at least threatens and frightens when he fails in doing mischief. And all times have their special trials which others have not. And so far I will admit that there were certain specific dangers to Christians at certain other times, which do not exist in this time. Doubtless, but still admitting this, still I think that the trials which lie before us are such as would appall and make dizzy even such courageous hearts as St. Athanasius, St. Gregory I, or St. Gregory VII. And they would confess that dark as the prospect of their own day was to them severally, ours has a darkness different in kind from any that has been before it. (SERMON 9, OCTOBER 2, 1873)

That a saint could so speak in the nineteenth century—and here we are a century and a half later, arguably tottering on the brink of a divine chastisement—is, for many of us, downright *discouraging*.

There it is. Discouragement. Our enemy's weapon of choice, one which he employs with devastating effect against Our Lady's children in the midst of the current crisis. And if this crippling if-I-cannot-succeed-so-why-try feeling of *discouragement* is the weapon, surely *weariness* is the wound inflicted by it.

WEARINESS — A CRISIS OF HOPE

We are not speaking of a physical weariness, such as may be brought on by a lack of sleep or an over-expenditure of energy or as the aftermath of an illness. Nor do we refer specifically to the mental weariness born of prolonged application of thought or the distastefulness of the subject under consideration. True, these may play their role, but, by and large, theirs is a transient presence. Spiritual weariness, on the other hand, with its sinister lethargy so convenient to the designs of the evil one, is a deeper reality, more difficult to eradicate, which comes upon us like a shadowy, hellish cloud, dulling the bright colors of our interior life, deadening its joyousness, and rendering insipid the sweetness of the Lord that we once tasted and savored with such delight. Spiritual weariness is brought on by suffering, yes, but not exclusively by suffering. We are weary from suffering *without hope of reprieve;* we are discouraged from fighting *with such seemingly scant hope of victory.*

Ours is a crisis of hope.

Why is this? Because knowing and *trusting* are two different things. We know very well that our glory as Catholic warriors is to rely on God's strength, not ours; to labor in His fields with no thought to the harvest His Providence may or may not bless us with; and to believe in the ultimate victory He has promised us time and time again. We know these things as we know that there is a God and we are loved by Him. We acknowledge on principle the gloriousness of the Cause to which we have committed our lives; and though we may tire of the battle, we know better than to dismiss the battle as a tired thing in itself. "To meditate on the magnificences of God," Fr. Faber assures us, can hardly be dull; to fight for our lives with the superior intellect and huge power of a fallen seraph can hardly be tame, whatever else it may be: to be all day receiving new actual graces, realizing new increments of sanctifying grace, listening to numerous and wonderfully diversified inspirations of the Holy Spirit, can hardly be uninteresting; to be changing in grace, and love, and knowledge, nearly every hour, cannot strictly be called uniform; and to be fighting God's battle even with the most importunate and dishonoring temptations cannot truly be a sickly thing, even though it may be fatiguing. Indeed, from an intellectual point of view it would not be easy to find any thing in the world so thoroughly refreshing, so actively full of changeful vitality, or so briskly interesting, as a spiritual life. It is the healthiest, manliest, completest, divinest thing on earth. Resolve it into its elements of prayer, of light, of love, of heavenly communications, and of the highest operations of a human will, and what more noble, more free, more wide, more magnificent?

Yet this knowledge does not allay our discouragement.

It is the hope we know we ought to have of triumphing in the here and now against our personal faults, our family difficulties, and our social deterioration—this is that goal that seems so far beyond our grasp that we are tempted to give it up altogether. In spite of all the Masses and Holy Communions we have received, still the desolation we are plagued with—the loneliness, the fear for the future or regret for the past, the crippling sense of our own inadequacy—remain. All the Rosaries we have said and the fervent novenas we have offered in the throes of setbacks or misunderstandings or even the obvious injustice of all-out persecutions, seem to have had such little effect. We would not think for one second that God has failed us; but we can scarcely help wondering from time to time why He takes so, so long to come to our rescue.

We know deep down, of course, that our weariness itself is but a temptation — another nasty little goblinlike creature to add to our list of the enemies we are bound to fight with all the ardor that grace has put at our disposal. The question is — *how?*

THE NEED FOR THIS PUBLICATION

How does a general rouse the fighting spirit of his troops on the eve of a great battle? *He reminds them of their purpose.* He recalls to them the strength of their allies, the weakness and wretchedness of their adversary. In a word — he gives them *hope.* This will be our solution, as well, for, according to Msgr. Jean-Joseph Guame,

> When Christian hope is lively, it influences and subjects every power of the soul and body. With the eyes of faith, it looks ever far beyond the narrow horizons of this present life, even on to that which God has prepared for those who love Him. It speaks, but its converse is of Heaven: its heart is on fire, but it burns at the thought of things unseen. It makes use of the body, of its hands and feet, and every member, but solely in the interest of the work of Christ. Having God for its object, it stoops to no lesser thing. All that is not Him, it esteems as nothing, as dust and ashes, as very dung. And yet, not blind, for it makes every means contribute to its One great End; with the mammon of iniquity, it buys for itself incomparable treasures. If a thing can serve as a help to salvation, well; but if not, hope disdains it and, passing by, pitilessly shatters every obstacle.

That is why we Catholic warriors — men, women, children, priests, religious, the learn*ed* and the learn*ing*, *all of us* — need a book like this one. *Spes Nostra* is not a how-to book but a *go-to book*. It is a book for those in our ranks for whom the temptation to be discouraged about themselves or their past or their future or their family or their country or their Church — basically life and the world in general — has reached an acute stage. Or, to put it another way, this is a book both for souls afflicted with the wound of weariness and for those who would come to the assistance of such souls.

Taken from sixty-nine canonized saints and ninety holy priests, religious, and lay people, each one of the more than 800 passages in this book comprises a most potent salve with which to treat and heal the wound of weariness. That salve is *hope*. "The Christian motto is Hope!" declares St. Theophane Vénard. "Hope on! Hope ever! O Christian hope, how beautiful thou art! How thou dost satisfy the heart of man, the creature of a day, and yet created for an eternity of bliss!" We are not made for this world. We are here for a brief moment only, a day *in via*. Heaven awaits us, and we would do well to remember the fact more often. "Dear mystery of [heavenly] glory!" Fr. Faber exclaims,

> Why do we not call thee to mind more often than we do? Surely we stand in need of it. How weary we grow in well-doing. What a strange life is the spiritual life; to overcome one obstacle is only a guarantee that a worse one will be given us to overcome; labor leads to labor and away from rest. A temptation vanquished is only the miraculous multiplication of temptations; and the devils, like the flies, come in greater crowds the more we beat them away. How long can we go on? It seems desperate, an affair of moments, like the

struggles of a drowning man to keep himself on the surface. The longer we persevere the more impossible does perseverance seem. Of many things it may be true that the first blow is half the battle: who will dare to say it is so with the spiritual life? Yet sometimes we turn from the thought of glory as if it were a selfish and unworthy thought, a not loving God for His own sake, nor an exclusive seeking of His sole glory. But is this wisdom? Is this humility? Not such was the lowly wisdom of the Psalmist, *I have inclined my heart to perform Thy justifications for ever, because of the retribution!* Set but the thought of Heaven to fight with the sight of earth, and we ourselves in our inmost souls shall have peace to think of God. (THE BLESSED SACRAMENT, 103–104)

Would we but think on Heaven, how well we would realize — *defeatism is not an option.*

MARY, OUR HOPE

We must take Our Lady at Her word when She told little Lucia dos Santos, "Only I can help you now." It is in Her that we place our hope of reaching union with Jesus in this life and the next. It is, therefore, to Her that this present endeavor is consecrated. Hear St. Alphonsus Maria de Liguori:

The holy Church wishes that we call this divine Mother our hope. The impious Luther said that he could not bear to hear the Church teaching us to call Mary our hope; God only, he said, is our hope; and God Himself curses those who place their hopes in any creature. Yes, God curses those that trust in creatures independently of Him, but we hope in Mary as a mediatrix with God. For, says St. Bernard, God has placed in the hands of Mary all the treasures of the goods that He wishes to dispense to men. Hence the Lord wishes us to acknowledge that all good comes from Mary; for He has ordained that all the graces that He will give us should pass through the hands of Mary. Hence St. Bernard called Her his greatest confidence, and the entire ground of his hope. St. Bonaventure called Mary the salvation of them who invoke Her. Whenever, then, the devil terrifies us with the fear of being lost, let us say to Mary with the same saint: *In thee, O Lady, have I hoped; may I not be confounded forever.*

God, through the power of the Virgin, can and will—absolutely *will*, if only we trust Him to do so—free us and our loved ones from the manifold evils afflicting us. Every line of this compilation is geared towards fostering this most necessary conviction: *We shall receive as much as we hope for.*

WHO WILL BENEFIT FROM THIS BOOK AND HOW

Priests who would sink the arrows of holy confidence deep into the minds and hearts of their flock will find here a priceless array of ammunition at their disposal. But not priests only! Religious superiors will discover herein exquisite material with which to nourish the interior lives of their subjects; teachers, profound words with which to stir the enthusiasm of their students; administrators, thoughts to rally their staff; doctors, their patients; parents, their children; spouses, each other. Indeed, any individual Catholic of whatever position in the Church or in society can appeal to this treasury on behalf of his friends, relatives, colleagues, and co-workers. Whether in a private letter or a public article; whether as the subject of an hour-long conference, a half-hour of mental prayer, or a ten-second Rosary meditation, the passages in this book—each and every one of them solid gold—cannot fail to remind their hearers of the consoling truths of our Faith that can never be too deeply appreciated, and to embolden them with that God-loving hope on which all our victories depend.

✝

PART ONE

Reasons for Hope

Sanctify the Lord Christ in your hearts, being ready always to satisfy every one that asketh you a reason of that hope which is in you.

(ST. PETER)

THE BLESSED VIRGIN MARY

He who loves the Immaculata cannot be damned.
(ST. MAXIMILIAN KOLBE)

THE POWER OF MARY

❧ Mary is the Queen of Heaven and earth by grace, as Jesus is the King of them by nature and by conquest. The will of the Most High, Who exalts the humble, is that Heaven, earth, and hell bend, with good will or bad will, to the commands of the humble Mary, whom He has made sovereign of Heaven and earth, general of His armies, treasurer of His graces, worker of His greatest marvels, restorer of the human race, mediatrix of men, exterminator of His enemies, and faithful companion of His grandeurs and His triumphs. (ST. LOUIS MARIE DE MONTFORT)

❧ Everything, even the Blessed Virgin, is subject to the power of God; and everything, even God, is subject to the power of the Blessed Virgin. (ST. ANSELM)

❧ Mary. When you follow Her, you will not go astray; when you pray to Her, you will not despair; when you think of Her, you will not err; when She holds you up, you will not fail; when She protects you, you will not fear; when She leads you, you will not be fatigued; when She favors you, you will arrive safely. (ST. BERNARD)

❧ This is why the Blessed Virgin is called powerful — nay, sometimes, all-powerful, because She has, more than anyone else, more than all angels and saints, this great, prevailing gift of prayer. No one has access to the Almighty as His Mother has; none has merit such as Hers. Her Son will deny Her nothing that She asks; and herein lies Her power. While She defends the Church, neither height nor depth, neither men nor evil spirits, neither great monarchs, nor craft of man, nor popular violence, can avail to harm us; for human life is short, but Mary reigns above, a Queen forever. (ST. JOHN HENRY NEWMAN)

THE HOLY NAME OF MARY

❧ There is not such powerful help in any name, nor is there any other name given to men, after that of Jesus, from which so much salvation is poured forth upon men as from the name of Mary. The devout invocation of this sweet and holy name leads to the acquisition of superabundant graces in this life and a very high degree of glory in the next. (RICHARD OF ST. LAWRENCE)

❧ Thy name, O Mary, cannot be pronounced without bringing some grace to him who does so devoutly. (ST. BONAVENTURE)

❧ There is not on earth a sinner, however devoid he may be of the love of God, from whom the devil is not obliged immediately to fly, if he invokes Mary's name with a determination to repent. (ST. BRIDGET OF SWEDEN)

❧ In the same way as the rebel angels fly from sinners who invoke the name of Mary, so also do the good angels approach nearer to just souls who pronounce Her name with devotion. (ST. BRIDGET)

❧ Oh, beast! How he must regret the fact that this young Virgin has crushed his head and taken away his power! He can do nothing further, and, from the moment that this Virgin chooses to invoke Her power and authority, he is like a poor, weak fly. Cursed and damned beast, he cannot prevent Her from being exalted, honored, and revered. He can do nothing against Her or against those who love Her and place their confidence in Her. I glory in Her power over him. I fear neither his deceit nor his violence, both now and at the hour of my death. For I hope then, as now, to bear Her holy name engraved upon my heart; and when he sees my heart covered by this divine seal, he will dare not approach it. (VEN. MARIE PETYT)

✣ Have always the sacred name of Mary in your heart, and often on your lips, and you will be more terrifying to all hell than an army, well ranged, well equipped, and well conducted, is to a small troop of feeble enemies. (ST. JOHN EUDES)

THE MOTHER OF GOD IS OUR MOTHER

✣ A soul is of more value through the love infused into it than through any activity it can produce by itself. For it belongs to the nature of love to unite the lover with the object of his love. And thus love so unites the lover and his beloved that they seem, in time, to become one single object. It is in this sense that love, tender and violent, burning and unifying, leads the soul who loves Mary to live in Her, to be dissolved in Her. And all of this happens in its fullest perfection when the Divine Spirit Himself directs this love and stimulates it.

Thus, when the Eternal Father sends the Spirit of His Son into our hearts, crying, "Abba, Father," and when this

Spirit produces a tender, childlike love for our Father in Heaven, then this same Spirit of the Son produces within us a tender and childlike love for our dearest, our most lovable Mother. And, in this sense, the Eternal Father also sends the Spirit of His Son into our hearts, crying, "Mary, Mother!" For it is one and the same Spirit, the Spirit of Christ, Who arouses in our hearts filial love for God and for Mary, in the same manner in which He aroused such love in the Heart of Jesus Himself. (VEN. MARIE PETYT)

☙ The Mother of God! In what surpassing heights is She sublimely throned! Yet not a day passes in which She does not interest Herself in us. A thousand times and more has She mentioned our names to God in such a sweet persuasive way that the Heart of Jesus sought not to resist it, though the things She asked were very great for such as we are. She has been in the secret of all the good things which have ever happened to us in life. She has our predestination at heart far more than we have ourselves. She is ever mindful of that second maternity which dates from Calvary, which has no fellow except the Sacrifice of Her Son, our Brother and our God. What a light does it not shed on life to think that the same love, the nameless love, the inexhaustible love wherewith the heart of Mary loved Her blessed Son, is for His sake and by His own command being poured out over us this very hour! We are living now on earth, dear to Heaven, because we are suffused with its pathetic splendors. Angels envy us a love which in their case cannot be, as ours is, identical in kind with that which the sinless Mother has for Her adorable Son. But it is not the poetry of this thought on which we need to dwell, bright revelation as it is of God's creative love; but on the real help, the substantial support, the immense solid advantages, the positive efficacy of this love of Mary in the matter of our salvation. (FR. FREDERICK FABER)

❧ The child, especially while very young, has even greater need of the mother than of the father. It is the mother's part to nourish and to clothe her little one; hers to hush it to sleep, to tend it in sickness, comfort it in pain, soothe its fears, help it to rise when it falls, warm it when chilled. With a wonderful instinct which is not given in the same degree to fathers, she foresees the desires of her child and anticipates its every want, providing for it with unwearied care; heedless of trouble or fatigue whether by day or by night, with a heart full of tender love, she sacrifices herself for her babe. To one who had never seen a mother occupied with her little one, the most touching form of human love would be a thing unknown. We ought to praise and thank God for having, in the person of our mothers, placed thus near to the cradle of each one of us a heart so loving, eyes bright with love, smiling lips, and helpful hands.

But still more must we praise and thank Him for having willed to provide for us in the supernatural order, help similar yet a thousand times more excellent, in giving to our souls regenerated by baptism, a Mother to love. And such a Mother! Not just anyone taken at random from amidst other women, but the Mother admirable amongst all mothers, She who Herself alone has more love to give us than all others together could give, the very Mother of His own Divine Son, the kindest, most loving, and most lovable Virgin Mary. (REV. GABRIEL MARTIN)

❧ Ah, most sweet Mary! Ah, most loving Mother! This is precisely what thou desirest: that we should become thy children, and call on thee in every danger, and at all times have recourse to thee, because thou desirest to help and save us, as thou hast saved all who have had recourse to thee. (ST. ALPHONSUS DE LIGUORI)

❧ Mary is a Mother. She will, then, educate us. When the child goes wrong in its work, the Mother is there to put it right. If it is sick, She cares for it. She never leaves Her child, for She must fulfill Her mission of teacher. It is Mary who will train you. Our Lord has given us Mary to be the bond of union between Him and us. Mary gives us the first attraction to Jesus. The child goes first to its mother, by instinct; the mother leads it to its father. But it does not run of itself to the father; at first it follows the mother. Our Lord has, then, given us Mary for Mother, that She may be for us a first center of easy attraction. (ST. PETER JULIAN EYMARD)

❧ It is not a matter of kneeling down a long time and praying, but of this relationship of a child to his mother. A loving glance at Her statue, the frequent repetition of the name, *Mary*, even if it be just in our hearts. Different prayers and formulas are good and beautiful, but the essential thing is this simple relationship of a child to his Mother, this sense of our need for this Mother, the conviction that without Her we can do nothing. (ST. MAXIMILIAN KOLBE)

❧ Blessed are the faithless children of the unhappy Eve, if only they attach themselves to the faithful Mother and Virgin. *She always loves those who love Her* (Prov. 8:17) — not only with an affective love, but with an effectual and efficacious one, by hindering them, through a great abundance of graces, from drawing back in the pursuit of virtue and from falling in the road and from losing the grace of Her Son. (ST. LOUIS MARIE DE MONTFORT)

SPES NOSTRA

✤ Let us be drawn to Mary by a certain very powerful impulse, and let us trust to Her confidently all that is ours — joys, if we rejoice; woes, if we are in trial; hopes, if we endeavor to rise to better things. If the Church falls on difficult times, if faith wanes and charity grows cold, if morals, private and public, grow worse, if any danger threatens the Catholic cause or civil society, let us have recourse to Her, begging help from Heaven; in the supreme trial of death, when all hope, all help, is gone, let us lift up our eyes in tears and trembling, imploring through Her: pardon from Her Son and eternal joy in Heaven. (POPE PIUS XI)

✤ Oh, if Mary were but known, there would be no coldness to Jesus then! Oh, if Mary were but known, how much more wonderful would be our faith, and how different our Communions would be! Oh, if Mary were but known, how much happier, how much holier, how much less worldly should we be, and how much more should we be living images of our sole Lord and Savior, Her dearest and most blessed Son! (FR. FREDERICK FABER)

✤ What shall bring you forward in the narrow way, if you live in the world, but the thought and patronage of Mary? What shall seal your senses, what shall tranquilize your heart, when sights and sounds of danger are around you, but Mary? What shall give you patience and endurance when you are wearied out with the length of the conflict with evil, with the unceasing necessity of precautions, with the irksomeness of observing them, with the tediousness of their repetition, with the strain upon your mind, with your forlorn and cheerless condition, but a loving communion with Her! She will comfort you in your fatigues, raise you after your falls, reward you for your successes. She will show you Her Son, your God and your All. When your spirit within you is excited, or relaxed, or depressed, when it loses its balance, when it is restless and wayward, when it is sick of what it has not, when your eye is solicited with evil and your mortal frame trembles under the shadow of the tempter, what will bring you to yourself, to peace and to health, but the cool breath of the Immaculate, and the fragrance of the Rose of Sharon? (ST. JOHN HENRY NEWMAN)

❧ You never think of Mary without Mary's thinking of God for you. You never praise or honor Mary without Mary's praising and honoring God with you. When we praise Her, love Her, honor Her, or give anything to Her, it is God Who is praised, God Who is loved, God Who is glorified, and it is to God that we give through Mary and in Mary. (ST. LOUIS MARIE DE MONTFORT)

❧ What we need most is not simply instruction or precept, but strength. We are weak, and our appetites, passions, propensities, are too strong for us, and enslave us. We feel ourselves sinking; the waves are closing over us, and in fear and agony we cry out: "Lord, save us, we perish!" "Holy Mother of God, pray for us, or we are lost!" The soul oppressed with a deep sense of its weakness, of its inability to conquer by its own strength in the battle of life, calls out for supernatural aid, and it is precisely this aid, so much needed, which enables us to resist and overcome our enemies, that I dare believe, and avow that I believe, the Blessed Mary can and *does* obtain for those who fly to Her protection. (ORESTES BROWNSON)

❧ Be consoled, ye afflicted; and rejoice, ye disconsolate; be raised up, ye fallen; come to rest, ye uneasy. Come, come, ye poor; approach, ye little ones, without fear; for in my arms, I bear the Lion made Lamb, the Almighty become weak, the Invincible subdued. Come to draw life, hasten to obtain salvation, approach to gain eternal rest, since I have all this for all, and it will be given to you freely. (OUR LADY TO VEN. MARY OF AGREDA)

TRUE DEVOTION TO MARY

❧ If we are to believe the revelations of the saints, God is pressing for a greater, a wider, a stronger, quite another devotion to His Blessed Mother. I cannot think of a higher work or a broader vocation for anyone than the simple spreading of True Devotion to Mary as expounded by St. Louis Grignion de Montfort. Let a man but try it for himself, and his surprise at the graces it brings with it, and the transformations it causes in his soul, will soon convince him of its otherwise almost incredible efficacy as a means of salvation of men and for the coming of the kingdom of Christ. (FR. FREDERICK FABER)

❧ Devotion to the Blessed Virgin will be your safeguard. If you are devoted to Her, She will not only shower you with blessings on earth, but through Her intercession, She will secure Heaven for you also. (ST. JOHN BOSCO)

❧ True devotion to Mary makes us give to Jesus and Mary, without reserve, all our thoughts, words, actions, and sufferings, every moment of our lives, in such wise that whether we do great actions or very little ones, it is always true to say that whatever we do, even without thinking of it — at least if it has not been intentionally retracted — is done for Jesus and Mary. What a consolation this is! (ST. LOUIS MARIE DE MONTFORT)

11

❧ True devotion to Our Lady confirms the soul in good and does not let it easily abandon its spiritual exercises. It makes it courageous in opposing the world in its fashions and maxims, the flesh in its wearinesses and passions, and the devil in his temptations. (ST. LOUIS MARIE DE MONTFORT)

❧ It is true that we can attain divine union by other roads; but it is by many more crosses and strange deaths, and with many more difficulties, which we find it hard to overcome. We must pass through obscure nights, through combats, through strange agonies, over craggy mountains, through cruel thorns, and over frightful deserts. But by the path of Mary we pass more gently and more tranquilly. (ST. LOUIS MARIE DE MONTFORT)

❧ He who is growing in devotion to the Mother of God is growing in all good things. His time cannot be better spent; his eternity cannot be more infallibly secured. (FR. FREDERICK FABER)

TOTAL CONSECRATION TO MARY

❧ We must put ourselves and leave ourselves in Her virginal hands like a tool in the grasp of a workman, like a lute in the hands of a skillful player. We must lose ourselves and abandon ourselves to Her, like a stone one throws into the sea. This can be done simply and in an instant by one glance of the mind, by one little movement of the will, or even verbally, in saying, for example, "I renounce myself. I give myself to thee, my dear Mother." We may not, perhaps, feel any sensible sweetness in this act of union, but it is not on that account any less real. It is just as if we were to say with equal sincerity, though without any sensible change in ourselves what — may it please God — we shall never say:

"I give myself to the devil;" we should not the less truly belong to the devil because we did not feel we belonged to him. The more often we renew this act of offering and union, the sooner we shall be sanctified and attain to union with Jesus Christ, which always follows necessarily on our union with Mary. (ST. LOUIS MARIE DE MONTFORT)

❧ The most holy Virgin, who is a Mother of sweetness and mercy, and who never lets Herself be outdone in love and liberality, seeing that we give ourselves entirely to Her, stripping ourselves of all that is dearest to us in order to adorn Her, meets us in the same spirit. She also gives Her whole self, and gives it in an unspeakable manner, to him who gives all to Her. She causes him to be engulfed in the abyss of Her graces. She adorns him with Her merits; She supports him with Her power; She illuminates him with Her light; She inflames him with Her love; She communicates to him Her virtues: Her humility, Her faith, Her purity and the rest. She makes Herself his bail, his supplement, and his dear all toward Jesus. In a word, as that consecrated person is all Mary's, so Mary is all his. (ST. LOUIS MARIE DE MONTFORT)

❧ Whence comes it that the majority of the conversions of sinners are not durable? Whence comes it that we so easily relapse into sin? Whence comes it that the greater part of the just, instead of advancing from virtue to virtue and acquiring new graces, often lose the little virtue and the little grace they have? This misfortune comes from the fact that man is so feeble and so inconstant, and yet trusts in himself, relies on his own strength, and believes himself capable of safeguarding the treasure of his graces, virtues, and merits.

By Total Consecration we entrust all that we possess to the Blessed Virgin, who is faithful; we take Her for the universal depositary of all our goods of nature and of grace. We say to Her as a good child to his mother, "I beseech you, receive in trust all that I possess, and keep it for me by your fidelity and power. If you keep it for me, I shall lose nothing; if you hold me up, I shall not fall; if you protect me, I shall be sheltered from my enemies." (ST. LOUIS MARIE DE MONTFORT)

❧ It seems to me that I can aptly compare directors and devout persons who wish to form Jesus Christ in themselves or others by practices different from that of Total Consecration to Mary to sculptors who trust in their own professional skill, ingenuity, or art, and so give an infinity of hammerings and chiselings to a hard stone or a piece of badly polished wood, to make an image of Jesus Christ out of it. Sometimes they do not succeed in giving anything like the natural expression of Jesus, either from having no knowledge or experience of the Person of Jesus, or from some blow awkwardly given which has spoiled the work. But those who embrace the secret of grace which I am revealing to them, I may rightly compare to founders and casters who have discovered the beautiful mold of Mary, where Jesus was naturally and divinely formed; and without trusting in their own skill, but only in the goodness of the mold, they cast themselves and lose themselves in Mary, to become faithful portraits of Jesus Christ. (ST. LOUIS MARIE DE MONTFORT)

❧ Mary is wise: let us place everything in Her hands. She knows how to dispose of us and all that we have for the greater glory of God. Mary is charitable: She loves Her children and servants. Let us offer everything to Her, and we will lose nothing by it; She will turn everything to our gain. Mary is liberal: She returns more than we give Her. Let us give Her unreservedly all that we own; She will give us a hundredfold in return. Mary is powerful: nothing on earth can take from Her what we have placed in Her keeping. Let us then commit ourselves to Her care; She will defend us against our enemies and help us to triumph over them. Mary is faithful: She will not permit anything we give Her to be lost or wasted. She stands alone as the Virgin most faithful to God and to men. She faithfully guarded and kept all that God entrusted to Her, never allowing the least bit to be lost; and She still keeps watch every day, with special care over all those who have placed themselves entirely under Her protection and guidance.

Let us, then, confide everything to the faithful Virgin Mary, binding ourselves to Her as to a pillar that cannot be moved, as to an anchor that cannot slip, or better still, as to Mount Sion which cannot be shaken. Thus whatever may be our natural blindness, our weakness, and our inconstancy, however numerous and wicked our enemies may be, we shall never go wrong or go astray or have the misfortune to lose the grace of God and that infinite treasure which is Eternal Wisdom. (ST. LOUIS MARIE DE MONTFORT)

꙳ Whoever is truly and totally consecrated to the Immaculata has already reached holiness; and the more perfectly a person lets himself be led by Her in the paths of interior and exterior life, the more fully will he share in Her spirit. (ST. MAXIMILIAN KOLBE)

II

LOVE

That soul is dearest to Me who loves Me the most.
(OUR LORD TO VEN. CONSOLATA BETRONE)

GOD LOVES US

❧ You ask me whether Our Lord thinks of you, and whether He looks upon you with love. Yes, He thinks of you, and not only of you but of the least hair of your head. This is an article of faith. We cannot doubt it. Tell me, do you not intend to belong to God? Do you not desire to serve Him faithfully? And who gave you this desire, this intention, unless Himself in His loving regard for you? But enough: live joyful. Our Lord looks upon you with love and with so much the more tenderness as you are the more feeble. Never permit your mind willingly to entertain thoughts to the contrary; and when they come, regard them not, turn your eyes away from their iniquity, and have recourse to God with a courageous humility, to speak to Him of His ineffable goodness by which He loves us, poor, abject, and miserable as we are. (ST. FRANCIS DE SALES)

❧ Our parents have been the first to love us in the world, but they have loved us only after they had known us, whereas God loved us before we had existence. Our fathers and mothers were not yet born, and God loved us; the world was not yet created, and God loved us; and how long before the creation of the world did He love us? It is useless to multiply years and ages, for God loved us as long as He has been God; He has loved us as long as He has loved Himself. (ST. ALPHONSUS DE LIGUORI)

❧ If all the affections of all men, of all the angels, and of all the saints were united together, they would not equal the smallest part of the love that God bears to a single soul. (ST. ALPHONSUS DE LIGUORI)

❧ Let us never doubt God's love for us. Let us put unfailing trust in the wisdom and power of our Father Who is in Heaven. No matter how numerous our difficulties, no matter how alarming events may be, let us pray, let us do all that prudence prescribes; but let us accept in advance whatever trials God may will, abandoning ourselves to the care of this good Master. Then everything, everything without exception, shall contribute to the profit of our souls. (REV. DOM VITALIS LEHODEY)

❧ No tongue can express the greatness of the love of Jesus for a soul in the state of His grace. (ST. PETER OF ALCANTARA)

❧ He is our Savior; that is something that must never be forgotten. It is as our Savior that He comes to us full of perfect knowledge and unlimited love. He knows exactly what we are, and He knows exactly what our life will be. He knows all our defects and weaknesses, those that are natural to us, those that are the result of circumstances, and those that are the result of our own sins. He knows all that has happened or will happen to us. He knows all that might have been done for us or by us, but which has been neglected. He knows all our mistakes and all our sins; He knows all these things in advance, but being the perfect Lover, He comes with the power of God to heal all these ills. He is perfectly prepared to repair our life completely if we do not prevent Him. (DOM EUGENE BOYLAN)

❧ In the case of a parent or a teacher, we judge of the value set upon a particular line of conduct by the greatness of the reward promised and actually conferred. Now, if we love God, the reward promised us is nothing less than the sight of God Himself, face to Face, not transiently, not as a glorious flash of light renewed once in ten thousand years to feed our immortality with contentment and delight, but an abiding Vision, a glory and a gladness, a marvelous rapture of the will, and an ecstasy of vast intelligence, for evermore. Think how such a reward transcends all the expectations, all the possibilities even, of our nature! How God must love us, and how too He must love our love, to have prepared for us such joys as these, which eye has not seen, nor ear heard, nor man's heart conceived! (FR. FREDERICK FABER)

GOD THIRSTS FOR OUR LOVE

❧ I ask your love, do not refuse it. It is so easy to love Love itself. (OUR LORD TO SR. JOSEFA MENÉNDEZ)

❧ Blessed, blessed God! Wonderful Father! Compassionate Creator! This mystery of His desiring our poor love should of itself be a lifelong joy to us in our time of pilgrimage. It puts a new face upon the world. All things glow with another light. A feeling of security comes upon us, like a gift from heaven, and wraps us round; and the cold chill goes from our heart, and its dark spots are illuminated; and we want nothing more now, nothing. Earth has nothing to give, which would not be a mere impertinence after this desire of God. Our hearts are full. We have no room for more. This desire of God solves all the problems of our inner life; for it at once calms us in our present lowness and spurs us on to higher things, and the name of that double

state—the calm and the spur—what is it but perfection?
(FR. FREDERICK FABER)

🕊 God loves me—God desires my love. He has asked for it, He covets it, He prizes it more than I do myself! I would fain tell the poor trees, and the little birds that are roosting, and the patient beasts slumbering in the dewy grass, and the bright waters, and the wanton winds, and the clouds as they sail above me, and that white moon, and those flickering far-off stars, that God desires my love, mine, even mine! And it is true, infallibly true. O God! O Thou Who in the world above givest us the light of glory that we may bear to see Thy beauty, give us now the strength of faith to endure these revelations of Thy love. (FR. FREDERICK FABER)

🕊 Every glance towards God, every virtuous act performed in grace, and every sigh of the soul that loves God, even though so light as a hair, becomes an arrow that wounds, not the unstable heart of man, but the eternal and constant Heart of God. Every step that you take in the pathway of grace is so beautiful and lovely that God, beholding you, exclaims, *How beautiful are thy steps in shoes, O prince's daughter!* (Cant. 7:1). Every word that you address to God is so dear and precious that it brings down upon you His richest blessings, as the Psalmist sings: *Grace is poured abroad in thy lips; therefore hath God blessed thee forever* (Ps. 44:3). Nothing in the beloved is insignificant to the lover; nothing in the beloved soul is insignificant to the loving God. Here each and every thing is great because it gains God's love for us.
(FR. MATTHIAS J. SCHEEBEN)

🕊 God is astonishing in His love. The more we love Him, the more He loves us. He pays us back tenfold the love which we have for Him. (FR. PAUL OF MOLL)

❧ In our journey Heavenwards, it is love which takes every step, and love alone. It is not the sharpness of the austerity which merits, but the love. It is not the patience in sickness, or the silence under calumny, or the perseverance in prayer, or the zeal of apostolic labor, which win the crown, but just the love, and the love only, that is in the patience and the silence and the prayer and the zeal. Martyrdom without love is unprofitable before God. He has no longing for anything but love. He puts no price on other things. His taste is exclusive. His covetousness is confined to that one thing. If we could be as simple and as single in our desires as God! He only wants our love, and more of it, and more, and more. Why should not we also want one thing only, to love Him, and to love Him more, and more, and more? Surely if we prayed only for that after which He longs so earnestly, our prayer would not wait for its answer long; and then in His eyes — and who would wish to be so in other eyes? — we should soon be like the saints. (FR. FREDERICK FABER)

❧ If I have chosen you who are poor and miserable, it is that all may realize that I want neither greatness nor holiness, but only love. I Myself will do all the rest. (OUR LORD TO SR. JOSEFA MENÉNDEZ)

LET US RETURN HIM LOVE FOR LOVE

❧ It is a great favor that God should call a soul to love Him. (ST. TERESA OF ÁVILA)

❧ On whom shall our poor heart lavish its love? Who shall be found that is great enough to be the recipient of its treasures? Will a human being know how to comprehend them? And, above all, will he be able to repay? There exists but one Being capable of comprehending love. It is Jesus.

He alone can give us back infinitely more than we shall ever give Him. (ST. THÉRÈSE OF LISIEUX)

❧ If there is one gift that is to be had for the asking—and there are many—it is the gift of love for God. (DOM EUGENE BOYLAN)

❧ It is not we who draw the love of God from our hearts; it is the Holy Ghost, Who is Love, Who pours it into our hearts. (PÈRE LOUIS LIAGRE)

❧ It is easy to please Jesus, to enrapture His Heart; you have only to love Him without looking at yourself, without spending too much time on your own faults. (ST. THÉRÈSE OF LISIEUX)

❧ Everything that is done for God is the love of God. (ST. FRANCIS DE SALES)

❧ The more a man loves God, the more beautiful he grows in the eyes of God. (FR. PAUL OF MOLL)

❧ If we follow God's will in everything, that is proof that we love Him perfectly. You have not, therefore, to be troubled or sad. (BR. MARCEL VAN)

❧ We cannot be sure if we are loving God, although we may have good reason to believe that we are, but we can know quite well if we are loving our neighbor. And be certain that the further advanced you find you are in this, the greater love you will have for God. (ST. TERESA OF ÁVILA)

THE LOVE OF OUR NEIGHBOR

❧ God appreciates the love we show our neighbor more than a whole morning of praying in church. (ST. CHARLES OF SEZZE)

❧ The love His Majesty has for us is so great that to repay us for our love of neighbor He will in a thousand ways increase the love we have for Him. I cannot doubt this. (ST. TERESA OF ÁVILA)

❧ It is not always within your power to control your feelings. You will recognize that you have love if, after having experienced annoyance or contradiction, you do not lose your peace, but pray for those who have made you suffer and wish them well. (OUR LORD TO ST. FAUSTINA)

❧ Love your neighbors because they need it to become better, as you yourself need to be loved to become better. A person who feels herself loved becomes capable of every form of generosity. (OUR LORD TO SR. MARY OF THE TRINITY)

❧ Human love opens hearts to divine love. (OUR LORD TO SR. MARY OF THE TRINITY)

THE IMPORTANCE OF LOVE

❧ A little pure love is more precious in the eyes of God and of more value to the Church than all other works put together. (ST. JOHN OF THE CROSS)

❧ Nothing is sweeter than love; nothing stronger, nothing higher, nothing more generous, nothing more pleasant, nothing fuller or better in Heaven or on earth; for love proceeds from God and cannot rest but in God. Love feels no burden, values no labors, would willingly do more than it can; complains not of impossibility because it conceives that it may and can do all things. It *is* able, therefore, to do anything. (FR. THOMAS À KEMPIS)

❧ Everything done with a pure intention is perfect love. (ST. TERESA OF ÁVILA)

❧ The smallest thing, when done for the love of God, is priceless. (ST. TERESA OF ÁVILA)

❧ If every good work — learning, faith, alms, sacrifice, and even martyrdom — is as nothing and has no value without love, it follows that only love counts, only love is in truth, everything. And so even a soul who has not been called to great exterior works is really giving everything to God when she loves Him with all her heart, mind, and strength. (FR. LORENZO SALES)

❧ *Eye hath not seen, nor ear heard, nor hath it entered into the heart of man, what things God hath prepared for them that love Him.* (ST. PAUL)

LET US GROW IN LOVE DAILY

❧ In proportion to the intensity of my love for God, my supernatural life may increase at every moment — every time there is a prayer to say, a Mass to hear, reading, work, or study to be done; or acts of patience, zeal, renunciation, struggle, confidence, or love to be produced. (DOM JEAN-BAPTISTE CHAUTARD)

❧ Let us unite ourselves to Him so that our days may be in continual communion with Him; let us awake in love, deliver ourselves to love all day by doing the will of the good God, in His sight, with Him, in Him, for Him alone; let us give ourselves incessantly in the way in which He wishes; then, when night comes, after a colloquy of love in our heart throughout the time, let us sleep again in love. Perhaps we may know of faults and infidelities on our part; let us abandon them to love which is a consuming fire, and thus we shall have our purgatory. (ST. ELIZABETH OF THE TRINITY)

❧ The heights of divine love are always accessible. But it takes us time to learn by experience what we should know by faith—that our hearts were made for God and will not rest until they rest in Him. It is only after many mistakes and failures that we realize our folly and find the right road. Still even these mistakes—even our sins—can be used for our good. Whether we think of them as gaps and empty places in our past which God can fill up—for all evil is lack of due entity—or as marks which, by changing the pattern, God can fit into the design according to which He is weaving our whole life; or as splashes of misapplied color, which the Divine Artist can employ to form part of a new picture; or as a dye which can be mixed with God's specially chosen coloring for our soul in order to give it the exact hue which He seeks; whatever view we take of the past, we must never, never, let any of our past sins, no matter how great or how grievous, interfere in the slightest with our unlimited hope and complete confidence in God, or with our aims and plans for the future. The heights of divine love are always accessible. (DOM EUGENE BOYLAN)

❧ If we were thus faithful from morning till evening in doing all for the love of God, each of our days would contain hundreds of meritorious acts, hundreds of acts of love of God and our neighbor, made on every painful or pleasant occasion; and when evening came, our union with God would be more intimate and much stronger. (FR. REGINALD GARRIGOU-LAGRANGE)

SUFFERING AS A MEANS TO LOVE

❧ Patient endurance is the perfection of charity. (ST. AMBROSE)

❧ One is committed to love only to the extent that one is committed to suffering. (ST. THÉRÈSE OF LISIEUX)

❧ Look, My child, and understand what love means. Do you see this Cross, these nails, these thorns, this livid Flesh, these bruises, these wounds? All is the result of love, infinite love. See, then, to what a degree I have loved you. And if you desire to love Me truly, learn first of all how to suffer, because in suffering you will learn how to love. (OUR LORD TO ST. GEMMA GALGANI)

❧ In suffering, love becomes crystallized; the greater the suffering, the purer the love. (ST. FAUSTINA)

❧ It is love that makes reparation, because that which offends God in sin is the absence of love. (OUR LORD TO SR. MARY OF THE TRINITY)

❧ Under the influence of fear, we bear the cross of Christ with patience; under the more inspiring influence of hope, we carry the cross with a firm and valiant heart; but under the consuming power of love, we embrace the cross with ardor. (ST. BERNARD)

❧ You need not be uneasy to see in your soul apparent contradictions: an ardent desire to love God and to suffer for Him, and then, when the opportunity comes, a shrinking from pain and even a refusal to bear it. Fortunately, we are dealing with Our Lord Who can read the heart and Who knows our protestations of love are sincere and genuine; with One, too, Who knows the weakness of our human nature and Who does not expect much from us. The very longing to love Him and bear much for His sake is dear to Our Lord, even if our courage fails when tested. (FR. WILLIAM DOYLE)

THE LOVE OF GOD DOES NOT
DEPEND ON FEELINGS

❧ Merit depends less upon the difficulty that may be entailed by an action, than upon the intensity of charity with which it is carried out. (DOM JEAN-BAPTISTE CHAUTARD)

❧ It sometimes happens that we have no consolation in the exercises of holy love; so much so, that, like deaf religious, we can neither hear our voice in the choir nor enjoy the sweetness of our chant. Moreover, we are annoyed with a thousand fears, disturbed by a tremendous hurly-burly which the enemy raises round our heart, suggesting to us that perhaps we are not agreeable to our Master, and that our love is useless, or even false and vain, since it produces no consolation. We labor, then, not only without pleasure, but with extreme difficulty, seeing neither the good of our labor nor any contentment that it can afford to Him for Whom we labor.

But what increases the misery is that the mind and reason cannot give us any kind of relief; for, the superior part of the soul, being completely surrounded by the suggestions of the enemy, is in the greatest alarm and is kept busy in guarding against being surprised by any consent to evil, so that it cannot make a sortie to set free the inferior part of the soul. And though it does not lose courage, yet it is so fiercely assaulted that, if it is without blame, it is not without pain; for, to fill up the cup of its misfortune, it is deprived of that general consolation which accompanies nearly all the other afflictions of this world, namely, the hope that they will soon end; the heart, in these spiritual conflicts, falling into a kind of inability to think of their termination, and, consequently, being unconsoled by hope. Faith, indeed, residing in the summit of the soul, assures us that this trouble will end, and that we shall one day enjoy repose; but the terrific noise and shout raised by the enemy throughout the inferior part of the soul almost drown the voice of Faith with its warnings and encouragements, leaving only on the imagination this sad reflection: "I shall never be happy."

Ah! What can the soul do in this state? It knows not how to exist amid so many enemies, and has strength only to let its will die in the will of God, imitating the sweet Jesus, Who, having arrived at the height of sufferings on the Cross which His Father had prepared for Him, having heaved His last sigh, with a loud cry and abundance of tears, said, *Father, into Thy hands I commend My spirit,* words which were His last, and by which the Well-Beloved Son gave the highest proof of His love to His Father.

When, then, everything fails us, when our exhaustion is extreme, these words, this abandonment of our soul into the hands of our Savior, cannot fail us. The Son recommends His Spirit to His Father in His last and incomparable distress; and we, racked in the convulsions of interior pains, destitute of comforts, unable to live, surrender our spirit into the hands of the Eternal Son, Who is our true Father, and bowing down our head in acquiescence to His good pleasure, resign our whole will to Him. (ST. FRANCIS DE SALES)

❧ The only important thing in good works is the amount of love which we put into them. The soul of an action is its motive. The power of an action is neither in its size nor in its duration, though both these are very considerable matters. But its power is in its intention. An intention is pure in proportion as it is loving. Thus, you see, what we want is not many actions, but a great momentum in a few actions. Momentum is purity of intention. Purity of intention is love.

We must not fall into a mistake here. It is true that, as a general rule, great love gives a facility in doing hard things. But I am not speaking of a heroic love. I am speaking of such a love as you and I may soberly persist in exacting from ourselves, considering all the grace we receive. Love which is sufficient to give momentum enough to an action to carry it to Heaven may not be accompanied by any sensible sweetness. Indeed, in most cases it is not. Nay, I will go further. It is not by any means clear that heroic love devours all the repugnances of nature with sufficient rapidity to give even saints a habitual facility of action in hard things, any more than it always makes the flames of the martyrs cool and refreshing and the teeth of the wild beasts as gentle embraces, although it has done so to some. But it is perfectly clear that even heroic love is by no means universally accompanied by sensible sweetness in its exercise. It is often very heroic when it is driest, and most heroic when it is not so much as conscious of its own existence. Hence we must not distrust our actions or devotions because they have not this sensible sweetness, neither must we make such sweetness the test of our purity of intention. It is no part of real momentum.

We must be the more careful to bear this in mind, because in mere natural activity facility and sweetness are full half the momentum. If this were to be the case in religion, piety must begin in sentimentality, grow in excitement, and perfect itself in frenzy. There would be no help for it. Christian enthusiasm is a very sober sort of determination. It does not consist in neglecting calculations, but in running immense risks in the face of very disheartening calculations. We agree, then, to throw sweetness overboard, wistfully indeed, but quite understanding what we are about. (FR. FREDERICK FABER)

❧ The more the soul loves, the less she seems to herself to love. (GOD THE FATHER TO ST. CATHERINE OF SIENA)

❧ Be certain that the more a soul loves God, the less he feels it. (ST. PIO OF PIELTRICINA)

❧ Among all the pleasures of perfect love, that which is found in the acquiescence of the soul to spiritual tribulations is unquestionably the purest and most refined. The soul is sometimes so pressed with interior afflictions that all its powers and faculties are crushed and desolated by the absence of everything that could solace it, as well as by the dread and apprehension of everything that could sadden it. To such an extent that, after the example of its Savior, it begins to grow weary, to fear, to shudder, then to be sad with a sadness like that of the dying, and can well exclaim, *My soul is sorrowful even unto death.* And, with the consent of its whole interior, it desires, implores, and beseeches that, if it be possible, this chalice may pass away from it, remaining attached only by the finest point of the spirit to the heart and good pleasure of God, and making one simple act of acquiescence: "O Eternal Father, may my will be never done, but Thine!" And it is remarkable that the soul makes this act of resignation in the midst of so much trouble, so many repugnances and contradictions, that it does not perceive itself doing so; at least it imagines that its acts are all so languid that they cannot come from the heart or be of any value because what is regarded then as the divine good pleasure is endured not only without pleasure of contentment, but even contrary to the pleasure and contentment of the heart, which love allows to utter all the lamentations of Job and Jeremias, but on condition that one act of acquiescence should be made in the inmost, in the purest part of the soul. And this acquiescence is not sweet or tender or sensible, though it is real and strong and loving; it seems to have retired into the furthest corner of the soul, or, as it were, into the citadel of the fortress, where it remains courageous, though all the rest has fallen and is overwhelmed with sadness. And the more removed this love is from aid, abandoned by the faculties of the soul, the more sublime is its constancy and the nobler its fidelity. (ST. FRANCIS DE SALES)

❧ He who abandons himself unreservedly to God on the most trying occasions, gives the highest testimony that a creature can give of a sincere love. To act in this manner is to become, in Jesus Christ, the beloved Son of God. Far from being compassionated, you are to be envied. Peace of heart and resignation change torments into delights. (ST. FRANCIS DE SALES)

❧ Do not be afraid to tell Our Lord that you love Him, even if you do not feel it; this will compel Him to come to your assistance, to carry you as though you were a little child unable to walk. If the little child is afraid of the darkness and troubled because he cannot see the One Who is carrying him, let him close his eyes; this is the only sacrifice Jesus asks of him. By remaining thus, the night will no longer frighten him because he cannot see it. Soon, peace, if not joy, will be restored to his soul. (ST. THÉRÈSE OF LISIEUX)

THE POWER OF AN ACT OF LOVE

❧ If you knew what great merit and reward is earned by one act of pure love for Me, you would die of joy. (OUR LORD TO ST. FAUSTINA)

❧ A single act of love is more glorious than all the apostolates in the universe. (ST. PETER JULIAN EYMARD)

❧ Multiplying our acts of love is a very holy and useful thing for the soul to do because it allows us to give the maximum value to every instant of our short earthly journey: glorifying God, sanctifying ourselves, and saving souls. (FR. LORENZO SALES)

❧ Just as one learns to read by reading, so does one learn to love by multiplying one's acts of love for Him. Each one of these acts is, as it were, an armful of kindling, to be thrown on the fire; it renders the flame of love more ardent. (VEN. ADOLPH PETIT)

❧ To make an act of love requires but a few seconds. We can make these acts at any hour, we can multiply them, and how wonderful is their effect! We delight the Heart of Jesus and cause Him to shed more abundant graces on the world. The Blessed Virgin rejoices, Her love for us increases, and She thanks us for them. Our guardian angel listens with emotion and comes closer to us as if to make us feel that we have done well. The angels regard us with ineffable tenderness and joy. The power of the demons is lessened, and for a moment their temptations cease. The choirs of the Blessed in Heaven redouble their canticles of joy. Who would not during the day multiply acts of love? You who are reading this, pause a minute and say, "My God, I love You! My God, I love You!" (FR. WILLIAM DOYLE)

THE ROLE OF LOVE IN THE WAY OF SPIRITUAL CHILDHOOD

❧ In the days of old, victims pure and without blemish were alone acceptable to the great and all-powerful God; to satisfy divine justice, perfect victims must be offered. But the law of fear has been succeeded by the law of love, and Love has chosen me, a weak and imperfect creature! And is this choice not worthy of Love? Yes, that Love may be fully satisfied, it must come down to nothingness and transform this nothingness into fire. (ST. THÉRÈSE OF LISIEUX)

❧ Brilliant deeds are not for me. How, then, shall I prove my love, for love is proved by deeds? By my little actions and my little sacrifices! The little child will cast her flowers to God, and these nothings, O Jesus, will give Thee joy! (ST. THÉRÈSE OF LISIEUX)

❧ How do little children show their love in the natural order? Through little things: a toy, a picture, a flower, a pretty rock. A mother has no need of these things, but she loves to receive them anyway because of the love that prompted them. The lesson is obvious. We who desire in the spirit of little children to offer our lives to God as one continual act of love, can only do so through the ordinary details that surround us in our daily lives. (MSGR. VERNON JOHNSON)

❧ The supernatural value of the smallest details of human life is one of the most profound of the many lessons which St. Thérèse teaches us. That alone would justify the title "The Little Way." "There is only one thing to do here below, namely to offer Our Lord the flowers of little sacrifices, to win Him by our caresses." Caresses — she is right. Just as in human love it is the little attentions which betray the depth of human feelings, so it is our little actions done for love which show the intensity of our devotion to Our Lord. (MSGR. VERNON JOHNSON)

UNION WITH MARY FOSTERS OUR LOVE
❖

❧ In the soul's union with Mary, love of God becomes continually more intense. Mary, the Mother of Jesus and our Mother, is pure love. You cannot live steadily near Her without also gradually becoming pure love. From another point of view, love of God is a grace, the greatest of graces. Will not the Distributrix of all graces be exceptionally profuse with the grace of love in favor of the soul who lives constantly in Her sight, desirous of doing all She wishes? (FR. EMILE NEUBERT)

❧ Union with Mary makes the soul loving because Mary, the sweet Virgin, the Mother of Jesus and our Mother, is all love. This union creates an affinity between the soul and the mysteries of faith, which are mysteries of love. To believe means to believe in love. (FR. EMILE NEUBERT)

❧ Union with Our Lord and with the Blessed Virgin should proceed from the heart rather than from the mind. We must consider each action in its relation to the will of Jesus and Mary, how through each action we can promote Their interests and show Them our love. As a result, our interest in the activity will be sharpened, even to the point of enthusiasm, because we will see it as an opportunity to please Jesus and Mary. When actions are directly concerned with the glory of God, the cause of religion, the salvation of souls, it will be easy to accomplish them joyously, but even when an action is mundane, or when it is some meaningless drudgery imposed on us, we can still make an act of love of it by considering it as a cross to bear in union with Jesus for the redemption of souls and the success of our apostolate. The more clearly we see the relation between our act and the love of Jesus and Mary, the more facility will we acquire in accomplishing it with enthusiasm and love. (FR. EMILE NEUBERT)

❧ With Mary we make more progress in the love of Jesus in one month than we could make in years of living less united to this good Mother. (ST. LOUIS MARIE DE MONTFORT)

III

MERCY

God's mercies are to our miseries what
the ocean is to a drop of water.
(BL. DOM COLUMBA MARMION)

THE MERCY OF GOD IS LIMITLESS

❧ I am God, but a God of love! I am a Father, but a Father full of compassion and never harsh. My Heart is infinitely holy but also infinitely wise, and, knowing human frailty and infirmity, stoops to poor sinners with infinite mercy. (OUR LORD TO SR. JOSEFA MENÉNDEZ)

❧ The character of the Incarnation is intrinsically one of mercy. Had man not fallen, God would indeed have loved him as He loves the angels, but He would not strictly have shown him mercy. The Incarnation has the character of a mother's pity for her child who has tumbled and hurt himself. She loved him before, but never so much as she does now. The caresses which she now lavishes upon him would have been mere extravagance before; now they are the spontaneous overflowing of a heart whose floodgates have been opened. (DOM BRUNO WEBB)

❧ The mercy of God is infinitely greater than your malice. (ST. PIO OF PIETRELCINA)

❧ The mercy of God is infinite and never refuses to forgive sinners, and more especially when there is question of a poor little creature like you. (OUR LORD TO SR. JOSEFA MENÉNDEZ)

❧ *Let the impious forsake his way, and the wicked man his thoughts, and let him return to the Lord, and He will have pity on him; for He is bounteous in mercy to forgive* (Is. 55:7). Observe that God not only says He will pardon the ordinary sinner, one who has been carried away by common passions, but even the impious, that is to say, the man without faith, without law, without religion; the man who has insolently risen up against God and His Christ, who has uttered a thousand blasphemies, who has outraged Heaven and scandalized earth by the frightful impiety of his language; who, even as Manasses, has destroyed the worship of God, overthrown its altars, erected idols in their place. This is the monster, the very thought of whom makes us tremble, that God promises to forgive, not after a long lapse of years spent in laborious penance, but on the very first day of his conversion, though it should be the last of his life, if his return to God is sincere. And you, souls of little faith, still doubt whether God pardons you your old wanderings, although for a long time you have wept over, or at least detested them. (ST. FRANCIS DE SALES)

❧ I want all souls to have confidence in My mercy, to expect all from My clemency, and never to doubt My readiness to forgive. This is what I wish all to know: the mercy of My Heart is inexhaustible. (OUR LORD TO SR. JOSEFA MENÉNDEZ)

❧ Let souls who are striving for perfection particularly adore My mercy, because the abundance of graces which I grant them flows from My mercy. I desire that these souls distinguish themselves by boundless trust in My mercy. I Myself will attend to the sanctification of such souls. I will provide them with everything they need to attain sanctity. (OUR LORD TO ST. FAUSTINA)

❧ Damnation is for the soul that wants to be damned; but for the one who desires salvation, there is an inexhaustible ocean of the Lord's mercy to draw from. (ST. FAUSTINA)

THE POWER OF REPENTANCE

❧ We have often need here to remember for our own comfort, that, if steps are irretrievable, nothing in the spiritual life is irremediable. Who could believe the opposite doctrine and then live? (FR. FREDERICK FABER)

❧ One tear of the sinner, produced by the sorrow of his heart, is capable of making God forgive many, even the most atrocious crimes. (FR. CORNELIUS À LAPIDE)

❧ There is not a page in the Gospel in which we do not see that Jesus has a certain tenderness for reconciled sinners more than for the just who persevere. Who does not know that the penitent Magdalen was His faithful and His well-beloved; that Peter, after having denied Him, was chosen to confirm the faith of his brethren; that He left the whole flock in the desert to run after His lost sheep; and that the one of all His children who most sensibly moved His Heart was the returned Prodigal? Hence we are to understand that while innocence has its tears, He esteems more precious those which sins cause to flow in the holy weepings of penance, and that justice recovered has something more agreeable in His eyes than justice preserved. (BISHOP JACQUES-BÉNIGNE BOSSUET)

❧ Such is the mercy of God toward men that He never rejects a sincere repentance. But if any should have fallen into the lowest depth of wickedness, and should desire to return thence to the path of virtue, He receiveth such a one and embraceth him, and leaveth nothing undone which may restore him to his first state. (ST. JOHN CHRYSOSTOM)

❧ I love those who after a first fall come to Me for pardon. I love them still more when they beg pardon for their second sin, and should this happen again, I do not say a million times but a million million times, I still love them and pardon them, and I will wash in My Blood their last sin as fully as their first. (OUR LORD TO SR. JOSEFA MENÉNDEZ)

❧ Never shall I weary of repentant sinners nor cease from hoping for their return, and the greater their distress, the greater My welcome. Does not a father love a sick child with special affection? Are not his care and solicitude greater? So is the tenderness and compassion of My Heart more abundant for sinners. (OUR LORD TO SR. JOSEFA MENÉNDEZ)

❧ I cannot punish even the greatest sinner if he makes an appeal to My compassion, but on the contrary, I justify him in My unfathomable and inscrutable mercy. (OUR LORD TO ST. FAUSTINA)

❧ I am more generous toward sinners than toward the just. It was for their sake that I came down from Heaven; it was for their sake that My Blood was spilled. Let them not fear to approach Me; they are most in need of My mercy. (OUR LORD TO ST. FAUSTINA)

❧ God is magnificent when He pardons: He does not reproach us for the faults over which we have already wept, nor does He keep any account of them; His pardon is so generous, so great and complete, that it not only annuls our debts, but destroys even the memory of them, as if they had never existed. It is enough for Him to see us repentant; then every wound, even the most grievous and repugnant, is completely healed by the Precious Blood of Jesus. (FR. GABRIEL OF ST. MARY MAGDALEN)

❧ Have you not for some time loved the Lord? Do you not love Him now? Do you not long to love Him forever? Therefore: do not fear! Even conceding that you had committed all the sins of this world, Jesus speaks to you: Many sins are forgiven thee because thou hast loved much! (ST. PIO OF PIETRELCINA)

❧ Do not think of your past sins, for that will harm you and favor your enemies; but make haste to go on your way as if nothing happened. Think only of Jesus and of your desire to gain His love, and nothing will harm you. (BL. HENRY SUSO)

GOD JUDGES US WITH LOVE AND COMPASSION

❧ Are you terrified, perhaps, because He is your Judge? Have confidence, my soul, because, if He is your Judge, He is also your Defender. He is your Defender to excuse you and justify you if you repent; and He is your Judge, not to condemn you, but to save you, if you are humble. His mercy is infinitely greater than all your iniquities. And I tell you this not that you will remain in sin and make yourself unworthy of His pity, but that you will drive away evil, and not despair of His clemency and pardon. (BL. LOUIS DE BLOIS)

❧ Love, we all know, is marvelously ingenious in finding excuses. The two subjective conditions of sin are knowledge and consent, and Our Lord defends us on both counts. It is the weakness of the flesh, He pleads, not the unwillingness of the spirit. In His prayer for those who crucify Him, He excuses us for our want of full knowledge: *Father, forgive them for they know not what they do.* Who can sound the depths of compassion in the heart of Christ? (FR. FRANCIS XAVIER LASANCE)

❧ It can hardly be denied that men's actions are often worse than their hearts, even when they proceed from the heart; and they have often less heart in them than they seem to have. For instance, a man commits a sin in a sudden outburst of passion, that passion may have felt some peculiar sting in the provocation which another would not feel, and it may have fallen upon him when he was physically agitated or when his nerves were unstrung. For all this the sin may remain a sin, and yet be no fair index of the sinner's heart. Or, again, men are propelled into sin not infrequently by false shame, by human respect, by bad companions, and the man's heart may be far better all the while than its outward actions testify. Many a man looks to his neighbors a very monster of depravity, while the priest, who heard his general confession, has been almost touched to tears with the spots of green verdure, the almost feminine sensibilities, the refined kindnesses, but above all with the moral shyness, the ground of so many virtues, which he found in that great rough nature. Are we not learning every day to be less surprised at finding how so very much good can dwell with so very much evil? Then, again, many have so many odd crossings in their minds which tell upon their motives and hamper the free action of their moral sense; and thus it is that cruelty in war, murders, and the like, are not on the whole such conclusive proofs of a depraved heart as they are commonly taken to be. Much crime lies at the door of a warped mind, and how much of that crime is sin can be known to God alone. The heart is the jewel which He covets for His crown, and if the heart which we do not see is better than the actions that we see, God be praised! For then the world is a trifle less dismal than it seems. (FR. FREDERICK FABER)

❧ Poor sinner, why despair of thy salvation, since all here speaks of mercy and of love? Behold the two Advocates Who plead thy cause before the tribunal of Divine Justice: a Mother and a Redeemer — Mary, who presents to Her Son Her heart transfixed with a sword of sorrow; Jesus, Who presents to His Father the Wounds in His feet and hands, and His Heart pierced by the soldier's lance. Take courage; with such a Mediator, with such an Intercessor, Divine Mercy cannot reject thee. (ST. ANTHONY OF PADUA)

THE TRIBUNAL OF MERCY
❖

❧ Tell souls where they are to look for solace; that is, in the Tribunal of Mercy, the Sacrament of Penance. There the greatest miracles take place and are incessantly repeated. To avail oneself of this miracle, it is not necessary to go on a great pilgrimage or to carry out some external ceremony; it suffices to come with faith to the feet of My representative and to reveal to him one's misery, and the miracle of Divine Mercy will be fully demonstrated. Were a soul like a decaying corpse so that from a human standpoint, there would be no hope of restoration, it is not so with God. The miracle of Divine Mercy restores the soul in full. (OUR LORD TO ST. FAUSTINA)

❧ Confession is an act of faith on the part of the creature. It is also an act of the most concentrated worship. It is a breaking with the world and a turning to God. It is a triumph over millions of evil spirits of huge power, and, comparatively with us men, of unbounded intellect. It is the beginning of an eternity of ineffable union with God, and confers the right of beholding the Invisible Face to face. A man sees in a fellow-creature as sinful as himself, perhaps even evidently more unworthy, the form and features and real jurisdiction of the Incarnate Son of God. He kneels at his feet as if he were divine. He narrates to him the most secret shames and hidden sins of his soul. He submits to his questioning, as if he were the absolute and ultimate judge of all the earth. He listens with meekness to his reproof, as if it were God Himself Who spoke. He leaves to him the fixing of his punishment. He gives him rights over the arrangement of much of his external life.

His act thus completed, with much help and interference on the part of God, God Himself begins His exclusive part. One of His creatures, a fallible and himself a guilty judge, pronounces some few words, and straightway, though invisibly and spiritually, there falls from the veins of Jesus a shower of the Precious Blood, shed hundreds of years ago and resumed three days after it was shed, and bedews the sinner's soul. All his guilt is done away with instantaneously. His state is completely changed. Manifold works are done in his soul, such as the reinfusion of certain supernatural habits, the revival of dead merits, and a communication of the divine nature. His change can only be paralleled with that of a devil into an angel. All Heaven is stirred at the event. It is the special subject of an angelic jubilee. No angel or saint could have done it. It is the immediate action of the Creator on the soul of His creature. (FR. FREDERICK FABER)

❧ That there should be such a sacrament at all, after the completeness and magnificence of Baptism, is a miracle of divine love. But that the Precious Blood of the Incarnate Word should be always at hand, like a public fountain at a roadside, open, gratuitous, and ever-flowing, for the convenience of all passers-by, could not be believed if the Church did not assure us of it. Our sheer inability to comprehend a love so great as God's would make simple Novatians of us, if we had not the Church to inform the littleness of our own conceptions by the magnificence of her dogmas. Is it easy to imagine the mercy which will absolve from different mortal sins the same soul perhaps five hundred times in ten or twenty years, and some thousands of times in the course of a long life? Yet this is not an extravagant or fabulous case. Then again think of the completeness of the absolution. Each time it destroys the guilt of the sin completely, so that it can never rise again, never bring back, even to the relapsed sinner, its consequences of everlasting punishment, while at the same time it wakens to vigorous life again the merits that have been killed a hundred times by sin. How special, how ingenious, how peculiar, how unlike anything human is this process; and yet on reflection how naturally outflowing from the Divine Perfections. (FR. FREDERICK FABER)

❧ At every confession, we seem to hear Jesus say to His Father: "O Father, I offer Thee, for this soul, the satisfactions and the merits of My Passion; I offer Thee the chalice of My Blood which has been shed for the remission of sins." Then, in exactly the same way as Christ ratifies the judgment and the pardon given by the priest, the Father in His turn confirms the judgment rendered and the pardon granted by the Son. He says to us: "I, too, pardon you." Those are the words which establish the soul in peace. This is what it is to receive from God an assurance of pardon. If I have insulted an upright man, and he, holding out his hand to me, says: "I've forgotten all about it," I do not doubt his forgiveness. In the Sacrament of Penance, it is Christ, the Man-God, Truth in Person, Who says to us: "I pardon you"—and are we to doubt His forgiveness? No, one cannot doubt it; this pardon is absolute, irrevocable. God says to us: "If your sins are glaring as scarlet, I will so wash your soul that they will be as resplendent as snow." He says again: "I have made your iniquities vanish like a cloud, your sins like a mist." God's pardon is worthy of Him. What a king does is kingly; what God does is divine. Let us believe in His love, His words, His forgiveness. Such an act of faith and of trust is extremely pleasing to God and to Jesus, for it is a homage given to the infinite value of the merits of Christ. It is declaring that the fullness and the universality of the pardon God accords to men here below is one of the triumphs of the Blood of Jesus. (BL. DOM COLUMBA MARMION)

❧ No kind, no number, no duration of sins impede the facility of absolution. Its efficacy is always instantaneous. The word is spoken, and the work is done. But what is still more marvelous is the little which is required for absolution, the ordinary fidelity of the confession, the positive imperfection of the sorrow, the moderate resoluteness of the purpose of amendment! Supernatural as all these must be, the confession, the sorrow, and the purpose, and depending for their validity on certain theological requirements, yet are they not among the commonest graces in the Church? Is attrition a romantic flight of generosity, or the purpose of amendment akin to the heroism of martyrdom? Surely these requisites for absolution seem completely within the compass of our infirmity. The habitual sinner and he who has once fallen, the sinner of a day and the sinner of half a century — to all, the simple requisites for absolution remain the same. If all this were not among God's daily mercies, how inscrutable would it not seem to us; but we are obliged without fault of ours to tread God's common mercies underfoot, because He has so profusely strewn the whole earth with them that there is not room to move. (FR. FREDERICK FABER)

❧ Is there any earthly joy like the sense of pardon? How

deep it goes down into our nature, unlocking such secret fountains of tears as were far beyond the reach of ordinary hopes and fears! There is also a satisfyingness about it, which seldom accompanies other joys. A void is filled up in our hearts which had ached before. Peace comes where before there was a trouble of uncertain fears, and love awakens with a keener, fresher appetite for its obedient work for God. In prosperity, in adversity, in the love of others, in the enmity of others, in hard work, in old age, in sickness, and in death, the state of grace seems just to add what was needed, to supply that the absence of which was regretted, to throw light upon the darkness or to subdue the glare, to level the rocks or fill in the sunken places, to drain what was marshy or irrigate what was dry. It has shed upon the whole of life repose, plenitude, satisfaction, contentment. It has positively given us this world, while it was in the act of transferring to us the other. (FR. FREDERICK FABER)

❧ Confession heals, confession justifies, confession grants pardon of sin. All hope consists in confession. In confession there is a chance for mercy. Believe it firmly. Do not doubt, do not hesitate; never despair of the mercy of God. Hope and have confidence in confession. (ST. ISIDORE OF SEVILLE)

THE MOTHER OF MERCY

❧ The multitude of our sins should not diminish our confidence that Mary will grant our petitions when we cast ourselves at Her feet. She is the Mother of Mercy; but mercy would not be needed did none exist who require it. (ST. ALPHONSUS DE LIGUORI)

❧ Then, O sinner, whoever thou mayest be, embedded in crime, grown old in sin, despair not. Thank thy Lord Who, that He might show thee mercy, has not only given His Son for thy Advocate, but, to encourage thee to greater confidence, has provided thee with a Mediatrix who by Her prayers obtains whatever She wills. Go, then, have recourse to Mary, and thou wilt be saved. (ST. BERNARD)

❧ How wonderful! It sometimes happens that salvation is obtained by the invocation of the name of Mary, rather than by that of Jesus. But how can that be? Is Mary greater and more powerful than Jesus? No, for Jesus has not received His greatness and power from Mary, but rather, Mary has received Hers from Jesus. But the Son of God, being Lord and Sovereign Judge, must necessarily treats each one according to his merits, and according to the order of justice, which demands that the prayers of a criminal shall not be heard; but if he invoke the Name of the Mother of Mercy, although his sins render him unworthy of all grace, he is, nevertheless, heard through the intervention of Mary. (ST. ANSELM)

❧ O Mary, how could you refuse to help us miserable wretches when you are the Queen of Mercy? The subjects of mercy are precisely the wretched. You are the Queen of Mercy, and I, being the last among sinners, am, therefore, the first, the greatest among your subjects. (ST. BERNARD)

❧ She is Queen of Mercy, and therefore patroness of all the wretched, the ne'er-do-wells, of all great sinners! The deeper one has fallen, the more right he has to count on Mary to help him out of sin. Be he the most leprous of sinners, the most infamous of evil men, even vomited from the mouth and the Heart of Jesus, even rejected and cursed by God, he always retains an immense hope: the Blessed Virgin, supreme hope of those who have no other. When nothing else remains, there is still Our Lady! (FR. LOUIS COLIN)

❧ When Mary sees a sinner at Her feet, imploring Her mercy, She does not consider the crimes with which he is loaded but the intention with which he comes; and if this intention is good, even should he have committed all possible sins, the most loving Mother embraces him and does not disdain to heal the wounds of his soul; for She is not only called the Mother of Mercy but is so truly and indeed. (ST. ALPHONSUS DE LIGUORI)

❧ Go to this Mother of Mercy and show Her the wounds which thy sins have left on thy soul; then She will certainly entreat Her Son to pardon thee all. And this Divine Son, Who loves Her so tenderly, will most certainly grant Her petition. (ST. BERNARD)

❧ If anyone falls into sin, falls deeply into bad habits, despises God and His grace, ignores good example, pays no attention to the inspirations that can save, and becomes unworthy of further graces, should he despair? Never, absolutely never! For from God he has a Mother who with a warm heart follows his every action, word, and thought. She does not look upon whether he is worthy of the grace of loving kindness and mercy. She is only a Mother of mercy, and hastens, even when not invoked, there where She finds the greatest misery in souls. She needs only to enter into a heart, though it still be filled with misery, sullied by sin and vice, and She cannot let it be lost, but begs God for the soul to be enlightened, to follow the light of grace and reason, and to take on strength of will, that it might come to its senses and rise again. (ST. MAXIMILIAN KOLBE)

❧ Let us never forget that She understands better than anyone else that what She does to us is done to Her Son. Let no one then say he is too befouled by sin to go to Mary. Was any child ever too dirty for its mother to wash it? And if that child were Christ — and we are Christ in Her eyes — and if that mother be Mary, is there any filth of sin which would deter Her from joyfully cleansing the dirt and foulness with which we have befouled the Body of Christ? Nor need we be afraid that Her immaculate purity will make Her repel us. She is the Refuge of Sinners; and despite Her purity, or perhaps because of it, She has a wonderful understanding and sympathy for the weakness of human nature. She is the Mother of Fair Love, and will give us a love of Her Son that will more than atone for any sin. (DOM EUGENE BOYLAN)

❧ However great a sinner may have been, if he shows himself devout to Mary, he will never perish. (ST. HILARY OF POITIERS)

❧ No one alive is so cast off by God that he will not return to Him and enjoy His mercy, if he invokes my aid. (OUR LADY TO ST. BRIDGET OF SWEDEN)

❧ As a mother on seeing her son in the midst of the swords of his enemies would use every effort to save him, so do I for all sinners who seek my mercy. (OUR LADY TO ST. BRIDGET OF SWEDEN)

❧ Let a sinner be ever so abandoned, if he come to me, I am ready to receive him the moment he returns. Nor do I attend to the sins he has committed, but only to the intention with which he comes to me. If he come with a desire to change his life, I will not disdain to apply a remedy and heal his wounds; for I am called, and truly am, the Mother of Mercy. (OUR LADY TO ST. BRIDGET OF SWEDEN)

IV

THE HOLY WILL OF GOD

*No obstruction in the whole world can possibly
prevent the will of God from being carried out.*
(ST. LOUIS MARIE DE MONTFORT)

THE OMNIPOTENCE OF GOD

❧ Know this, My child: all creatures, whether they know
it or not, and whether they want it or not, always fulfill
My will. (OUR LORD TO ST. FAUSTINA)

❧ It is one of the most firmly established and most consoling of the truths that have been revealed to us that nothing
happens to us in life unless God wills it so. (ST. CLAUDE DE
LA COLOMBIÈRE)

❧ It is certain that whatever happens takes place by the
Divine Will. (ST. ALPHONSUS DE LIGUORI)

❧ When we realize that the will of God has been ruling the
universe since the day of creation, and will continue to rule
it long after we are gone; that victory is already guaranteed
and prophesied; that our only legitimate worry is to see
to it that we are on the side of victory; it is then that we
begin to do our immediate daily duties, leaving the issue
to God. In this is peace. (BR. FRANCIS MALUF)

GOD WILLS ONLY OUR HAPPINESS

❧ God's will is always most holy, tender, and merciful
towards His servants, always guided by infinite love and

wisdom. What can be more just and reasonable than for us earnestly to commend ourselves to His mercy and to acquiesce with thanksgiving and confidence in all His appointments? This conformity to His holy will, if it be courageous, constant, and universal, is the most perfect sacrifice of our will, of ourselves, of all that we possess to Him; it is the entire reign of grace in our souls, the victory over our most dangerous spiritual enemies, the firm anchor of our souls amidst the inconstancy of human affairs, and a source of unalterable peace and secure joy, with which the heart rests in the sweet bosom of Divine Providence, and drowns all distrustful and disquieting fears which passions are so apt to raise. (REV. FR. ALBAN BUTLER)

⁂ Oh, how they should bless the Lord, they who have learned to love Him and to follow Him with affectionate confidence withersoever He leads them! And how miserably are they deceived who do not sufficiently trust their God, their Father, their Savior, their Friend of friends, to allow Him to sanctify them and to make them happy! Let us, at least, love our sweet Master, so wise and so good; let us courageously accomplish whatever He wills; and let us accept with confidence all that He appoints for us: this is the way of lofty virtues, the secret of happiness for time and eternity. (REV. DOM VITALIS LEHODEY)

⁂ Turn to God with blind trust and surrender yourself unconditionally and unreservedly to Him; entirely resolve to put aside your own hopes and fears; in short, determine to wish nothing except what He wishes and to wish all that He wishes. From this moment you will acquire perfect liberty and will never again be able to feel troubled or uneasy, and there will be no power on earth capable of doing you violence or giving you a moment's unrest. (ST. CLAUDE DE LA COLOMBIÈRE)

❧ To love God and do His holy will: is this not the only essential thing and even our ultimate end? Everything besides is but a way leading to this — consolations as well as aridities, peace as well as war, light as well as darkness. Which way will be best for us? We cannot tell. But God knows, and He loves us tenderly. Let us therefore permit Him to dispense of us according to His beneficent designs. Our happiness is a thousand times safer in His hands than it would be in our own. (REV. DOM VITALIS LEHODEY)

❧ He who practices holy abandonment, whether in choir or at manual labor or spiritual reading, whether working for himself or for others, whether enjoying leisure or busily occupied, has never more than one thing to do: his essential duty, the holy will of God. He will pass through seasons of health and sickness, aridities and consolations, peace and conflict; but amidst all this variety of events, he sees only one thing: the God of his heart Who directs them and employs them to manifest to him His divine good-pleasure. Around him, men come and go and busy themselves about sundry affairs. Whether they approve or blame or forget him, he lifts his gaze above them and sees only God Who guides them, Who makes use of them to instruct him as to what he ought to do. In all occurrences, therefore, he attends to God alone and His adorable will. This is what gives his life a marvelous simplicity and extremely simple unity. (REV. DOM VITALIS LEHODEY)

DISCERNING GOD'S WILL

❧ What is the will of God? Our salvation, our happiness, our eternal union with Him. How can we discover it where it is hidden, how can we fathom its infallible directions?

What is the will of God for me in this particular matter? How can I be *sure*? Will I, in spite of my best intentions, make a mistake about His will and wander off the road?

His encompassing love has left little grounds for our uneasiness. There are the explicit statements of His will in the divine prohibitions, precepts, and counsels. For judgments in the entangling circumstances of particular occasions, He has given us minds of our own, imaging and sharing the divine light of His own mind, and therefore to be followed confidently; and there is the advice of those wiser than ourselves. Beneath, behind, and through it all there is the stupendous truth that no man loses God by accident; no man wanders off the road home in spite of himself; no man is in rebellion against the will of God except by his own open declaration of war. Perhaps the months or years will show us that we have taken a round-about path; but if our heart is right, our feet will find the ultimate goal of God: our salvation. (FR. WALTER FARRELL)

PERFECTION CONSISTS IN CONFORMITY TO THE DIVINE WILL

❧ Holiness consists simply of two things, two endeavors — the endeavor to know God's will, and the endeavor to do it when we know it. (FR. FREDERICK FABER)

❧ God's will is the sanctification of souls. Always and everywhere, this is the work that exclusively occupies Him. It is the purpose underlying all occurrences, great and small, which agitate in different ways nations, families, and the lives of individuals. It explains why God wills that I should be sick today, contradicted, humbled, forgotten; why He has prepared this happy event for me, faced me with this difficulty, caused me to hurt my foot against this stone, exposed me to this temptation. It is His love for me, His desire for my happiness that regulates all His actions. With what confidence and docility we should submit and correspond to His guidance if we better understood His merciful ways! (REV. DOM VITALIS LEHODEY)

❧ A single act of uniformity to the divine will suffices to make a saint. (ST. ALPHONSUS DE LIGUORI)

❧ Desire only what God has willed from all eternity; accept the place which in His most amiable will He has decided should be yours. My children, it is by complete renunciation of self and of all that one possesses that one goes to God. One drop of this renunciation, one rill of it, would better prepare a man and lead him nearer to God than the most absolute exterior denudation. A short moment in these dispositions would be more useful for us than forty years following practices of our own choice. (FR. JOHANNES TAULER)

❧ Since it is the most perfect act of charity and the most pleasing and acceptable sacrifice that is given to man to offer to God, there can be no doubt that whoever practices entire submission to His will lays up inestimable treasures at every moment and amasses more riches in a few days than others are able to acquire in many years and with great labor. (FR. JEAN BAPTISTE SAINT-JURE)

❧ This holy and adorable will, if we knew how to recognize it always, to approve it always, to embrace it always, and always to accomplish it with our whole hearts and with love and fidelity, as the angels and saints do in Heaven: this divine will, I say, would quickly transform the face of the world. Sanctity would flourish everywhere, there would be a constant abounding joy in all hearts, charity would reign amongst men and peace in families and nations. Notwithstanding trials, our lives would flow on in sweetness and happiness, perfumed with confidence and holy love, enriched with virtues and merits. Gladly, when our last moment came, we should quit this exile for our homeland; and far from fearing a stern judge in God, we should be impatient to go to our Heavenly Father. Earth would thus become an anticipated paradise, and in the real paradise would await us a superabundant wealth of glory and bliss. (REV. DOM VITALIS LEHODEY)

꙳ Everything we do derives its value from our conformity to the will of God. Hence even eating, if done because such is the will of God, is more meritorious than death would be without that intention. Fix this principle firmly in your mind, and in your every action keep it before your eyes. Thus you will do your work with perfection. (ST. FRANCIS DE SALES)

OBEDIENCE TO MARY IS OBEDIENCE TO GOD

꙳ She is our Mother. She helps everyone but especially those who commit themselves completely to Her. Jesus is our best example. He was the first to commit Himself to the Immaculata, and He was obedient to Her. Obedience to the Immaculata is nothing but the faithful fulfilling of God's will. Such obedience leads to sanctity. We need not flagellate ourselves. Jesus didn't. He faithfully fulfilled His Father's will. (ST. MAXIMILIAN KOLBE)

꙳ What would happen if a soldier, who doesn't always know the plan of the general, began to act on his own and open fire when he must remain silent and hidden, or march forward when he must retreat? And even more: the difference between the scope of the military knowledge of a soldier and his leader is limited, and his leader can make errors. The will of God, however, is infinite and infallible. He, then, who perfectly accomplishes the will of God does something infinitely great for the happiness of souls. And this is the most perfect way because Jesus Himself showed us this way. If there had been another more perfect, He would certainly have shown us that way. Behold, for thirty years He was obedient to the Most Holy Mother and St. Joseph, and He said that He always fulfills the will of His Father. (ST. MAXIMILIAN KOLBE)

V

DIVINE PROVIDENCE

Our sanctification is God's aim in all His dealings with us.
(FR. JEAN BAPTISTE SAINT-JURE)

THE GOODNESS OF GOD'S PROVIDENCE

❧ God cast His divine gaze upon you from all eternity; He looked upon you with the eye of mercy; He thought of you tenderly and ardently; He disposed and ordained, with wondrous kindness, everything that was to happen to you in body and soul and in every circumstance, development, and event of your existence and life, even to the hairs of your head; He formed great designs concerning you. He deigned to create you with all the natural advantages He has given you. He deigned to preserve you as He does every moment of your life. He deigned to create the world and keep it in existence for love of you. (ST. JOHN EUDES)

❧ God takes extraordinary care of your life. You were yet an infant, borne in the bosom of your mother, and without distrust of her, affectionate as she was, He carried you in His arms. He aided you to form your first steps and has always led you by the hand. If He permitted you to fall, it was to teach you your own weakness; the fall has not been fatal; you fell under His hand, and He has raised you up.

If you are tempted, He assists you; if shaken, He steadies you; if in sin, He endures you; if penitent, He forgives you. You retire to rest; He watches over you. Are you sick? He is around your bed, on the right hand and on the left, to comfort you, whichever way you turn. For you He tempers the heats of the day and the evil influences of the night. Never did father so much love his children as God loves you. Your defects disfigure you in the eyes of men; but our Heavenly Father finds His children amiable. He loves all His works; but He singularly loves you, made to His image. (ST. FRANCIS DE SALES)

❦ *All things are yours,* says the Apostle to us. The saints are ours, in order to help us; sufferings and temptations, in order to free us from imperfections; trials are ours in order to strengthen us in virtue; the world, in order to give us the means to serve God and to lighten our goal; life is ours in order to make us happy in God; death, in order to lead us to God. O happy and secure position! Only adhere to God, and you will be lord over all things; for the Lord, the Friend, the Father, cannot permit anything to be wanting to His servant, friend, and child. (FR. MATTHIAS J. SCHEEBEN)

❦ Remember that He has always infinite power and infinite wisdom employed in the service of His paternal goodness. He knows the particular end appointed for each soul, the degree of glory He has destined for her in Heaven, the measure of sanctity He has prepared for her. In order that she may attain her end and become perfect, He knows what paths she must follow, what trials she must endure, what humiliations she must undergo. His Providence has control of the myriad events which make up the course of our earthly existence, and directs them all to the appointed end. On the side of God, with Whom rests ultimately the disposal of all things, there is nothing but light, wisdom, grace, love, and salvation. (REV. DOM VITALIS LEHODEY)

❦ Our Lord loves with an extremely tender love those who are so happy as to abandon themselves entirely to His paternal care, letting Divine Providence govern them, without amusing themselves with considering whether the effects of this Providence will be useful, profitable, or injurious to them; being well assured that nothing detrimental can be sent them from that paternal and most amiable Heart, and that He will permit nothing to happen to them but what will prove good and useful to them. (ST. FRANCIS DE SALES)

WE MAY CONFIDENTLY RELY ON GOD'S CARE

❧ You must believe that we have a God Who has cared for us in every minute of the past and Who will continue to do so in the future. (ST. MARIE OF THE INCARNATION)

❧ Put your trust often in the Divine Providence of God, and be certain that rather will Heaven and earth pass away than that Our Lord should fail to protect you. (ST. PIO OF PIETRELCINA)

❧ God would sooner work miracles than leave without assistance, either spiritual or temporal, those who trust entirely in His Divine Providence. (ST. FRANCIS DE SALES)

❧ A thousand details of daily life will escape the notice of the father of a family and the most attentive of mothers, but God in His infinite intelligence possesses the secret of providing without effort for the most trivial as well as for the most important events. Thus can each of us say: "When I am hungry, God thinks of it; when I am thirsty, God thinks of it; when I undertake any work, God thinks of it; when I have to choose a state in life, God thinks of it; when difficulties arise in that state, God thinks of them; in order to resist a temptation or fulfill a duty I need such and such a grace, God thinks of it; in my journey to eternity I require the daily bread of soul and body, God thinks of it; when death approaches and I need to have my graces multiplied, God thinks of it; I am now on my deathbed, at my last gasp, and unless I am helped, I shall be lost eternally, God thinks of it." And thus I, an insignificant atom in the great world, occupy day and night, always and everywhere, the mind and heart of my Father in Heaven. Oh, how infinitely touching is this truth of our holy Faith; how touching and how consoling! (REV. DOM VITALIS LEHODEY)

❧ When one places all his confidence in God, God protects him in a special way at all times, and thus he can rest assured that nothing evil will befall him. (ST. VINCENT DE PAUL)

❧ Nothing whatsoever can happen without Divine Providence having foreseen it and having made it fit into His plans beforehand. (ST. LOUIS MARIE DE MONTFORT)

❧ Suppose You were to say to us: "There are a few, a very few, whose salvation is so dear to Me that I will trust the choice of means to no one. I will plan and arrange all Myself. Nothing shall happen to them but what has been foreseen and prepared from all eternity by My infinite Wisdom and Goodness. No one shall touch them, no joy or sorrow shall come in their way, no, nor a hair of their head fall to the ground without My knowledge and permission." Should we not cry out: "My God, I hardly dare ask it, but O that I might be one of those happy chosen few, for surely they are safe!"

You check me by a warning: "These souls will not have their own way in life. Their road will sometimes be hard and rugged. They will see things prosper in the hands of others and fail in theirs. They will be harshly used by those around them—misjudged, set aside, unjustly treated; life to many of them will be uphill work." Do I draw back now, or do I cry out again: "No matter that, no matter that at all! What will they care when they know Your arm is around them as they go uphill; Your hand sends the cross and the failure and the pain! No, my God, that does not frighten me. Let me be only one of those whose lot is altogether in Your hands, and I will fear nothing; nay, I will be grateful for all that comes to me. I will kiss Your hand even when You strike me. I shall feel peaceful and happy always in the thought that it is the wisdom of my God that orders all for me, and the love of my Heavenly Father that provides everything to help me. Let me be one of those chosen ones, and You will see how I value my privilege, how I prize whatever You send."

Suppose—I have been saying. But this is no supposition. I am that privileged one whose life in its minutest details is Your ordering and Your care. How can I complain, my God? How can I be mistrustful or even anxious? *My lots are in Thy hands.* (REV. DANIEL CONSIDINE)

❧ I will protect you. My Providence shall never fail you in the slightest need. (OUR LORD TO ST. CATHERINE OF SIENA)

❧ Let us place our confidence in God and set ourselves in complete dependence upon His Providence. Then we need not worry about what others say of us or do to us, for it will all turn out to our advantage. (ST. VINCENT DE PAUL)

❧ Think of Me, and I will think of thee. I will take complete care of everything that pertains to thee. (OUR LORD TO ST. CATHERINE OF SIENA)

❧ Divine Providence is never wanting where necessity is concerned. (ST. ROSE PHILIPPINE DUCHESNE)

❧ God, in the perfection of His Providence, leads us on a long journey, and often through winding paths and inextricable labyrinths, but He knows by what way to guide us to the heavenly pastures. Why, therefore, do we murmur against this most watchful Leader? If anyone sets out on a journey with a companion who is thoroughly acquainted with the road, and when rough, difficult, and marshy parts come in sight, begins to complain and says, "By what a round-about way are you leading me, my friend? Unless I am much mistaken, we have long ago left the proper path;" his guide will quickly reply—"Do not be alarmed, but leave it all to me. I have led you by a circuitous path, I allow; but if we had kept a straight course we should have fallen into those quagmires from which we should never have extricated ourselves. Trust yourself to me, and I will guide you in such a way that you shall not be sorry for having had me for a companion." And in this way Divine Providence guides us. We must go, indeed through many by-paths and long circuitous windings of the road; but why are we angry with our most excellent Guide? Only let the road be safe, and what does it matter if it is rough? (FR. JEREMIAS DREXEL)

TRUSTING GOD IN THE MIDST OF TRIALS

❧ As My Providence provides your daily bread that your body may live, so it is My very tender Providence which provides you with fresh sacrifices and occasions for practicing the virtues you have asked of Me, so that you may be living souls, growing daily in My knowledge and My love. Think of this when suffering comes. (OUR LORD TO SR. MARY OF THE TRINITY)

❧ The same Everlasting Father Who cares for you today will take care of you tomorrow and every day of your life. Either He will shield you from suffering, or He will give you unfailing strength to bear it. Be at peace, then, and put aside all anxious thoughts. (ST. FRANCIS DE SALES)

❧ Whatever men may do or say, they certainly can do nothing except what God wills or permits, nothing that He cannot utilize for the accomplishment of His mysterious purposes. Let us, therefore, banish all fears and surrender ourselves unreservedly to the guidance of His Providence. He has at His disposal many secret but infallible expedients. He is not less able to accomplish His designs by means in appearance the most contrary than He was to refresh His servants in the midst of a raging furnace or to make them walk upon the waters. We shall experience for ourselves this paternal protection of Divine Providence in the measure in which we trust our all to it with filial abandonment. (REV. DOM VITALIS LEHODEY)

❧ It is a consoling thought that God watches over us with unceasing care; that no matter where we may be — alone in our room or passing through the crowded streets of a feverish panting city — the hand of God is over us and sheltering us from a thousand unknown dangers, guiding us safely along the path of life. Wicked men may plot evil things against us, around us, but harm us they cannot without His consent Who directs all things for His own wise ends. Poverty may be our lot, sickness may lay its heavy hand upon us, and misfortunes thickly strew our path. But welcome be they all! They are precious gifts from the hand of a loving Savior. (FR. WILLIAM DOYLE)

❧ If we could discover the designs of Providence, it is certain we would ardently long for the evils we are now so unwilling to suffer. We would rush forward to accept them with the utmost gratitude if we had a little faith and realized how much God loves us and has our interests at heart. (ST. CLAUDE DE LA COLOMBIÈRE)

❧ When calamity falls upon ourselves, our families, or our communities, we should endeavor to see God in it, God paternally occupied with the concerns of our souls. The death of a beloved friend appears to me disastrous. But perhaps if that friend had been allowed to live longer, he would have died in the state of sin. I may owe thirty or forty years of life to this very malady I have supported with so little patience. The eternal salvation of my soul may have depended on the humiliation which has cost me so many tears. I should perhaps have been spiritually ruined had I not lost that money. Why, then, do we complain? God Himself has undertaken to conduct us to our destiny, and still we are full of anxiety! Oh, if only we better understood His loving designs for us, we would bless Him even when He treats us with seeming severity. Such filial abandonment would multiply our merits, establish us in peace, touch the heart of our Heavenly Father, and would often be the best means of temporal success. (REV. DOM VITALIS LEHODEY)

❧ To live constantly in devotion, we have only to establish sound principles or maxims in our soul.

The first which I desire you to adopt is that of St. Paul: *All things work together for good to those who love God.* And truly, since God is able and understands how to draw good from evil, for whom will He be disposed to do so, if not for those who give themselves unreservedly to Him? Even sins, which God in His goodness has forbidden, are changed by the Divine Providence to the good of those who belong to Him. David would not have been so full of humility if he had not sinned, nor Magdalen of love for her Savior if He had not forgiven her many sins: and never would He have forgiven them if she had not committed them.

Behold the great dispense of mercy: He changes our miseries into favors, and from the adder of our iniquities, makes a salutary balm for our souls. Tell me, then, what will He not do with our afflictions, our labors, our persecution? If it happens that something grieves you, no matter from what quarter it comes, be assured that while you love God, all will turn to your good. And though you cannot see the means by which this good will come, be assured that it will come. If God places the bandage of ignominy over your eyes, it will be to render you an admirable sight, a spectacle of honor. If He permits you to fall, like St. Paul, whom He cast to the earth, it will be to raise you up with glory. (ST. FRANCIS DE SALES)

❧ If you would be convinced that in all He allows and in all that happens to you God has no other end in view but your real advantage and your eternal happiness, reflect a moment on all He has done for you. You are now suffering, but remember that the Author of this suffering is He Who chose to spend His life suffering to save you from everlasting suffering; Whose angel is always at your side, guarding your body and soul by His order; Who sacrifices Himself daily on the altar to expiate your sins and appease His Father's anger; Who comes lovingly to you in the Holy Eucharist, and Whose greatest pleasure is to be united to you. Let us not be ungrateful enough to mistrust Him after He has shown such proofs of His love. (ST. CLAUDE DE LA COLOMBIÈRE)

GOD WORKS WONDERS WITH SOULS ABANDONED TO HIM

❧ God alone, in truth, knows the way that each soul should follow here below. There is nothing more admirable than the variety of the ways by which He leads His elect. But one thing remains invariable, and that is the particular love with which He directs, governs, and protects the soul which, entrusting herself to Him without reserve, leaves Him completely free to lead her on according to His wisdom. At every instant, both outwardly by the course of events and inwardly by the promptings of His grace, He procures for her what is most useful and best for her just at the moment. And so the soul which is most completely given up to abandonment is always the most tenderly fondled, the most powerfully succored, the most constantly laden with the favors of Divine Goodness. (REV. GABRIEL MARTIN)

❧ Our Lord needs nothing more than your abandonment to bring about the divine wonders that His Heart has prepared for you from all eternity. (FR. JEAN C.J. D'ELBÉE)

❧ Oh, how much I desire that you would have more confidence in God, more abandonment to His wise and omnipotent Providence! It is Providence that regulates all events, even to the very least, of this life. It turns everything to the advantage of those who put perfect confidence in it and abandon themselves unreservedly to its paternal control. Oh, what fruits of interior peace such confidence and abandonment yield! How quickly and thoroughly they would deliver you from the tyranny of cares, multiplied to infinity, always disquieting and tormenting! However, you cannot hope to reach at a single bound such a height of perfection, but gradually, step by step, and by almost imperceptible progress. Yet you must always aspire to this filial abandonment; you must implore it of God and exercise acts of it. Occasions will not be lacking. Avail yourself of them, and on each, endeavor to say: "Yes, my God, Thou willest or permittest this. Very well! I also will it for the pure love of Thee. Help and sustain my weakness." (FR. JEAN PIERRE DE CAUSSADE)

❧ We understand now why so many Communions — each of which should be capable of transforming us into great saints — why they do not bring us all the supernatural fruits they should. We open our arms to Him, yet we close the doors of our intelligence, of our will, of our heart, by not living in abandonment. We bid Him come, but we do not permit Him to enter. But if, in receiving Him, we grant Him, by perfect abandonment, all the controls, all the keys to the house, that He may be Master in us with full liberty to act, then, oh! what marvels will His omnipotence not accomplish in our souls in the service of His love! (FR. JEAN C.J. D'ELBÉE)

TRUST IS ESSENTIAL IN THE WAY
OF SPIRITUAL CHILDHOOD

❧ Abandonment alone really surrenders the soul into the arms of Jesus and thus allows His love to act freely and according to the full extent of its force. That is why, in her challenge to the soul weaker than her own, St. Thérèse confidently asserts that it will receive favors still greater than those showered on herself, provided the soul abandon itself with full confidence to the infinite mercy of God. (SISTERS OF CARMEL)

❧ A little soul ought to believe, for it is true, that everything Providence sends her is the work of Love — everything is determined, willed, chosen by Love. Consequently, the good pleasure of God should appear to her all radiant with love, and she must surrender herself to it filially, lovingly, and also with confidence, her eyes closed, without seeking to penetrate the secrets that her Father in Heaven wishes to keep hidden from her. Let her only consider it as certain that He in His infinite wisdom and goodness will never require of her sacrifices above her strength. (REV. GABRIEL MARTIN)

❧ Let yourself be led blindfolded. My eyes are wide open to lead you, and am I not your Father? (OUR LORD TO SR. JOSEFA MENÉNDEZ)

❧ Rely on Me with closed eyes, without anxiety, content; yes, like a babe sleeping in its mother's arms. (OUR LORD TO SR. MARY OF THE TRINITY)

❧ Yes, I attend to these details of your life—you are amazed at it! As a mother interests herself in all that concerns her newborn infant, I interest Myself in all that affects you. I do not lower Myself by doing so because I am not a degree of greatness; I am Love, and Love remains great when manifesting itself among little things as well as among great things. (OUR LORD TO SR. MARY OF THE TRINITY)

VI

THE PASSION

The Cross is the standard of the elect. Let us always keep close to it, and we will succeed in conquering in everything and over everyone.

(ST. PIO OF PIETRELCINA)

CONTEMPLATING THE PASSION

❧ By simply thinking of or meditating on the Passion of Our Lord Jesus Christ, a Christian gains more merit than if he had fasted on bread and water every Friday for a whole year, or had beaten himself with his discipline once a week till blood flowed, or had recited the whole book of Psalms every day. (ST. LOUIS MARIE DE MONTFORT)

❧ There is more merit to one hour of meditation on My sorrowful Passion then there is to a whole year of bloody scourging. The contemplation of My painful Wounds is of great profit to you, and it brings Me great joy. (OUR LORD TO ST. FAUSTINA)

❧ When a man earnestly turns himself towards the thought of the Passion and dwells in it, God reveals to him the fruit of His suffering, which is so great that it flows out upon and around the man, and he is thus forcibly drawn through the rushing of grace towards God. (FR. JOHANNES TAULER)

❧ Whenever anyone sighs towards Me with love in meditating on My Passion, it is as though he gently touched My

Wounds with a fresh-budding rose, and I wound his heart in return with the arrow of My Love. Moreover, if he sheds tears of devotion over My Passion, I will accept them as if he had suffered for Me. (OUR LORD TO ST. MECHTILDE)

❧ If anyone looks at the image of the Cross of Jesus Christ with a holy intention, God rewards him with such goodness and mercy that he receives in his soul, as in a spotless mirror, an image which is so agreeable that the whole court of Heaven delights therein, and this serves to increase his eternal glory in the life to come in proportion as he has practiced this act of devotion in this life. (REVELATION TO ST. GERTRUDE THE GREAT)

❧ I wish all men to do their utmost to sorrow in their hearts through veneration for My Passion, as if compassionating Me. If they shed one little tear over It, they may be sure they have done a great thing, for the tongue of man cannot tell what joy and satisfaction that one little tear causes Me. (OUR LORD TO BL. VERONICA OF BINASCO)

❧ They who occupy themselves with the sufferings of Jesus do not walk in the spiritual life but run as fast as men who have enemies behind them. They never stand still, they never go backwards, but ever without intermission advance forwards. This however comes not from their own strength, but it is heavenly power lent them through the contemplation of the Passion of Our Lord. (FR. JOHANNES TAULER)

THE EFFICACY OF THE PASSION

❧ I will grant all that is asked of Me through the invocation of My Holy Wounds. You will obtain everything because it is through the merit of My Blood, which is of infinite price.

With My Wounds and My Divine Heart, everything can be obtained. (OUR LORD TO SR. MARY MARTHA CHAMBON)

❧ At three o'clock, implore My mercy especially for sinners; and, if only for a moment, immerse yourself in My Passion, particularly in My abandonment at the moment of agony. This is the hour of great mercy for the whole world. In this hour, I will refuse nothing to the soul that makes a request of Me in virtue of My Passion. (OUR LORD TO ST. FAUSTINA)

❧ Happily, joyfully, with flaming desire, take up the standard of the most Holy Cross so that no blow can pierce you. Never fear that you will not be able to persevere in the life you have begun. If you keep Christ's Blood in mind, you will be victorious. (ST. CATHERINE OF SIENA)

❧ There is no fault, no want of fidelity, no evil tendency, no sin, which, if sincerely detested, cannot be cleansed, purified, and pardoned by the Blood of Jesus; there is no weakness which He cannot cure, strengthen, and transform. (FR. GABRIEL OF ST. MARY MAGDALEN)

❧ Christ's Blood is like an immense sea which has the power to cleanse and destroy the sins of all mankind, provided they are sincerely repented of. Every minute of every day we can take the burden of our sins and infidelities, heavy or light as it may be, and make it disappear in this ocean of grace and love, certain that not one trace of it will remain. (FR. GABRIEL OF ST. MARY MAGDALEN)

MAKING REPARATION FOR ALL OUR LORD SUFFERED

❧ If anyone sacrifices his own way of thinking or acting in order to conform to another's opinion, he makes reparation for the thongs which bound Me and the injuries which I received in prison during the first hours of My Passion. He who humbly avows his faults, atones for the false accusations made against Me and for My condemnation to death. To deprive the senses of what gratifies them repays Me for what I endured by the cruel scourging; while to obey those who are fretful and exacting, consoles Me for the pain of wearing the crown of thorns.

In dispute, or when anyone is offended, he who makes the first advance towards reconciliation helps Me to carry My Cross; while anyone who exerts himself beyond what he can ordinarily do to help others by works of charity, repays Me for what I suffered when, as I was being nailed to the Cross, My muscles were stretched and My bones dislocated in order to make My hands reach the places prepared for the nails. Not to shrink from pain or trouble when it is a question of rescuing another from sin, makes up to Me for My death for man's salvation; and returning a meek answer to reproaches or unkindness, is as pleasing to Me as the act of those who took My Body down from the Cross.

Finally, he who prefers his neighbor to himself, acknowledging that he has a better right to honors, comforts, or other advantages, acts as if he placed Me in the tomb with all honor and reverence. (OUR LORD TO ST. GERTRUDE THE GREAT)

VII

THE HOLY MASS

Holy Mass is the golden key to paradise; and,
since the Eternal Father gives us this key, which
of all His other benefits can He refuse?

(ST. LEONARD OF PORT MAURICE)

THE GREATNESS OF HOLY MASS

❧ One single Mass gives more honor to God than all the penances of the saints, the labors of the Apostles, the sufferings of the martyrs, and even the burning love of the Blessed Mother of God. (ST. ALPHONSUS DE LIGUORI)

❧ He who hears Mass devoutly gains more than he who performs some arduous work for the love of God or goes on a distant pilgrimage. And no wonder, for what is nobler, more precious, more divine than the Sacrifice of the Mass! (BISHOP FORNERUS)

❧ We can do as much to please Our Lord and acquire merit for ourselves when we hear Mass as we should have done had we been present on Calvary, if we are no less devout and recollected than we should have been standing beneath the Cross. We are fortunate indeed, in that we can stand in spirit beneath the Cross of the dying Savior, that we can behold Him with our eyes, speak to Him with our lips, tell Him our troubles, obtain from Him help and consolation, just as those did who were present in person at the Crucifixion. How highly we ought to prize the favors Christ thus daily places within our reach; how anxious we should be to claim a share in the graces He thus holds out to us! (FR. MARTIN VON COCHEM)

❧ Just as when we climb a mountain, we reach a greater elevation at every step, so each time we hear Mass, we rise to a higher place in Heaven, and the height which we attain is greater or less in proportion to the fervor of our devotion. The greater our degree of grace, the nearer we are to God, the clearer will be our knowledge of Him, the more ardent our love of Him, the more unbounded our enjoyment of Him. Each degree we rise will increase our beauty, our nobility, our riches, our glory, and the esteem in which the Saints hold us. (FR. MARTIN VON COCHEM)

THE EFFICACY OF HOLY MASS

❧ The efficacy of the Mass is so wonderful, God's mercy and generosity are then so unlimited, that there is no moment so propitious to ask for favors as when Jesus is born on the altar. What we then ask for, we shall almost certainly receive. (FR. PAUL O'SULLIVAN)

❧ Assuredly, no human tongue is capable of telling how abundant are the fruits to be derived from the Holy Sacrifice of the Mass, how great the gifts and graces that flow from it. The sinner is reconciled with God, the just is confirmed in his justice. Transgressions are forgiven, vices exterminated, virtues multiplied, merits augmented, temptations overcome. (ST. LAWRENCE JUSTINIAN)

❧ All the favors I ask of God in the Mass are finite, whereas the Gift which I offer to Him is uncreated and infinite; and so, the account being rightly summed, I am the creditor, and He the Debtor. And you — why do you not demand great graces? Take my advice, in every Mass, ask God to make you a great saint. Does this seem too much? It is not too much. Is it not our good Master Who protests in the Holy Gospel that for a cup of cold water given out of love for Him, He will, in return, give Paradise? How then, while offering to God the Blood of His most blessed Son, should He not give you a hundred Heavens, were there so many? How can you doubt but that He wishes to give you all the perfections which are required to make you a saint and a great one? (ST. LEONARD OF PORT MAURICE)

❧ What graces, what virtues, what gifts Holy Mass calls down! In the first place, it calls down all spiritual graces: repentance for sins and victory over temptations. It calls down the aid of grace, so necessary for enabling us to rise up, stand upon our feet, to walk forward in the ways of God. It calls down many good and holy inspirations and many internal impulses, which dispose us to shake off tepidity and spur us on to work our best with greater fervor, with a will more prompt, and an intention more upright and pure. But further still, it calls down temporal blessings such as health, abundance, peace, with the exclusion of the evils which are their opposites, such as pestilences, hatreds, calumnies, injuries. In fine, here at Mass we may find liberation from all evils; here we may find enrichment by every sort of benefit. (ST. LEONARD OF PORT MAURICE)

❧ The wants of souls are almost infinitely various. Some have the grace to feel the want of much and to be ever wanting more; others unhappily want little and can be contented with almost less. But just as the running stream fills the vessels great or small which are dipped into its abundance, and just as the sun gives full light to the various powers of vision of different men and animals, so it is with the Mass. It is coextensive with the wants of all, embraces all, satisfies all, stimulates all. Our all is there: our bread for the single day, our viaticum for the journey to eternity. In the same way that all souls are equal, so the Mass is equal to all; and in the same way that every degree of mental power and glorious giftedness, from the sublimest intelligence of the theologian to the limited understanding of the peasant, is secured and sustained, as much as it wants and no more, by the immortal soul, so the broad edifice of the saint's sanctity and the small beginnings of the sinner's efforts have all they want and no more in the Sacrifice of the Mass. The adorable Sacrifice fills all spiritual depths and shallows: it is its gift that it should fill wherever it is. Fullness is its prerogative. (FR. FREDERICK FABER)

❧ Holy Mass is never offered in vain. If we do not receive the very thing for which we asked, we infallibly receive something else that is more beneficial for us. (CARDINAL GIOVANNI BONA)

CHRIST PRAYS WITH US AND FOR US IN THE MASS

❧ The prayers said at Mass, offered in union with the Holy Sacrifice, have infinitely more value than any other prayers, however long, however fervent, in virtue of the merits of Christ's Passion, the power of which is manifested in Holy Mass by a superabundance of celestial gifts and graces. (BISHOP FORNERUS)

❧ If we unite our poor petitions which we offer during the Mass to the perfect prayer of Our Lord, they will, like a copper coin immersed in gold, be beautified and ennobled. Prayers said at Mass time have far more value than more fervent prayers said at home. (FR. MARTIN VON COCHEM)

❧ How much is done for our welfare by Christ's prayers from the altar! How often would calamities have befallen us had they not been averted by His prayers! How many thousands of the blessed, now happy in Heaven would be in Hell, had not Christ by His intercession saved them from that place of torment! Let us, therefore, go frequently and gladly to Mass, in the hope that we may, through that omnipotent Mediator, obtain from God that which of ourselves we cannot obtain. (FR. MARTIN VON COCHEM)

❧ If our sins render us unworthy of being heard, the holiness of Jesus and the fervor with which He prays for us makes His Father forget our unworthiness, and He only considers that One Whom He has made to be our Advocate. (BL. DOM COLUMBA MARMION)

THE POWER OF THE MASS TO CONVERT POOR SINNERS

❧ Believe and doubt not that every day I desire, with the same love and strength of desire, to be sacrificed for every sinner upon the altar, as I sacrificed Myself upon the Cross for the salvation of the world. Therefore, there is no one, however heavy the weight of sin wherewith he is burdened, who may not hope for pardon, if he offers to the Father My sinless Life and Death, provided he believes that thereby he will obtain the blessed fruit of forgiveness. (OUR LORD TO ST. GERTRUDE THE GREAT)

❧ Such is My long-suffering when I come at the time of Mass that there is no sinner present, howsoever great, to whom, provided he desire it, I do not gladly grant forgiveness of sin. (OUR LORD TO ST. MECHTILDE)

✢ If we draw nigh unto God, contrite and penitent, and with sincere heart and upright faith, with fear and reverence, offer the Holy Mass to God, the Lord, appeased by the oblation thereof and granting the grace and gift of penitence, forgives even heinous crimes and sins. Listen, O sinner, to this consoling truth! Take from it fresh hope of your salvation, fresh courage for the amendment of your life; disentangle yourself from the net of despair and trust in this all-powerful Sacrifice of Atonement. Go diligently to church and there join in offering the Holy Sacrifice to God. (FR. MARTIN VON COCHEM)

VIII

THE HOLY EUCHARIST

*Each look of love to the Tabernacle causes a
beat of grace-laden love in the Sacred Heart.*

(FR. WILLIAM DOYLE)

THE PRESENCE OF OUR LORD
IN THE BLESSED SACRAMENT

❧ The perpetual Real Presence of Jesus with His faithful, His
perseverance in the obscure Tabernacle, and His frequent
Benedictions which preside over the evenings of our toil-
some days, just as the Mass so beautifully fills the morning
with its light and love — it is Jesus all day long, courting our
society and mingling with us with an intimacy we get to
understand less and to prize more the longer it is vouchsafed.
Surely this is enough to supernaturalize the whole world, to
make hard things easy, and dark things bright, and throw an
invisible armor round us which will charm our lives against
the weapons and the wiles of hell. (FR. FREDERICK FABER)

❧ The Blessed Sacrament is the invention of Love. It is
life and fortitude for souls, a remedy for every fault. In It
sinners recover life for their souls; tepid souls, true warmth;
fervent souls, tranquility and the satisfaction of every longing; saintly souls, wings to fly towards perfection; pure
souls, sweet honey and rarest sustenance. (OUR LORD TO SR.
JOSEFA MENÉNDEZ)

❧ It is love for souls that keeps Me a Prisoner in the Blessed
Sacrament. I stay there that all may come and find the

comfort they need in the tenderest of Hearts, the best of Fathers, the most faithful of Friends, Who will never abandon them. (OUR LORD TO SR. JOSEFA MENÉNDEZ)

❧ Poor pitiable sinners, do not turn away from Me. Day and night I am on watch for you in the Tabernacle. I will not reproach you; I will not cast your sins in your face, but I will wash them in My Blood and in My Wounds. No need to be afraid. Come to Me. If you but knew how dearly I love you! (OUR LORD TO SR. JOSEFA MENÉNDEZ)

❧ And you, dear souls, why this coldness and indifference on your part? Do I not know that family cares, household concerns, and the requirements of your position in life make continual calls upon you? But can you not spare a few minutes in which to come to Me in the Tabernacle and prove your affection and your gratitude? Were you weak or ill in body, surely you would find time to see a doctor who would cure you? Come, then, to One Who is able to give both strength and health to your soul; bestow the alms of love on this Divine Prisoner Who watches for you, calls for you, and longs to see you at His side. (OUR LORD TO SR. JOSEFA MENÉNDEZ)

❧ That you are unworthy I well know, but not for that would I turn away from you. On the contrary, with anxious solicitude I look for your coming to Me in the Blessed Sacrament, that I may not only ease your troubles but also grant you many favors. (OUR LORD TO SR. JOSEFA MENÉNDEZ)

❧ Do we realize the infinite possibilities of grace which lie hidden in the Tabernacle? Jesus only awaits our coming, and even before we have begun to beg His help, He has opened the treasures of His Sacred Heart and filled our hands with priceless gifts. What monarch ever rewarded his subjects as Jesus repays us for the little trouble it costs us to visit Him even for one short moment? (FR. WILLIAM DOYLE)

❧ As often as you lift your eyes to the Sacred Host, or supposing you cannot see It, as often as you represent to yourself the presence of your Lord upon the altar, you practice a lofty virtue, meriting a great increase of grace in life, and after your death, a higher place in Heaven. (FR. MARTIN VON COCHEM)

❧ Each time a soul in the state of grace looks upon the Most Blessed Sacrament with love, his place in Heaven is raised forever. (OUR LORD TO ST. GERTRUDE THE GREAT)

❧ Real devotion to the Blessed Sacrament is only to be gained by hard, grinding work of dry adoration before the Hidden God. But such a treasure cannot be purchased at too great a cost, for once obtained, it makes of this life as near an approach to Heaven as we can ever hope for. (FR. WILLIAM DOYLE)

❧ You say that you cannot remain in the presence of Jesus Christ because you know not what to say to Him. O God! And why do you not employ yourself in asking the graces of which you stand in need? Beg of Him to give you strength to resist temptations, to correct the faults into which you always relapse, to rescue you from the passion that keeps you in chains and hinders you from giving yourself entirely to God. Entreat Him to give you aid to suffer all insults and contradictions in peace, to increase in your heart His divine love, and entreat Him particularly to make you live always united with His holy will. When you feel disturbed on account of having committed any fault, go instantly to the Holy Sacrament to ask pardon, and then calm your mind. When you receive any offense or when you meet with a heavy cross, go and offer it to Jesus Christ and ask His aid to embrace it with resignation. Oh if all souls acted in this manner and knew how to avail themselves of the presence of their Savior, they would all become saints. Let it be your care to become a saint by adopting this practice. (ST. ALPHONSUS DE LIGUORI)

THE POWER OF HOLY COMMUNION

❧ When Christ desires to conduct a soul to the summit of perfection, He offers her the cross and the Eucharist. These two complete each other. The cross makes you love and long for the Eucharist. The Eucharist makes you first accept then love, and, therefore, long for the cross. The cross purifies and disposes the soul and prepares her for the Divine Banquet. The Eucharist nourishes and fortifies the soul, helps her to carry the cross, and supports her on the weary way to Calvary. What precious gifts are the cross and the Eucharist! They are the gifts which God bestows on His true friends. (REV. DOM VITALIS LEHODEY)

❧ Holy Communion is the shortest, surest way to Heaven. There are others: innocence, for instance, but that is for little children; penance, but we are afraid of it; a generous endurance of the trials of this life, but when they approach us, we weep and pray to be delivered. Once and for all, beloved children, the shortest, easiest, surest way is by the Holy Eucharist. (ST. PIUS X)

❧ This Sacrament infuses into the soul great interior peace, a strong inclination to virtue and great willingness to practice it, thus rendering it easy to walk in the path of perfection. Thus he who communicates most frequently will be freest from sin and will make farthest progress in Divine Love. (ST. ALPHONSUS DE LIGUORI)

❧ One of the most admirable effects of Holy Communion is to preserve souls from falling and to help those who fall from weakness to rise again. Therefore, it is much more profitable to approach the Divine Sacrament frequently, with love, respect, and confidence, than to keep back from an excess of fear. (ST. IGNATIUS OF LOYOLA)

❧ The Savior instituted the most Holy Sacrament of the Eucharist, really containing His Body and His Blood, in order that they who eat It might live for ever. And therefore whosoever receives it frequently and devoutly, so strengthens the health and life of his soul that it is hardly possible for him to be poisoned by any evil desires. We cannot be fed by that Living Flesh and hold to the affections of death; and just as our first parents could not die in Paradise, because of the Tree of Life which God had placed therein, so this Sacrament of Life makes spiritual death impossible. The most fragile, easily spoilt fruits, such as cherries, apricots, and strawberries, can be kept all the year by being preserved in sugar or honey; so what wonder if our hearts, frail and weakly as they are, are kept from the corruption of sin when they are preserved in the sweetness of the Incorruptible Body and Blood of the Son of God. (ST. FRANCIS DE SALES)

❧ All graces are contained in You, O Jesus in the Eucharist, our celestial Food! What more can a soul wish when it has within itself the One Who contains everything? If I wish for charity, then I have within me Him Who is perfect charity, I possess the perfection of charity. The same is true of faith, hope, purity, patience, humility, and meekness, for You form all virtues in our soul, O Christ, when You give us the grace of this Food. What more can I want or desire, if all virtues, graces, and gifts I long for are found in You? (ST. MARY MAGDALEN DEI PAZZI)

❧ We shall have a greater capacity to receive the Bread of Life to the extent that our faith in that Life becomes greater, our trust firmer, our desire more ardent. *Open your mouth wide, and I will fill it*, Christ says to us, as God said of old to the Psalmist. "Open up yourself by faith, by trust, by love, by holy desires, by abandonment to Me, and I will fill you." "With what, Lord?" "With Myself. I will give Myself to you, whole and entire, with My Humanity and My Divinity, with the fruit of My mysteries, the merit of My labors, the satisfaction of My sufferings, and the price of My Passion. I will come down within you, as of old I came down upon the earth, to destroy the works of the devil there; to render there, with you, a divine homage to My Father. I will make you partake of the treasures of My Divinity, of the eternal life which I have from My Father, which My Father wants Me to communicate to you in order that you may resemble Me. I will shower My grace upon you so as to become, Myself, your wisdom, your sanctification, your way, your truth, your life. You shall become another Myself, and—like Me, and because of Me—be the object of My Father's delight. (BL. DOM COLUMBA MARMION)

OUR LADY OF THE BLESSED SACRAMENT

❧ Our Lord left His Mother on earth after His Ascension because He distrusted our weakness and inconstancy. Our Lord feared that men, not knowing how to find and adore Him in His Sacrament, would become discouraged and forget Him. The child, as we know, does not search long. If he does not at once find what he wants, he changes his desire and runs after something else. This is what Our Lord feared from us. He left His Mother, whose whole mission it would be to take us by the hand and lead us to His Tabernacle. The Blessed Virgin, then, became our Mother in view of the Eucharist. It is for Her to show us how to find our Bread of Life, to make us appreciate and desire It. (ST. PETER JULIAN EYMARD)

IX

PRAYER

God is so good and so merciful, that to obtain Heaven
it is sufficient to ask it of Him from our hearts.
(ST. BENEDICT JOSEPH LABRE)

WHAT PRAYER IS

❧ Prayer is the illumination and nourishment of the soul, the source of all virtues, the fountain of divine graces, the foretaste of future glory. (ST. JOHN CLIMACUS)

❧ Prayer is an outburst from the heart; it is a simple glance darted upward to Heaven; it is a cry of gratitude and of love in the midst of trial as in the midst of joy. In a word, it is something exalted, supernatural, which dilates the soul and unites it to God. (MOTHER AGNES OF JESUS)

❧ Because it is called meditation, many feel that they must think about God and not talk to Him; even because it is called mental prayer, many come to the same conclusion. That is sheer nonsense. Whenever a man is talking to God in a rational way, he is praying. Whenever a man is looking at God and loving Him or adoring Him, even though no word pass his lips or form itself at all — he is praying. The essence of prayer is the interior action of the soul; whether its acts find external expression in words or not does not make any essential change in it. (DOM EUGENE BOYLAN)

❧ True prayer lies in whatever unites us to God, whatever enables us to enjoy Him, to appreciate Him, to rejoice in His glory, and to love Him as one's very own. (BISHOP JACQUES-BÉNIGNE BOSSUET)

❧ If thou dost love God, thou wilt understand the great art of prayer; and if thou dost pray aright, God will love thee more and more. Prayer is, therefore, the divinest virtue, because it is the expression of perfect love. (ST. NILUS)

❧ The graces and favors of prayer are not earthly but heavenly waters, which all our efforts cannot acquire, but for which indeed we must dispose ourselves with humble and tranquil care. We must hold up our heart open to Heaven and await the sacred dew. And never forget to carry this consideration to prayer: that therein we approach to God for two principal reasons. The first is to render to God the honor and homage which we owe Him, and this can be done without His speaking to us, or our speaking to Him, acknowledging by our presence that He is our God and we His creatures, and remaining prostrate in spirit before Him, awaiting His commands. How many courtiers are there who appear a hundred times before the king, not to speak to him or to hear him, but simply to be seen by him and to testify by their assiduity that they are his servants! This motive of presenting ourselves before God merely to attest our engagement to His service is most pure, worthy, and excellent, and, consequently, of the highest perfection. The second reason for which we come before God is to speak to Him, and to hear Him speak to us by His inspirations and interior motions, and this is usually performed with a delicious pleasure because it is a great happiness to speak to so mighty a Lord. And when He answers, He is accustomed to pour out such precious balm and unction as fill the soul to overflowing with sweetness.

One of these reasons may sometimes fail us, but both

never. If we can speak to Our Lord, let us speak to Him, praise Him, beseech Him, listen to Him; if we cannot, because we are hoarse, let us remain in His chamber and pay Him reverence; He will observe us there, regard our patience, and be pleased with our silence. Another time we shall be amazed when He takes us by the hand and shows us everything, making a hundred turns along the beautiful walks of the garden of prayer. (ST. FRANCIS DE SALES)

THE POWER OF PRAYER

❧ Prayer is the best weapon we possess, the key that opens the Heart of God. (ST. PIO OF PIETRELCINA)

❧ In prayer the soul cleanses itself from sin, charity is nourished, faith is strengthened, and hope is made secure. In prayer the spirit rejoices, the soul grows tender, the heart is purified, truth discovers itself. In prayer are brought forth flashes of heavenly desire, and in these fires, the flame of divine love burns up. In prayer temptation is overcome, sadness takes to flight, the senses are renewed, failing virtue is made good, tepidity disappears, and the rust of sin is rubbed away. (ST. LAWRENCE JUSTINIAN)

❧ Consider the efficacy of prayer. We have only to pray for lawful things, to pray for them often and perseveringly, and to believe we shall receive them — and receive them, too, not according to the poverty of our poor intentions, but according to the riches and wisdom and munificence of God — and it is an infallible truth that we shall receive them. God is at our disposal. He allows us this almost unbounded influence over Him not once or twice, not merely on feasts or great occasions, but all our lives long. Are there any of the mysteries of grace sweeter than this? (FR. FREDERICK FABER)

❧ Those who pray well never fall into heresy. Those who pray sincerely cannot fail to find the way of salvation. Those who pray unceasingly never lose sight of their complete dependence on God, and never fail to correspond to His grace. (BR. FRANCIS MALUF)

❧ Pray, pray, never cease to pray; for if you pray, your salvation will be secure; but if you leave off praying, your damnation will be certain. There is no doubt of this truth: he who prays obtains grace and is saved. (ST. AUGUSTINE)

❧ We must convince ourselves that all our good depends on prayer. On prayer depends the change of life; on prayer depends the triumph over temptations; on prayer depends the grace of divine love, of perfection, of perseverance, of eternal salvation. Experience proves this. He who has recourse to God triumphs. (ST. ALPHONSUS DE LIGUORI)

❧ He who prays most receives most. (ST. ALPHONSUS DE LIGUORI)

❧ It is the issue of faith that we can achieve more by prayer than by any other kind of activity. (BR. FRANCIS MALUF)

ON PRAYING WELL

❧ He prays best who does not know that he is praying. (ST. ANTHONY OF THE DESERT)

❧ Look at the incredible ease of prayer. Every time, place, posture is fitting; for there is no time, place, or posture in and by which we cannot reverently confess the Presence of God. Talent is not needed. Eloquence is out of place. Dignity is no recommendation. Our want is our eloquence, our misery our recommendation. Thought is quick as lightning, and quick as lightning it can multiply effectual prayer.

Actions can pray; sufferings can pray. There need be no ceremonies; there are no rubrics to keep. The whole function is expressed in a word; it is simply this — the child at his Father's knee, his words stumbling over each other from very earnestness, and his wistful face pleading better than his hardly intelligible prayer. (FR. FREDERICK FABER)

❧ Do not put yourself in misery by forcing yourself to any kind of exercise while praying. If you are tired on your knees, sit down; if you have not enough attention to pray for half an hour, pray a quarter of an hour. Do not worry that you do not perform well the acts of the virtues because your acts are still very good even though they are done without fervor, tardily, and, as it were, through force. You can give nothing to God except what you have. Do not torment yourself by trying to do a great deal, but dispose yourself to do with love that which you do. (ST. FRANCIS DE SALES)

❧ Let us think of where we pray. Whether it is in a consecrated place or not, it is in God Himself. We are in the midst of Him, as fish are in the sea. His immensity is our temple. His ear lies close upon our lips; it touches them. We do not feel it; if we did, we should die. It is always listening. Thoughts speak to it as loudly as words, sufferings even louder than words. His ear is never taken away. We sigh into it even while we sleep and dream. (FR. FREDERICK FABER)

❧ Prayer consists not in much thinking, but in much loving. (ST. TERESA OF ÁVILA)

❧ Neither feeling, nor consolation, nor sighs, nor transports, nor the continual attention of the imagination are needed to pray well; faith and good intentions are quite enough. (ST. LOUIS MARIE DE MONTFORT)

❧ Weary not, neither be slothful, but be ever strong in thy combats, call constantly upon the heavenly King for help, and thou shalt have God Himself for a Teacher in thy prayer. We cannot procure for ourselves the gift of sight by our own exertions, for it is a gift of nature. So also in the science of prayer God is Himself our Teacher, and gives the gift of prayer to him who is faithful in prayer. (ST. JOHN CLIMACUS)

❧ There are very few invariable rules in the spiritual life, but this is one: pray in the way that you like best. (REV. DANIEL CONSIDINE)

❧ Remember that every time you are filled with extraordinary sentiments, either of thanksgiving, or the love of God, or of admiration for His kindnesses, or of desire to please Him, or of contempt for the things of earth, or finally, of His presence, you should make them the subject of your prayers, and busy yourself in relishing these feelings and strengthening them.

Enjoy, prolong, increase the desire God gives you of doing something for Him. Make that the subject of your prayer as often as you feel moved by these thoughts. Do not take any other except when your heart is empty of all good thoughts. If it is always occupied with movements — now of admiration, now of desire, of shame, of sorrow, of submission, of contempt for the world, of love of God, of reverence for His presence — you will be able to do without books, and you will be right. (ST. CLAUDE DE LA COLOMBIÈRE)

❧ It is easy to live in My intimacy by conversing with Me. I desire that of each soul. (OUR LORD TO SR. MARY OF THE TRINITY)

PRAYING WITH CONFIDENCE

❧ Whatsoever things ye seek, when ye pray, believe that ye shall receive them, and they shall be given you. (OUR LORD JESUS CHRIST)

❧ Ask little and thou shalt obtain much. God does not stoop to measure His gifts, nor to proportion them to our merits, or even to our prayers. He gives freely, without stint. He loves to give what man has not even thought of asking. For God is good, and He is generous. He is almighty, and His mercy knows no bounds. (MSGR. JEAN-JOSEPH GUAME)

❧ The more we submit to God's will, the more He tries to meet our wishes. It would seem that as soon as we make it our sole aim to obey Him, He on His part does His best to try and please us. Not only does He answer our prayers, but He even forestalls them by granting the very desires we endeavored to stifle in our hearts in order to please Him, and in a measure we never imagined. (ST. CLAUDE DE LA COLOMBIÈRE)

❧ When we pray and are heard, it seems to us that the will of God inclines toward us; on the contrary, it is *our* will which rises; we begin to will in time what God willed for us from all eternity. (FR. REGINALD GARRIGOU-LAGRANGE)

❧ If you want God to give you what you ask, either for yourself or for anyone else, love Him ardently, and ask always for what is to His greater glory. Love your neighbor and the welfare of your own soul, and be sure He will grant you all you need, for He loves us with an infinite love, and knows what we need. So that, really, we hardly require to ask or to wish for anything, but we can leave the care of ourselves to God, and everything will go right. (ST. ALPHONSUS RODRIGUEZ)

❧ Pray quite definitely and absolutely, for whatever you think God wishes you to pray for, whether for yourself or others; and make up your mind that you will get it, not because you deserve it, but because God is so good. (DOM JOHN CHAPMAN)

❧ God will never refuse a confident prayer. Our hope and confidence are, as it were, the coins by which we can purchase all His graces. God Himself values our confidence exceedingly and bestows His gifts on us in proportion to our confidence. (FR. MICHAEL MÜLLER)

❧ The graces of My mercy are drawn by means of one vessel only, and that is — trust. The more the soul trusts, the more it will receive. Souls that trust boundlessly are a great comfort to Me because I pour all the treasures of My graces into them. I rejoice that they ask for much because it is My desire to give much, very much. (OUR LORD TO ST. FAUSTINA)

❧ Pray, hope, and don't worry. Anxiety doesn't help at all. Our Merciful Lord will listen to your prayer. (ST. PIO OF PIETRELCINA)

❧ We ought to be persuaded that what God refuses to our prayer, He grants to our salvation. (ST. AUGUSTINE)

PRAYING WITH PERSEVERANCE

❧ It is a strange fact that although Christ repeatedly and solemnly promised to answer our prayers, most Christians are continually complaining that He does not do so. We cannot account for this by saying that the reason is because of the kind of things we ask for, since He included everything in His promise — *All things whatsoever you shall ask.* Nor can we attribute it to the unworthiness of those who ask, for His promise extended to everybody without exception—"Whosoever asks shall receive." Why is it, then, that so many prayers remain unanswered? Can it be that, as most people are never satisfied, they make such excessive and impatient demands on God that they tire and annoy Him by their importunity? The case is just the opposite. The only reason why we obtain so little from God is because we ask for so little and are not insistent enough. (ST. CLAUDE DE LA COLOMBIÈRE)

❧ If you want all your prayers to be answered without fail, if you want to oblige God to meet all your wishes, the first thing is never to stop praying. Once we have really understood just how far God's goodness extends, we can never believe that we have been refused or that He wishes to deprive us of hope. Rather, the more He makes us keep on asking for something we want, the more confident we should feel that we shall eventually obtain it. (ST. CLAUDE DE LA COLOMBIÈRE)

❧ I address myself to those faithful souls kneeling in prayer before the altar of God and asking for the graces He is so pleased to hear us asking for: you who are happy that God has shown you the vanity of the world, you who groan under the yoke of your passions and beg to be delivered from them, you who burn with desire to love God and serve Him as He would be served, you who intercede with God for the sake of one who is dear to you — do not grow weary of asking, but be steadfast and tireless in your demands. If you are refused today, tomorrow you will obtain everything; if this year brings nothing, the next will bring you abundance. Never think your efforts are wasted. Your every word is numbered, and what you receive will be in measure of the time you have spent asking. Your treasure is piling up, and suddenly one day it will overflow to an extent beyond your dreams. (ST. CLAUDE DE LA COLOMBIÈRE)

❧ God's munificence is shown in His making us seek and ask for, over a long period of time, the grace which He wishes to give us, and quite often, the more precious the grace, the longer He takes to grant it. There are three reasons why He does this: first, to increase the grace still more; second, to make the recipient more deeply appreciate it; third, to make the recipient very careful indeed not to lose it — for people do not appreciate things they get quickly or with very little trouble. (ST. LOUIS MARIE DE MONTFORT)

❧ When God delays in giving, He does not deny the gifts but makes them more agreeable. Things long desired are sweeter; those that are quickly given, spoil. By asking and seeking, the desire of attaining grows. (ST. AUGUSTINE)

❧ God deferred for twenty years to hear the prayers of St. Joachim and St. Ann. In the end He accorded them more than they had asked of Him. For they prayed only to be delivered from the confusion caused by their barrenness, and He honored them with the most glorious fecundity ever known upon earth. They asked of Him but one child, and He gave them an innumerable multitude, making them father and mother of all the faithful. They sought of God a child who would comfort and sustain their declining years; and He gave them a daughter who would be the honor, the joy, the love, and delight of all Heaven and earth. They asked for a child like unto all other children of Adam, and He granted them a daughter like unto the angels in purity and sanctity; one who, from the first moment of Her life, should be more ardent in Her love for God than the highest seraph. They asked of God a child to bring up in His holy fear, that might become a worthy servant of the Most High; and they received a daughter who would be Mother of the Son of God and Queen of all creation. (ST. JOHN EUDES)

❧ Consider the workings of Divine Providence, and think that the refusal you meet with is only God's stratagem to increase your fervor. With what tenderness does He repulse those whom He wishes most to be indulgent to, hiding His clemency under the mask of cruelty! Take care not to be deceived by it. The more He seems to be unwilling, the more you must insist. (ST. CLAUDE DE LA COLOMBIÈRE)

❧ Do not lose courage when you have begun so well to struggle with God. Do not give Him a moment's rest. He loves the violence of your attack and wants to be overcome by you. Make importunity your watchword; let persistence be a miracle in you. Compel God to throw off His mask and say to you with admiration, "Great is thy faith! Be it done as thou wishest. I can no longer resist you; you shall have what you desire in this life and the next." (ST. CLAUDE DE LA COLOMBIÈRE)

❧ I always end by yielding to those who ask with perseverance. (OUR LORD TO SR. MARY OF THE TRINITY)

❧ Providence defers its assistance only to excite our confidence. If our Heavenly Father does not always grant what we ask, it is to keep us near Him and to give us occasion of pressing Him by a loving violence. (ST. FRANCIS DE SALES)

❧ The Lord often denies what we wish for, that He may give us what we would prefer. (ST. AUGUSTINE)

❧ How often have we murmured against the good God because He has refused our petitions or frustrated our plans. Can we look into the future as God can do? Can we see now and realize the full effect our request would have if granted? God loves us; He loves us too dearly to leave us to the guidance of our poor judgments; and when He turns a deaf ear to our entreaties, it is as a tender Father would treat the longings of a child for what would work him harm. (FR. WILLIAM DOYLE)

PRAYING WITH CHILDLIKE SIMPLICITY

❧ Speak to Me about everything in a completely simple and human way; by this you will give Me great joy. This simple language of your heart is more pleasing to Me than the hymns composed in My honor. Know, My child, that the simpler your speech is, the more you attract Me to yourself. (OUR LORD TO ST. FAUSTINA)

❧ Hold converse with God, the Blessed Virgin, and the saints; speak to them of all your affairs; ask with trust for what you need. I am often faced with difficulties, sometimes of such a nature that I cannot ask the advice of others. At such times I wait impatiently for the time of meditation, and then I make the difficulty the subject of my prayer. I speak to God and the Blessed Virgin about it, just as if I saw Them. I explain my difficulty, and then I ask Them how I am to solve it. With Them I discuss the pros and cons, and when meditation comes to an end, I see very clearly what I am to do. Above all, act with deep simplicity with Our Lord and all the heavenly court; make known to Them your needs and anxieties. They know our difficulties, but They act as did the risen Christ with the disciples at Emmaus. He wished to hear from their own lips the story of their doubts and worries. (VEN. ADOLPH PETIT)

❧ We ought to pray like little children of four years old, who have no guile. They tell their Mother everything. (ST. JOHN MARIE VIANNEY)

PRAYING TO OUR LADY

❧ The life of union with Mary, especially when it includes the communication of our thoughts and feelings to Her, develops naturally into a life of evangelical childhood. (FR. EMILE NEUBERT)

✾ Tell your Mother everything that disturbs or impresses you. She understands the turmoil in the depth of your heart; She understands what you yourself cannot understand. Are you sad? Share your affliction with Her, and She will help you to endure it or will change it into joy. Are you happy? Tell Her your happiness, and She will intensify and purify it. Do you feel discouraged? Lay your fears and failures before Her, and She will obtain real success for you. Have you been successful in an enterprise? Go and thank Her for it and ask Her to assure the fruits of your labor. Are you unable to make a choice in the midst of your perplexities? Consult Her; She will enlighten and guide you. Are you without strength and willpower? Come closer to Her and renew your energy. (FR. EMILE NEUBERT)

✾ Tell Her not only your profound emotions but even the simple impressions and reflections which your ordinary occupations suggest. Does not a child act in that way with its mother? And do you not believe Christ acted in that way when He was near His Mother?

In these incessant communications with Mary, you do not need many words. How often does it not happen that children let their mother know their feelings and their needs by just crying, "Mother!" and then looking at her with pleading eyes. On such occasions a mother has a wonderful intuition of what is meant. Better than any other mother, Mary knew what the Child Jesus meant when He uttered Her name or looked at Her. And Her look answered His. Oh, what infinite joy it was for Her and for Him!

In order to tell Mary your needs or your feelings, say to Her simply, "Mother!" and look at Her a moment, put-

ting into that name all you wish to tell Her: a protesta-
tion of love, an offering of your work, a cry of distress, a
word of gratitude, your joy or your sorrow. Your Mother
will understand and answer as only She can. (FR. EMILE
NEUBERT)

❧ Know that I promise graciously to hear all those who
ask any favor of Me in Mary's name, though they may be
sinners, if only they have the will to amend their lives. (OUR
LORD TO ST. BRIDGET OF SWEDEN)

❧ Let us not doubt whether Mary will hear us when we
address our prayers to Her. It is Her delight to exercise Her
powerful influence with God in obtaining for us whatever
graces we stand in need of. She is very desirous that we
should have recourse to Her that She may save us. (ST.
ALPHONSUS DE LIGUORI)

❧ You may be absolutely sure that any favor you ask of
Mary will be granted unless it might prove harmful. (ST.
JOHN BOSCO)

❧ It is sufficient to ask favors of Mary to obtain them. (ST.
ALPHONSUS DE LIGUORI)

❧ Every time you desire something, ask your Mother to
make Her intentions in the matter come true, and rest
assured, infallibly so, that you will either get what you desire
or something better; and that you will get it not according
to your own narrow views, but according to those of Her
immense love. (FR. EMILE NEUBERT)

❧ A prayer raised up to God through the hands of the
Immaculata cannot possibly remain unanswered. (ST. MAX-
IMILIAN KOLBE)

X

THE HOLY ROSARY

*I want you to know that no one can please me
more than by saying the salutation which the
Most Adorable Trinity sent to me, and by which
He raised me to the dignity of the Mother of God.*

(OUR LADY TO ST. MECHTILDE)

THE HAIL MARY

❧ The Hail Mary, said with attention, devotion, and modesty, is, according to the saints, the enemy of the devil which puts him to flight and the hammer which crushes him. (ST. LOUIS MARIE DE MONTFORT)

❧ The Hail Mary is the sanctification of the soul, the joy of the angels, the melody of the predestinate, the canticle of the New Testament, the pleasure of Mary, and the glory of the Most Holy Trinity. (ST. LOUIS MARIE DE MONTFORT)

❧ The Hail Mary is a heavenly dew which fertilizes the soul; a chaste and loving kiss which we give to Mary; a vermilion rose we present to Her; a precious pearl we offer to Her; a chalice of divine ambrosial nectar we proffer to Her. (ST. LOUIS MARIE DE MONTFORT)

❧ The Hail Mary is a blessed dew that falls from Heaven upon the souls of the predestinate. It gives them a marvelous spiritual fertility so that they can grow in all the virtues. The more the garden of the soul is watered by this prayer, the more enlightened one's intellect becomes, the more zealous his heart, and the stronger his armor against his spiritual enemies. (ST. LOUIS MARIE DE MONTFORT)

❧ Let the pious lover of your holy name listen and attend, O Virgin Mary. The heavens rejoice and all the earth ought to stand still when I say, *Hail Mary*. Satan and hell tremble when I say, *Hail Mary*. Sorrow is banished and new joy fills my soul when I say, *Hail Mary*. My languid affection is strengthened in God, and my soul is refreshed when I say, *Hail Mary*. So great is the sweetness of this blessed salutation that it is not to be expressed in words but remains deeper in the heart than can be fathomed. (FR. MICHAEL MÜLLER)

❧ When combined with the pure contemplative prayer of the Rosary meditations, the Hail Mary becomes the most powerful weapon ever placed in the hands of man — a weapon which, through God and His most Blessed Mother, will someday change the face of the earth. (VEN. PATRICK PEYTON)

THE NATURE OF THE ROSARY

❧ The Rosary is the great propagator of Christianity; the sweet nurse and sure preserver of faith, hope, and charity; the indomitable expeller of unbelief, the quick extinguisher of heresies. (FR. MICHAEL MÜLLER)

❧ The Rosary is the infallible remedy for sadness and despair, the universal appeaser of the anger of God, the fruitful mother of tears, the entertaining companion on journeys, the irresistible destroyer of vice, the easy bridge over the high waters of temptation, the impregnable bulwark against all assaults and afflictions, the glorious standard and trophy in war. (FR. MICHAEL MÜLLER)

❧ The Rosary is the substantial food of souls; the fertile source of all virtues; the wide and deep channel of all blessings, spiritual and temporal; the powerful lever of the spiritual life. (FR. MICHAEL MÜLLER)

❧ The Rosary is the patent medicine of the sick, the bright light of understanding, the best riches of the poor, the inexhaustible treasure of all Christians, the never-failing support of widows, the reliable protection of the just. (FR. MICHAEL MÜLLER)

❧ The Rosary is the insupportable torment of the devil, a most acceptable homage to God and the most Blessed Mother of God, the safe seal of virginity, the strong safeguard of nuptial fidelity, the safe harbor in the storms of this life. (FR. MICHAEL MÜLLER)

❧ The Rosary is the city of refuge for sinners, the faithful friend and physician of the dying, the sweet milk of little children, the beautiful crosier of bishops, the unconquerable strength, courage, and persuasive power of priests. (FR. MICHAEL MÜLLER)

❧ The Rosary is the golden key to Heaven, the mother of good counsel, the celebrated school of eloquence, a pious, gentle tyranny towards God, the impenetrable armor of all the faithful, who, when shielded by this heavenly armor, courageously fight and gloriously overcome all their enemies. (FR. MICHAEL MÜLLER)

❧ The Rosary is the scourge of the devil. (POPE ADRIAN VI)

THE POWER OF THE ROSARY

❧ Being human, we easily become tired and slipshod — but the devil makes these difficulties worse when we are saying the Rosary. Before we even begin, he makes us feel bored, distracted, or exhausted—and when we have started praying, he oppresses us from all sides. And when, after much difficulty and many distractions, we have finished, he whispers to us: "What you have just said is worthless. It's only a waste of time to pray without paying attention to what you are saying: half an hour's meditation or some spiritual reading would be much better."

Dear child, do not listen to the devil, but be of good heart even if your imagination has been bothering you throughout your Rosary, as long as you really tried to resist these temptations and get rid of them as soon as they came. Prayer is all the harder when it is (naturally speaking) distasteful to the soul and filled with those annoying little ants and flies running about in your imagination against your will, scarcely allowing you time to enjoy a little peace and appreciate the beauty of what you are saying. But always remember that there is more merit in praying when it is hard than when it is easy. (ST. LOUIS MARIE DE MONTFORT)

❧ When you look at the rosary in your hand it appears very simple, that little string of beads, yet how far that short chain reaches, what a cosmos it encircles, how closely it binds us to God and to Mary. You hold the power to change your lives. (VEN. PATRICK PEYTON)

❧ The decades of the Rosary are like the belt of a machine gun: every bead is a shot, every affection of the soul is an explosion of faith that frightens off the devil, and Mary once more crushes his head. (FR. DOLINDO RUOTOLO)

❧ The Most Holy Virgin, in these last times in which we live, has given a new efficacy to the recitation of the Rosary, to such an extent that there is no problem, no matter how difficult it is, temporal or especially spiritual, in the personal lives of each one of us, of our families, of the families of the world or of religious communities, or even of the lives of peoples and nations, that cannot be solved by the recitation of the Rosary. There is no problem, I tell you, no matter how difficult it is, that we cannot resolve by the prayer of the Holy Rosary. (VEN. LUCIA DOS SANTOS)

⚜ With the Holy Rosary, we will save ourselves. We will sanctify ourselves. We will console Our Lord and obtain the salvation of many souls. (VEN. LUCIA DOS SANTOS)

⚜ You shall obtain all you ask of me by the recitation of the Rosary. (OUR LADY TO BL. ALAN DE LA ROCHE)

⚜ The Rosary shall be a powerful armor against hell; it will destroy vice, decrease sin, and defeat heresies. It will cause virtue and good works to flourish; it will obtain for souls the abundant mercy of God; it will withdraw the hearts of men from the love of the world and its vanities and will lift them to the desire of eternal things. O that souls would sanctify themselves by this means! (OUR LADY TO BL. ALAN DE LA ROCHE)

⚜ Devotion to my Rosary is a great sign of predestination. (OUR LADY TO BL. ALAN DE LA ROCHE)

⚜ If you say the Rosary faithfully until death, I assure you that, in spite of the gravity of your sins, you shall receive a never-fading crown of glory. (OUR LADY TO BL. ALAN DE LA ROCHE)

⚜ When the Rosary is said properly, my power is behind it. Say it with my Divine Son and me in mind, and ask me to bring about the true value of this devotion; then each bead said well can conquer a host of men. (OUR LADY TO VEN. MARY OF AGREDA)

❧ The Rosary is what sustains the little flame of faith that still has not been extinguished in many consciences. Even for those souls who pray without meditating, the very act of taking up the Rosary to pray is already a remembrance of God, of the supernatural. A simple recollection of the mysteries of each decade is one more ray to sustain in souls the still smoldering wick. (VEN. LUCIA DOS SANTOS)

❧ After the Holy Sacrifice of the Mass, there could not be a finer devotion or one of greater merit than that of the Rosary. (OUR LADY TO BL. ALAN DE LA ROCHE)

❧ You will never pray the Rosary in vain. (ST. BERNADETTE)

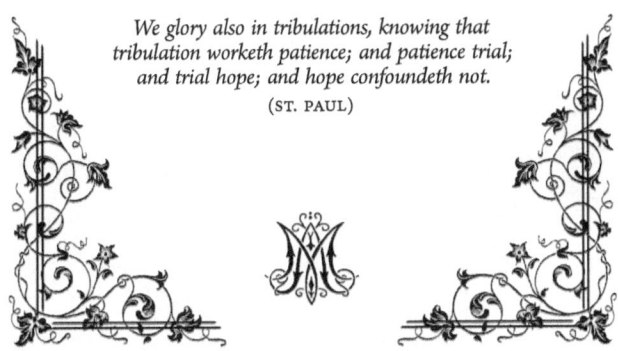

PART TWO

The Perfecting of Hope

*We glory also in tribulations, knowing that
tribulation worketh patience; and patience trial;
and trial hope; and hope confoundeth not.*

(ST. PAUL)

XI

SUFFERING

*The more intense the suffering and the less
apparent to human eyes, the more lovingly
dost Thou smile upon it, O my God.*

(ST. THÉRÈSE OF LISIEUX)

THE VALUE OF SUFFERING

❧ Because nothing about men can escape the universal
contagion of His redeeming grace, there is in mere suffering, in the simple pressure of pain, in the sheer tortures of
mental anguish, in the very weight of labor and weariness
of endurance, a secret underground virtue which is not
without its own peculiar acceptableness to the justice of
God. It is not that He loves to see His creatures suffer,
it is not that His glory can feed itself on mere torments,
which are but irregularities we have brought into His glad
creation, and which formed no part in the primeval plan of
Him Who is Himself an uncreated ocean of joy, a glorious
abyss of unutterable beatitudes. His love gives an inward
dignity even to the most inevitable suffering of the creature. Who can doubt that it is because of Christ and the
luminous shadow of His redeeming Passion, which falls
with a soft light on every human woe and mortal pain
and so mellows them into that beautiful landscape of earth
which God once looked at and blessed for its exceeding
loveliness? Thus He, Who made Mary merit even while
She slept, communicates to us wretched sinners some faint
similitude of that astonishing privilege. Even while we are

concentrated in our sufferings, while pain absorbs us in itself or else distracts us by its vehemence, some sort of dumb sacrifice to the justice of our Creator is rising up from our clouded minds, as if our bed of pain were an altar to His purity, or our broken heart gave out a faint odor of Christ, or our aching limbs were as cinnamon burning in the fire. (FR. FREDERICK FABER)

❧ The souls most pleasing to My Heavenly Father are those that suffer the greatest afflictions and tribulations. (OUR LORD TO ST. TERESA OF ÁVILA)

❧ Suffering itself passes, but the fact of having suffered remains forever. Look at the Blessed Virgin at the foot of the Cross, and you will understand this even better. (CARDINAL MERRY DEL VAL)

❧ Be sure, in My Cross there is salvation. The devil has no real power against those who suffer for My sake. My child, many would have been lost had I not crucified them. (OUR LORD TO ST. GEMMA GALGANI)

❧ There is no exercise more profitable and useful for the soul than to suffer: for suffering gives light, undeceives, detaches the heart from visible things, and raises it up to the Lord. He will come to meet those in suffering, because He is with the afflicted and sends to them His protection and help. (OUR LADY TO VEN. MARY OF AGREDA)

❧ Let us imagine our confusion when we appear before God and understand the reasons why He sent us the crosses we accept so unwillingly. The death of a child will then be seen as its rescue from some great evil had it lived; separation from the woman you love, the means of saving you from an unhappy marriage; a severe illness, the reason for many years of life afterwards; loss of money, the means of saving your soul from eternal loss. So what are we worried about? God is looking out for us, and yet we are full of anxiety! If we could see all He sees, we would unhesitatingly wish all He wishes. We would beg Him on bended knees for those afflictions we now ask Him to spare us. (ST. CLAUDE DE LA COLOMBIÈRE)

❧ Since the Son of God obtained our salvation through suffering, He willed to teach us that there is nothing more fitting than suffering to give glory to God and to sanctify our souls. Yes, suffering for the love of God is the right road. Let us suffer as much as we can, for we will be that much more fortunate. (ST. TERESA OF ÁVILA)

❧ Oh, my children, how can you wish to be freed from your sufferings? Do you not yet know that no mortification is so pleasing to God as the joyful, or at least patient, acceptance of the crosses He imposes? Fasting, watching, and mortifying the flesh are good kinds of penance, but suffering in union with our suffering Lord is incomparably better. (ST. PACHOMIUS)

❧ Look at My whole life, full of suffering, and be persuaded that they whom My Father loves most dearly shall receive from Him the heaviest crosses. The measure of His love is also the measure of the sufferings He sends. How could I better prove My affection for you than by desiring for you that which I desired for Myself? (OUR LORD TO ST. TERESA OF ÁVILA)

❧ A day of suffering born with resignation is worth more than a month of hard work. (ST. FRANCIS DE SALES)

❧ God often grants many and great graces out of regard for the souls who are suffering, and He withholds many punishments because of them. (ST. FAUSTINA)

❧ We ought to conform to God's will in all public calamities such as war, famine, and pestilence, and reverence and adore His judgments with deep humility in the firm belief that, however severe they may seem, the God of infinite goodness would not send such disasters unless some great good were to result from them. Consider how many souls may be saved through tribulation who would otherwise be lost, how many persons through affliction are converted to God and die with sincere repentance for their sins. What may appear a scourge and punishment is often a sign of great grace and mercy. (FR. JEAN BAPTISTE SAINT-JURE)

❧ The everlasting God has, in His wisdom, foreseen from eternity the cross He now sends you as a gift from His inmost Heart. This cross He now sends you, He has considered with His all-knowing eyes, understood with His Divine Mind, tested with His wise justice, warmed with His loving arms, and weighed with His own hands to see that it be not one inch too large and not one ounce too heavy for you. He has blessed it with His Holy Name, anointed it with His grace, perfumed it with His consolation, taken one last glance at you and your courage, and then sent it to you from Heaven, a special greeting from God to you, an alms of His all-merciful love. (ST. FRANCIS DE SALES)

❧ We can imagine the grief of a farmer when a hailstorm has ruined his vineyard. But suppose it was a hailstorm of gold, would his distress still be reasonable? Now, the contempt and other afflictions which fall upon us like showers of hailstones are really showers of gold for the soul that is truly patient. What she gains is infinitely more valuable than what she has lost. Heaven is the home of the tempted, the afflicted, and the despised. (FR. DIEGO ALVAREZ)

SUFFERING WINS HEAVEN FOR US

❧ Lift up thy eyes and see where thou dost belong. Thou dost belong to the Fatherland of the celestial paradise. Thou art here as a stranger guest, a miserable pilgrim; therefore, as a pilgrim hastens back to his home where his dear friends expect him and wait for him with great longing, so shouldst thou desire to hasten back to thy fatherland, where all will be glad to see thee, where all long so ardently for thy joyous presence, that they may greet thee tenderly and unite thee to their blessed society forever. And didst thou but know how they thirst after thee, how they desire that thou shouldst combat devoutly in suffering, and behave chivalrously in all adversity, even such as they have overcome, and how they now with great sweetness remember the cruel years through which they once passed, truly, all suffering would only be the easier to thee, for, the more bitterly thou shalt have suffered, the more honorably wilt thou be received. (BL. HENRY SUSO)

❧ Why do you fear to take up the cross when through it you can win a kingdom? In the cross is salvation; in the cross is life; in the cross is protection from your enemies; in the cross is infusion of heavenly sweetness; in the cross is strength of mind; in the cross is joy of spirit; in the cross is the height of virtue; in the cross is the perfection of sanctity. There is no health of soul, nor hope of eternal life but in the cross. Take up, therefore, your cross and follow Jesus, and you shall go into life everlasting. (FR. THOMAS À KEMPIS)

❧ The sorrows we endure for the love of God are like contracts that we make with Him. For wounds and bruises, He obliges Himself to clothe us with a shining robe; for affronts, He will give us a crown of glory; for prison, the vast empire of Heaven; for the wicked sentence passed against our innocence, we shall hear the praises and benedictions of angels and saints forever. (ST. FRANCIS DE SALES)

✤ If we shall have anything to regret at the moment of death, it will be that the time of suffering for God has passed and, consequently, the means of enriching ourselves are gone. The privilege of suffering is perhaps the only advantage we have above the angels. They may indeed be the companions of Our Lord, but they cannot be the companions of His death. Those blessed intelligences may well appear before the Face of God as victims burning with an ardent charity, but their impassible nature prevents them from giving one generous proof of their affection in the midst of anguish, or receiving that honor which is so sweet to him who loves, to love even to die, and even to die of love. Oh, how great a grace it is to love and to suffer, to love while suffering, and to suffer while loving! Let us never lose one of our crosses, but let us often say to ourselves: "Courage! The time of suffering is short; the love that suffering merits is eternal." (BISHOP JACQUES-BÉNIGNE BOSSUET)

✤ Think not only of the road through which thou art traveling, but take care never to lose sight of that blessed country in which thou art shortly to arrive. Thou meetest here with passing sufferings but wilt soon enjoy everlasting rest. When thou lookest up to the recompense, everything thou dost or sufferest will appear light and no more than a shadow; it bears no proportion with what thou art to receive for it. Thou wilt wonder that so much is given for such trifling pains. (ST. AUGUSTINE)

✤ The longest day has its evening; the hardest work, its ending; and the sharpest pain, its contented and everlasting rest. (FR. FREDERICK FABER)

❧ For one pain endured with joy, we shall love the good God more forever. (ST. THÉRÈSE OF LISIEUX)

❧ Contradictions bring us to the foot of the cross and the cross to the gates of paradise. To arrive there, we must be trampled on, scorned, despised, broken to pieces. Suffering! What does it matter? It will be all over in a moment. If we could only go and spend eight days in heaven, we should understand the value of this momentary suffering; we should find no cross too heavy, no trial too bitter. The cross is the present which God makes to His friends. Let us pray for a love of the cross, then it will become sweet. Oh, when the day of judgment comes, how happy we shall feel on account of our misfortunes in this life, how proud of our humiliations, how rich by reason of our sacrifices! (ST. JOHN MARIE VIANNEY)

❧ The cross is the pledge of happiness. Should I have to support the efforts of the most terrible enemies, to engage in a combat of blood, how long could it last? What sort of fight would it be? A moment of slight contest, almost nothing; and then, a weight of glory, but a weight, the value of which measures an eternity! O my heart, expand thyself at this hope! Not only shalt thou be resigned in thy different trials, but thou shalt exalt with joy at them. I sow, thou shalt say, but what a lovely harvest do I secure! Scepters and crown I shall one day reap. Let my tears flow, since to them is promised so valuable a consolation. Sorrows, avoid me not, as after ye the sweetest joys will come! Let me embrace you, O penance, O mortification, as you are the seed of a glorious resurrection. Yes, I desire to suffer in order to enjoy; I wish to fight in order to conquer. I wish to die to the world, to sin, to myself, that I may live to God, in God, and with God for all eternity. (DON FRANCESCO DE LUCIA)

❧ Blessed are You, O my God, because You have not demanded from us, as the price of Your Kingdom, a long period of suffering, but a very brief one, a moment compared with an eternity of happiness! Truly, if for love of You, we had to endure for hundreds of thousands of years, sufferings a thousand times harder, more painful and severe, we should have accepted Your decree with immense desire and longing, and thanked You on our knees with our hands joined. How much more, then, should we thank You now that, in Your mercy, You have deigned to give a time as short as a life! Short as an instant, as nothing, for life is nothing compared with eternity. (ST. ANGELA OF FOLIGNO)

❧ Judge now whether you should regret the time you spend under the pressure of suffering, since in each one of those moments you may earn an eternal crown. How many crowns in an hour! How many in a day! How many in a year! Oh, what treasures! What glory for Heaven! When we think on eternity, where there will be nothing more to suffer, where we can give nothing more to God, and where God will have nothing more to do but to load us with His gifts, all the miseries of this life appear infinitely amiable, and there is not a moment which we ought not wish to be a moment of the cross or humiliation. How precious then is the time of this life, and how holy is its use, when joined with pain and bitterness! (ST. FRANCIS DE SALES)

SUFFERING AS A MEANS TO HOLINESS

❧ When the wish for suffering comes upon you strongly and without previous effort on your part, it is from God. Do not resist it. (VEN. CORNELIA CONNELLY)

❧ Christian perfection consists in suffering well. To acquire solid virtues, complain not of your pains. Endure contradictions patiently. God gives you an occasion of practicing patience; would you wish to let it escape? Perhaps in your life, you will never meet the like of it again; perhaps it may be the last service you will render to His Divine Majesty. Be constant, and He will bless you in your affliction. (ST. FRANCIS DE SALES)

❧ Suffering is a great grace; through suffering, the soul becomes like the Savior. (ST. FAUSTINA)

❧ If God sends you many sufferings it is a sign that He has great plans for you and certainly wants to make you a saint. If you desire to become a great saint, ask Him to send you much suffering. (ST. IGNATIUS OF LOYOLA)

❧ It would be a very serious illusion to despise or underestimate our daily crosses because they are small. Individually, they are indeed small, but occurring, as they do, almost every instant, by their very multiplicity they provide the faithful soul with an immense sum of merits and sacrifices. Besides, there is nothing to prevent us from welcoming them with extraordinary faith, love, and generosity; and the sanctity of our dispositions will invest them with inestimable worth in the eyes of God. (REV. DOM VITALIS LEHODEY)

❧ Our Lord never sends a cross without rewarding us with some favor when we accept it with resignation. (ST. TERESA OF ÁVILA)

ON SUFFERING WELL
❧

❧ To suffer peacefully, it is enough to really want everything that Jesus wants. (ST. THÉRÈSE OF LISIEUX)

❧ We do not have to like suffering; we do not have to get impatient with ourselves for not wanting it. All we have to do is to *take* it, take it for the good it can do to our lives and for the benefit of those desperate, lonely, totally unhappy men and women who walk so far away from God. (FR. WALTER CISZEK)

❧ You should feel at home with the sufferings which it pleases Jesus to send you, since you always have to live with them. Acting thus, you think less of being freed from them. Jesus, Who cannot bear long to keep you in affliction, will come to relieve and comfort you by infusing fresh courage into your soul. (ST. PIO OF PIETRELCINA)

❧ This blow is a cruel one, you will say; He strikes too hard. *Yet* what do you have to fear from a hand that was pierced and nailed to the Cross for you? The path I tread is full of thorns, you will say. Yet is it not the same path He trod before you out of love for you? Is there a thorn in it that He has not reddened with His own Blood? (ST. CLAUDE DE LA COLOMBIÈRE)

❧ The chalice He offers you is a bitter one. But remember that it is your Redeemer Who offers it. Loving you as He does, could He bring Himself to treat you so severely if the need were not urgent, the gain not worthwhile? (ST. CLAUDE DE LA COLOMBIÈRE)

❧ If we could discover the designs of Providence, it is certain we would ardently long for the evils we are now so unwilling to suffer. We would rush forward to accept them with the utmost gratitude, if we had a little faith and realized how much God loves us and has our interests at heart. (ST. CLAUDE DE LA COLOMBIÈRE)

※ We should even make an effort to mount so high as to love our crosses, since it is God Himself Who has fashioned them for us, and Who still fashions them for us every day. Let us leave ourselves completely in His hands: He alone knows what is suitable for each of us. If we remain thus steadfast, submissive, and humble under all the crosses He sends us, we shall find in them at last, if He judges proper, the true rest of our souls. Then shall we enjoy an imperturbable peace when, by our docility, we shall have merited that God should make us experience the altogether divine unction attached to the cross since the hour Jesus Christ died upon it for the salvation of us sinners. (FR. JEAN PIERRE DE CAUSSADE)

※ It is for us to console Our Lord, and not for Him to be always consoling us. His Heart is so tender that if you cry, He will dry your tears; but afterwards He will go away sad, since you did not suffer Him to repose tranquilly within you. Our Lord loves the glad of heart, the children that greet Him with a smile. When will you learn to hide your troubles from Him, or to tell Him gaily that you are happy to suffer for Him? (ST. THÉRÈSE OF LISIEUX)

FINDING JOY IN THE CROSS

❊

※ Though we would strenuously deny it if charged with it, we do in fact behave as if God Himself had been taken off His guard by the Fall, as if He had not quite got the situation in hand. To be more than resigned, to embrace the cross with joy, we must not see it as an emergency measure, but as part of the eternal rhythm of the invincible will of the Father Who ordains all things, even the most minute and insignificant, with fatherly love. (MSGR. VERNON JOHNSON)

✛ We never have a greater reason to rejoice than when we are oppressed and burdened by sufferings and afflictions, because these render us similar to Christ Our Lord, and this resemblance is a true sign of our predestination. (ST. VINCENT DE PAUL)

✛ When God wills you to begin truly to suffer and sends you what you would most avoid suffering, then you may be confident that you are loved by Him and may hope with joy to see the face of the Lord. (ST. JOHN OF ÁVILA)

✛ If anyone be afflicted with Christ, Christ will most lovingly smile upon him; if with Christ he be nailed to the cross, Christ, extending His arms most tenderly, doth embrace him; if he bow down his head in compassion with Christ, Christ, raising His head most sweetly, doth console him. (ST. BERNARD)

✛ Oh, if only the suffering soul knew how it is loved by God, it would die of joy and excess of happiness! Someday we will know the value of suffering, but then we will no longer be able to suffer. The present moment is ours. (ST. FAUSTINA)

✛ He who embraces the cross and bears it with patience lightens the weight of the cross. Indeed, the weight itself becomes a consolation; for God abounds with grace to all those who carry the cross with good will in order to please Him. (ST. ALPHONSUS DE LIGUORI)

✛ As valiant knights of our Imperial Lord, let us not lose heart. As noble followers of our Venerable Leader, let us be of good cheer and rejoice to suffer. For if there were no other profit and good in suffering than that we became more like the fair, bright mirror, Christ, our sufferings would be well laid out. (BL. HENRY SUSO)

❧ Trials, disappointments, failures, humiliations, sufferings of body and soul may crowd upon you, at least from time to time; but if you welcome them all as coming directly from His hand, you will find a sweetness and a delight in these things you never tasted before. (FR. WILLIAM DOYLE)

❧ We are on earth to suffer. The more we suffer, the happier we are. (ST. THÉRÈSE OF LISIEUX)

❧ O you who want to walk in security and in consolation, if you only knew how pleasing suffering is to God, and how helpful it is in acquiring other benefits, you would never seek consolations in anything, but rather would deem it a great joy to carry the cross in the footsteps of Jesus. (ST. JOHN OF THE CROSS)

❧ What Jesus prefers above all are the roses of suffering; and your preoccupation must be to collect many of these roses to offer to Him. My child, I am going to tell you a secret so that little Jesus will prefer your roses above all others: each time you pick a flower, do it always in such a way that there is nothing lifeless or faded; take care that it is always very fresh. My child, I mean that at times of suffering, of whatever nature, you must remain always joyful. Should it happen that you shed tears, that is not important. If you love Jesus in peace and joy, the flowers that you will gather for Him will sparkle by their beauty and freshness. What is more, these flowers kept in the fire of love will last a long time, and little Jesus will be able to make use of them when He wishes to enjoy them. My child, is that not worthwhile? (OUR LADY TO BR. MARCEL VAN)

THE LITTLE VICTIMS OF GOD'S MERCIFUL LOVE

❧ Will not Almighty God, to Whom we surrender ourselves by the oblation to Merciful Love, at least avail Himself of it to send crosses and trials without measure?

Without measure? Certainly not! The trials willed by the Almighty are never willed without measure, but always proportioned to the supernatural energies which an ever-preventing grace has been careful to develop previously in the soul. There is always proportion between the trial and the divine help. (REV. GABRIEL MARTIN)

❧ The designs of Providence are not the same for all the little victims of Merciful Love, and there are some amongst them who shall know neither those great trials nor those great desires of suffering. They shall be none the less true victims of holocaust, most pleasing to God, for, according to the judgment of St. Thérèse, it is not these desires which delight the Heart of Our Lord. What most pleases Him in a soul is to see her love her littleness; it is the blind trust she has in His goodness. Love of suffering is merely an accidental effect of the martyrdom of Love. (REV. GABRIEL MARTIN)

❧ Pain makes a small child run to its mother more quickly than anything else. In her arms, its pain, although not taken away, becomes the means of his experiencing an especially tender embrace that he otherwise would not have known. In terms of St. Thérèse's teaching, the parallel is clear. So far from trying to meet pain with his own strength, or imagining that God has abandoned him, the childlike soul immediately relates his suffering to his Father's love and throws himself into the divine arms, where he finds himself drawn very close indeed to his Crucified Lord. (MSGR. VERNON JOHNSON)

MARY'S ROLE IN OUR SUFFERING

❧ Mary, the Mother of the living, gives to all Her children portions of the Tree of Life, which is the Cross of Jesus. But along with their crosses, She also imparts the grace to carry them patiently, even cheerfully. And thus it is that the crosses which She lays on those who belong to Her are rather steeped in sweetness than filled with bitterness. (ST. LOUIS MARIE DE MONTFORT)

❧ Hear and let it penetrate into your heart: Let nothing discourage you, nothing depress you. Let nothing alter your heart or your countenance. Also, do not fear any illness or vexation, anxiety or pain. Am I not here who am your Mother? Are you not under my shadow and protection? Am I not your fountain of life? Are you not in the crossing of my arms? Is there anything else you need? (OUR LADY OF GUADALUPE)

XII

SACRIFICE

*I can do all things in Him Who strengthens
me and through the Immaculata.*

(ST. MAXIMILIAN KOLBE)

LET US BE GENEROUS WITH GOD

❧ I think it evident that, in these awful days of sin and
hatred of God, our Blessed Lord wants to gather round
Him a legion of chosen souls who will be devoted, heart
and soul, to His interests, and upon whom He may always
count for help and consolation. Souls who will not ask,
"How much *must* I do?" but rather "How much *can* I do for
His love?" A legion of souls who will give and not count
the cost, whose only pain will be that they cannot do more
and give more and suffer more for Him Who has done so
much for them. In a word, souls who are not as the rest of
men, for their watchword is *sacrifice* and not self-comfort.

Now, my dear child, our Divine Savior seems to have
turned His eyes of love upon you, and asked if you are
willing to join. It should make your heart bound with joy
to think that He has given you such a loving call; for if
only you are faithful to Him and exact in following His
inspirations, He will raise you to a height of sanctity you
do not dare to dream of now. (FR. WILLIAM DOYLE)

❧ If I ask you for things that cost, know that at the same
time I will give you all the grace and strength you need
to conquer yourself. (OUR LORD TO SR. JOSEFA MENÉNDEZ)

❧ Those who wish to follow My way must renounce their own will everywhere and in everything. Do what you do not wish to do; leave undone that which you wish to do. One act of violence to oneself of this kind is much more pleasing to Me than an entire year of penances. (OUR LORD TO BL. ANNA MARIA TAIGI)

❧ How I hunger for souls, for their fidelity, for their generosity. Would they satisfy that eager hunger by a little victory over self or by a slight mortification? Would they comfort Me in My sorrow by their tenderness and compassion? In some hard moment, would they endure the pain, neglect, scorn, oppositions, grief of soul? Would they come to Me and say: "This I offer Thee to console Thy sadness, to keep Thee company in Thy solitude"? Oh! If they would thus unite themselves to Me, with what peace would they face difficulties, how much fortitude they would win, and how they would gladden My Heart! (OUR LORD TO SR. JOSEFA MENÉNDEZ)

❧ The more sacrifices cost you, the more you must concentrate on making them cheerfully. Never miss an opportunity. If you only knew the value Jesus sets on even the tiniest act of self-denial, you would grasp at every opportunity like a miser going after treasure. (ST. THÉRÈSE OF LISIEUX)

❧ The more this generous spirit of self-sacrifice springs up in your heart, the nearer and dearer will you become to Jesus. Love for Love. Blood for Blood. Life for Life. Will you give Him all? What do the sacrifices of the past cost you now? The future may never come, and so you have only the suffering of the moment to bear for His dear sake. (FR. WILLIAM DOYLE)

❧ We must not turn away from the opportunities of little daily martyrdom which present themselves. We run away when we do not do all that God asks of us, when we resist His grace and inspirations, when we close our eyes so as not to see the light which clearly reveals some sacrifice to be made, some duty to perform. Take the sword bravely; give yourself neither rest nor truce in the battles of life. This is how we obtain true peace, and how our secret martyrdom will become glorious. (MOTHER AGNES OF JESUS)

❧ If only you knew how much you gain by every act of sacrifice. What you gain is not lost, but the enjoyment—increased a thousandfold—is only postponed. (FR. WILLIAM DOYLE)

❧ As a rule, you will find that when you do the hard thing just because it is hard, great consolation and love always follow. (FR. WILLIAM DOYLE)

❧ If you do a bad thing with pleasure, the pleasure passes and the badness remains; if you wearily do a good thing, the weariness passes and the good remains. (ST. CAMILLUS DE LELLIS)

❧ Remember that sacrifice exists in the will; although force of habit may dull the sting of sacrifice, the merit lasts and increases with the repetition of the sacrifice. (ST. PETER JULIAN EYMARD)

NO SACRIFICE IS TOO SMALL

❧ The smallest thing, when done for the love of God, is priceless. (ST. TERESA OF ÁVILA)

❧ Be generous with God. The good Master will, even in this life, generously repay the little sacrifices you make for His love. (SR. LOUISE VANDERSCHRIEK)

🕸 Try to remember that nothing is too small, too small to offer to Him—that is, the tiniest act of self-conquest is of immense value in His eyes, and even lifting one's eyes as an act of love brings great grace. (FR. WILLIAM DOYLE)

🕸 Look upon nothing as too small to offer to God. Big sacrifices do not come very often, and generally we are too cowardly to make them when they do. But little ones are as plentiful as blackberries in September and stiffen the moral courage by the constant repetition of them, to do, in the end, even heroic things. (FR. WILLIAM DOYLE)

🕸 Remember above all that even one small victory makes up for a hundred defects. (FR. WILLIAM DOYLE)

THE IMPORTANCE OF SACRIFICE IN THE WAY OF SPIRITUAL CHILDHOOD

🕸 True love thrives on sacrifice. The more the soul denies itself its natural inclinations, the stronger and more disinterested becomes its tenderness. (ST. THÉRÈSE OF LISIEUX)

🕸 Calls to little sacrifices also come by way of our dealing with others: the call to sacrifice our own point of view when no principle is at stake; the failure of the hopes we had placed in others; their lack of gratitude, lack of response; the spoiling of what we imagined God's will to be by other people's mistakes or lack of vision. As these things are inescapable and painful to self-love, we often let them rankle in our minds; we wrap ourselves up in a garment of self-pity and become irritable and discontented. St. Thérèse liberates us from all this. She shows us that these occasions of sacrifice, far from being things to avoid, are providentially arranged by Our Lord and carefully proportioned to our powers to be opportunities to be snatched up as a means to show our love and gratitude to our Heavenly Father. (MSGR. VERNON JOHNSON)

❧ Offer to God the sacrifice of never gathering any fruit off your tree. If it be His will that throughout your whole life you should feel a repugnance to suffering and humiliation — if He permits all the flowers of your desires and of your good will to fall to the ground without any fruit appearing, do not worry. At the hour of death, in the twinkling of an eye, He will cause rich fruits to ripen on the tree of your soul. (ST. THÉRÈSE OF LISIEUX)

XIII

TRIALS

Great trials prepare us for the reception of great graces;
the latter never come except in the wake of the former.
(ST. BERNARD)

SEEING OUR TRIALS IN LIGHT OF ETERNITY

❧ Do you know why God keeps you under such difficulties and afflictions? It is because He intends to make you rich in Heaven. Short and momentary is this suffering, but the joy will be eternal. (ST. PAUL OF THE CROSS)

❧ We say sometimes that God chastises those whom He loves. That is not true. Trials are not chastisements; they are graces to those whom God loves. We must not consider so much the labor but the recompense. What are twenty, thirty years compared to eternity? What then have we to suffer? (ST. JOHN MARIE VIANNEY)

❧ Generally speaking, one day of adversity can be of more profit to us for our eternal salvation than years of untroubled living, whatever good use we make of the time. (ST. CLAUDE DE LA COLOMBIÈRE)

❧ The best passport to Heaven is trial accepted with resignation, because when one knows how to suffer, one loves very much, and it is love which merits from Our Lord the best recompense. (VEN. MOTHER CATHERINE AURELIA)

❧ Look up to Heaven every day, especially in time of trial or temptation. Heaven is well worth every suffering and every sacrifice and every combat required of us, and even a thousand times more! Life is short; its trials, its sufferings, its labors, its combats, its crosses also are short and transitory; but Heaven and its joys are inconceivable, never-ending, and satiating every desire of the heart. (FR. MARTIN VON COCHEM)

GOD WILL NEVER TRY US
BEYOND OUR STRENGTH
❧

❧ If the most ignorant men know the burdens that their poor horses or asses are able to carry and do not put on too heavy a load for fear of overpowering them; if the potter knows how long the clay should remain in the furnace in order to be heated to that degree which renders it fit for use, and does not leave it for a moment more or less; we cannot possibly have reflected, or we should not dare to say that God, Who is wisdom itself, and Who loves us with an infinite love, lays upon our shoulders a weight that is too heavy, or leaves us too long in the fire of tribulation. Let us then be without uneasiness. The fire will not be greater nor of longer duration than is required to heat our clay to the necessary degree. (ST. EPHREM)

❧ God measures our affliction to our need. (ST. JOHN CHRYSOSTOM)

GRATITUDE AND RESIGNATION
IN THE MIDST OF OUR TRIALS
❧

❧ Be grateful to God for coming to you by trials, for you are very fortunate. If only we knew the value of suffering, we would fall on our knees and with suppliant hands ask it of God. (ST. ANDRÉ BESSETTE)

❧ If some great misfortune should actually happen, instead of wasting time in complaint or self-pity, go throw yourself at once at the feet of your Savior and implore His grace to bear your trial with fortitude and patience. Let this be your first thought. Go and report to Him what He has done to you. Kiss the hands of God crucified, the hands that have struck you and caused you to suffer. Repeat over and over again to Him His own words to His Father while He was suffering: *Not My will, but Thine be done.* Only wait awhile and you will see that by this misfortune God is preparing you to receive the greatest marks of His favor. (ST. CLAUDE DE LA COLOMBIÈRE)

❧ Accept your trial willingly. Shut your eyes and go ahead from moment to moment, trusting in the mercy of the Lord, without looking ahead and without questioning anything. Your virtue will, as a result, be much more solid and meritorious than it would be in moments of comfort. Let Jesus work in your soul in whatever way He desires, while you remain at His feet, resigned and satisfied. (CARDINAL MERRY DEL VAL)

❧ Surrender yourself completely to the divine will of God, without setting limits either to the duration or the nature of your trials. Let your patience be long-suffering and trustful because, although you truly suffer, these sufferings do not come to you from an enemy, but from your greatest Friend — from God, Who loves you so much more than you could love yourself, Who wills your good, your happiness, your sanctification much more than you could ever desire them. Hope in Him blindly, and you will never be confounded; entrust yourself to Him blindly, and you will have nothing to fear. (FR. GABRIEL OF ST. MARY MAGDALEN)

❧ *My eyes are always on the Lord, for He will free my feet from pits and snares.* Have you fallen into the snares of trials? Regard not your misfortune; look only to God; He will have care of you. *Cast thy care on Him, and He will provide for thee.* Why trouble yourself by sighing or pining about the accidents of this world, since you know not what you ought to wish for, and God will always wish what is best for you? Await, then, in repose of spirit, the effects of the divine good pleasure, and let it suffice for you since it is always good. (ST. FRANCIS DE SALES)

❧ Be it known that, in the eyes of God, one gains more merit in a single day through trials given us by God and neighbor, than in ten years of penances and other practices chosen by us. (ST. TERESA OF ÁVILA)

TRIALS PERFECT
OUR UNION WITH CHRIST

❧ Do you doubt for a moment that God has great designs upon your soul? The clear and consoling proof is the terrible trial you are going through. (FR. WILLIAM DOYLE)

❧ The longer the trial to which God subjects you, the greater His goodness in comforting you during the time of trial and in exalting you after the combat. (ST. PIO OF PIETRELCINA)

❧ What a joy to remember that every tiny thing done for God — an act, a word, a glance, even — brings fresh grace to the soul, makes it partake more and more of the nature of God. Our Lord longs for this transformation, and so He sends us many hard trials to hasten the day of this perfect union. Let Him, then, have His way. You can have perfect confidence that He is doing the right thing ever and always.

Holiness is really nothing more than perfect conformity to God's will, and so every step in this direction must please Him immensely. (FR. WILLIAM DOYLE)

❦ How much we need trials to do the work of God within our soul! The good God has an immense desire to enrich us with His graces, but we regulate their measure which is in proportion to our submission to His immolation of us — a joyful immolation, and a thankful one, like that of Jesus, in which we say with Him, *The chalice which My Father hath given Me, shall I not drink it?* The Divine Master called the hour of the Passion *the cause for which He had come* and for which He had longed. When some great suffering or insignificant sacrifice offers itself, let us think at once that this is our hour, the hour in which we are to prove our love for Him Who has loved us with an *exceeding charity*. (ST. ELIZABETH OF THE TRINITY)

❦ Never does our good God leave us save to hold us tighter; never does He let go of us save to keep us closer; never does He wrestle with us save to give Himself up to us and bless us. (ST. FRANCIS DE SALES)

❦ God's arms are more closely folded round us in interior trials than in the sensible sweetnesses of His consoling visitations. (FR. FREDERICK FABER)

MARY WILL AID US IN OUR TRIALS

❦ If, for awhile, Mary's children feel the bitterness of the cup which one must drink in order to be the friend of God, the consolation and joy which this good Mother sends after the trial encourage them exceedingly to carry heavier and more painful crosses. (ST. LOUIS MARIE DE MONTFORT)

❧ Have no confidence in yourself, but in all your temptations and trials surrender yourself to the Immaculata, and surely you will triumph. (ST. MAXIMILIAN KOLBE)

❧ Mary wills that we accept trials with complete resignation to the will of God, believing in God's and Her own wisdom and goodness. But resignation will not be enough. Are we satisfied to be resigned to the favors our Heavenly Mother obtains for us? We should submit rather with joy and thankfulness because it is love that has sent us a trial for our greater spiritual profit. No matter what the trial, we will smile at the test, perhaps even as we weep bitterly, but smile nevertheless, believing in the love of Her who, through ways mysterious and supremely wise, leads us to union with Her Son. (FR. EMILE NEUBERT)

XIV

TEMPTATIONS

*All the temptations of hell cannot stain
a soul that does not love them.*

(ST. FRANCIS DE SALES)

TEMPTATIONS ARE NOT
SINFUL IN THEMSELVES

❧ Temptation is a horrible thing. It makes an impression on you; you actually feel an inclination for the evil suggested. No matter. The impression is only a sentiment. It humbles you, but it does not make you guilty. To be sensible of evil is not to consent to it. All that happens in the inferior part of the soul—imaginations, memories, feelings, irregular motions, etc.—all that is *in* us but not *from* us. Of itself it is indeliberate and involuntary. It can only become sin by our free consent. (REV. DOM VITALIS LEHODEY)

❧ However strong may be the suggestions of the demon, in whatever form appear the phantoms that flit through the imagination, so long as your will rejects them, instead of soiling your soul, they rather make it more pure and pleasing to God. (REV. DOM VITALIS LEHODEY)

❧ It is often the purest souls who are the most assailed by temptations and kept in spiritual darkness. They think that they have lost their spotless purity, and that the thorns that surround them have torn their petals. But it is the lilies among thorns that are the most carefully guarded, and in whom Our Lord takes delight. (ST. THÉRÈSE OF LISIEUX)

❧ You experience a profound interior affliction in the temptations to impurity, hatred, aversion, and such-like. The fear of having succumbed to them disturbs and distresses you. That is an evident sign that you have a great fear of God, a horror of sin, and the will to resist. Now, it is morally impossible for a soul in such dispositions to change suddenly so far as to give full and entire consent to a mortal sin without being clearly aware of it. (REV. DOM VITALIS LEHODEY)

❧ For one who loves God, there can be nothing more afflicting than the fear of offending Him, nothing more horrible than to have the mind filled with evil thoughts and to feel the heart drawn away by the force of temptation, despite one's best efforts. But have you never meditated on the numerous passages of Holy Scripture where the Spirit of God teaches us the necessity of temptations and the precious advantages they procure for souls that do not allow themselves to be overcome? Do you not know that temptations are compared to the furnace where clay acquires its firmness and gold its splendor; that they are represented as a subject for joy, as a sign of God's friendship, as lessons indispensable for the acquisition of the science of the saints? If you bore these consoling truths in mind, how could you allow yourself to fall into the gulf of sadness? True, such temptations never come from God, but is it not He Who always permits them for our good? And ought we not to adore these holy permissions in everything outside of sin, which He detests and which we also should detest? Be careful, then, not to let yourself be troubled or disquieted by temptations. That would be much worse than the temptations themselves. (FR. JEAN PIERRE DE CAUSSADE)

❧ Take notice of this: so long as the temptation displeases you, there is nothing to fear; for why does it displease you but because you do not approve of it? These importunate temptations come from the malice of the devil; but the pain we feel on their account comes from the mercy of God, Who, in opposition to the will and from the wickedness of our enemy, draws a holy tribulation by which He refines the gold intended for His treasury. I say, then, that your temptations are from the devil and hell, but your afflictions are from God and Heaven. Despise the vain allurement; embrace the precious tribulation. (ST. FRANCIS DE SALES)

❧ God wishes that we should have enemies; God wishes that we should repel them. Let us, then, live courageously in the accomplishment of the divine will, suffering with patience to be assaulted and with bravery resisting the assaults. (ST. FRANCIS DE SALES)

❧ When temptations come, we do not have to be — because we cannot be — as strong as was Christ in the desert. All we have to do is fight them. Sometimes it will seem as though we are fighting a losing battle. Sometimes we will come so close to the edge of sin that we will feel the hot breath of hell and almost taste the sin in our lives. But as long as we fight, we will be alright. To be impatient with our weakness, to curse ourselves and our human nature because the thought of the temptation delighted us, to feel shame and sorrow because we were on the verge of sin is all wrong. For all Christ asks is that we fight. This and this only is enough to win His love, no matter what our feelings. (FR. WALTER CISZEK)

❧ Do not grow weary through temptations but resist them

always, without letting yourself be overcome, and do not fear; if you resist temptation, and persevere in resistance, the battle *will* bring you victory. (OUR LORD TO ST. GEMMA GALGANI)

WE OUGHT NOT FEAR THE DEVIL WHEN HE TEMPTS US

❧ The soul that is united with God is feared by the devil as though it were God Himself. (ST. JOHN OF THE CROSS)

❧ I do not understand the fears of certain persons who say, "The devil, the devil," when we can say, "God, God," and make satan tremble. (ST. TERESA OF ÁVILA)

❧ The servant of God must not fear anything. He must not even pay much attention to the demons, for when they are disregarded, they are powerless. If God is powerful and the demons are His slaves, what harm can they do those who are the servants of so great a King and Lord? (ST. TERESA OF ÁVILA)

❧ The devil and his demons are put like scorpions and snakes to be trodden underfoot by us Christians. A proof of this is our now living this life in spite of him. For he that threatened to wipe up the sea and to grasp the world, now, behold, cannot hinder our devotion, cannot even stop me from speaking about him. The reason they do nothing is because they can do nothing. If they could, they would not wait but would do evil at once since their wills are quite ready for it, especially against us. We must not fear them, though they seem to assault us or threaten death, for they are powerless and can do nothing but threaten. (ST. ANTHONY OF THE DESERT)

❧ The devil is like a dog on a chain. Beyond the range off the chain he cannot bite anyone. And you, therefore, keep your distance. (ST. PIO OF PIETRELCINA)

❧ The powers of hell are a pack of furious dogs that would tear us to pieces. Each of them, however, has a chain to its neck, and God leads them about as He pleases. Against His good pleasure, they are powerlessness itself. He allows them no liberty to tempt, or He leaves them some latitude, more or less, as He judges fit, with regard to what persons He pleases, in the manner and for the time that He considers best. So the choice of the temptation, the time, the degree of its violence, and the period of its duration: all are in the hand of God, our Father, our Savior, our Sanctifier. This surely ought to encourage us. (REV. DOM VITALIS LEHODEY)

❧ Temptations, discouragement, and unrest are the wares offered by the enemy. Remember this: if the devil makes noise, it is a sign that he is still without and not yet within. (ST. PIO OF PIETRELCINA)

❧ Our enemy is a mighty blusterer. But do not let him frighten you. He has raised many an uproar and many a tumult around the saints, but, for all that, you see how they now occupy the place which he, miserable one, has lost forever. Let us pay no heed, then, to his fanfares, for he can do us no harm. This is why he wishes at least to terrify us, and by this terror to disturb our peace, and by this disturbance to weary us, and by this weariness to make us give up. Let us have no fear but of God, and even of Him only a loving fear. Let us keep the gates securely closed and the walls of our resolutions in good repair, and then let us live in peace. (ST. FRANCIS DE SALES)

❧ Remember that the devil has only one doorway by which to enter your soul: your will. There are no secret or hidden doors. (ST. PIO OF PIETRELCINA)

❧ The very attacks of the tempter ought to be a big joy for you since they show how much the evil one fears what you are going to do for our Blessed Lord and poor perishing souls. If you were not a dangerous "enemy," he would leave you alone. Besides, I promise you this, that if you fight the temptations for a little while, great peace will soon come. (FR. WILLIAM DOYLE)

❧ In a word, be not vexed because you have been vexed; nor troubled because you have been troubled; nor disquieted because you have been disquieted by those annoying passions; but resume control over your heart, and place it lovingly in the hands of Our Lord, begging of Him to heal it: on your part, doing as much as you can for this purpose by the renovation of your resolutions, perusal of good books, and other such means. Acting thus, you will gain considerably by your loss and become much healthier by your sickness. (ST. FRANCIS DE SALES)

❧ His Majesty knows how to draw good from evil. The road on which the devil wanted to make you go astray will be to your greater gain. (ST. TERESA OF ÁVILA)

THE VALUE OF TEMPTATIONS

❧ With regard to your temptations, don't be over-anxious to be set free of them. You desire most ardently that God would leave you in peace in this respect, whereas it is my desire that God Himself should be left free in all respects, that none of our desires should be in opposition to His.

Our Lord will give us His peace when we have humbly resigned ourselves to live meekly in a state of war. Be of good courage. Our Lord will help us, and we shall love Him dearly. (ST. FRANCIS DE SALES)

❧ You should consider that your temptations, in God's merciful design, are but trials well calculated to make your love for Him appear to best advantage; lessons to teach you compassion for those who, like yourself, are a target for the shafts of the enemy; means to expiate your past sins and to prevent fresh faults in the future; and a pledge of more abundant graces. (BL. LOUIS DE BLOIS)

❧ The temptations of blasphemy, despair, and interior shame place, to a certain degree, those who resist them in the rank and prerogatives of martyrs; for the servants of God would much prefer to yield with one blow their heads, their blood, their life, for Jesus Christ, than to endure such painful temptations for months and even for years. Let us conclude, then, that persons afflicted with scruples are the most favored by divine love and traverse the surest way to arrive at Heaven; because, by enduring their pains with patience and humility, and thus dying to themselves, they live in a continual purgatory, and leave this earth only to fly to Heaven, purified from every matter of expiation. (BL. HENRY SUSO)

❧ Let us fear neither temptation (when we resist it, God will make profit come out of it for us, because it is the occasion of a victory which strengthens us in the love of God); nor trials either. We can go through great difficulties, suffer grave contradictions, endure deep sufferings, but from the moment that we set ourselves to serve God through love, those difficulties, those contradictions, those sufferings, serve as the food of love. When one loves God, one can still feel the cross; God will even make us feel it more in the measure that we advance, because the cross establishes in us a greater likeness to Christ: but one loves, then, if not the cross itself, at least the hand of Jesus that places the cross on our shoulders. For this hand gives us also the unguent grace for bearing our burden. Love is a powerful weapon against temptation and an invincible force in adversity. (BL. DOM COLUMBA MARMION)

❧ If we never really have the opportunity of a temptation, then we could never have the opportunity of fighting. Yes, opportunity; for every temptation is an opportunity offered to us to grow in virtue: in kindness or thoughtfulness, or prayer, or zeal, or purity, or obedience, or trust. Each time we conquer a temptation, no matter how unclean we feel, no matter how close we have come to sin because of the strength of the temptation, we have grown in virtue, grown closer to Christ, and Christ simply will not take such an opportunity from our life. (FR. WALTER CISZEK)

❧ We shall obtain no recompense without victory, no victory without war. Have courage, then, and by converting your pain, which is without remedy, into merit, make a virtue of necessity. Look often to Our Lord Who regards you, poor little creature as you are, amid your labors and distractions. He will send you aid and will bless your afflictions. You should, on this consideration, take patiently and quietly the tediousness that grieves you, and bear it meekly for the love of Him Who only permits it for your good.

Elevate, then, your heart frequently to God, beg His assistance, and let your chief consolation be the happiness of belonging to Him. Every object of displeasure will be of little account when you remember that you have so kind a Friend, so great a Support, so excellent a Refuge. (ST. FRANCIS DE SALES)

❧ If the soul would know the merit which one acquires in temptations suffered with patience and conquered, it would be tempted to say, "Lord, send me temptations." (ST. PIO OF PIETRELCINA)

❧ Offer your temptations for the conversion of sinners. When the devil sees you doing this, he is beside himself with rage and makes off, because then the temptation is turned against himself. (ST. JOHN MARIE VIANNEY)

HAVE RECOURSE TO PRAYER AND THE SACRAMENTS WHEN TEMPTED

❧ Invoke the help of God and continue praying as long as the temptation lasts. The Lord often grants victory, not to the first petition, but to the second, the third, or the fourth. We must convince ourselves that all our good depends on prayer. Experience proves this. He who has recourse to God in temptation triumphs. (ST. ALPHONSUS DE LIGUORI)

❧ *Father, not My will but Thine be done.* These words of our Divine Master are the salvation of His whole Mystical Body, the Church. These words have instructed all the faithful, inspired all the confessors, crowned all the martyrs. Let all the Church's children, redeemed at so high a price, justified without any deserving on their part, learn these words, and, using them as a safe defense when they are assailed by any strong temptation, they will resist the attacks of nature and suffer tribulation with courage. (ST. LEO THE GREAT)

❧ I see now that I need never yield if only I pray for strength. (FR. WILLIAM DOYLE)

❧ Whosoever thou art who laborest under the fever of concupiscence, I do not say that thou shouldst embrace a monastic life or that thou shouldst macerate thy body by hair shirts or the scourge, or drink nothing but water. I suggest an easy and efficacious remedy: frequently receive Holy Communion, and, by so doing, receive Christ into the house of thy soul. He is a virgin, and the Son of a virgin, and by His own virgin flesh He will extinguish this fire. This assuredly is the most powerful medicine against lust, as the Holy Scripture teachers, and the holy Fathers testify, and daily experience confirms. (FR. CORNELIUS À LAPIDE)

❧ Are we in affliction? We shall find all manner of consolation at Mass. Are we tempted? Let us hear Holy Mass, and we shall find there a way of overcoming the devil. (ST. JOHN CHRYSOSTOM)

❧ When you have no time to go to Jesus, and temptations assail you, and you do not know what to do — hold the cross to your heart, kiss His holy Wounds, and He will support you. (ST. MAXIMILIAN KOLBE)

FLY TO OUR LADY IN TIME OF TEMPTATION

❧ Temptations to vanity and self-complacency endeavor to insinuate themselves into the soul because of the very perfection to which it aspires. But the soul discovers them easily by telling Mary all its emotions, of joy or of discontent, and it sees their inanity without trouble. (FR. EMILE NEUBERT)

❧ If you invoke the Blessed Virgin when you are tempted, She will come at once to your aid, and satan will leave you. (ST. JOHN MARIE VIANNEY)

❧ When assailed by temptations, when doubtful as to how you should act, remember that Mary can help you. If you but call upon Her, She will instantly help you. (ST. ALPHONSUS DE LIGUORI)

❧ The devils fear the Queen of Heaven to such a degree that only on hearing Her great name pronounced, they fly from him who does so as from a burning fire. (FR. THOMAS À KEMPIS)

❧ This good Mother and powerful Princess of the heavens would rather dispatch battalions of millions of angels to assist one of Her servants than should it ever be said that one who trusted in Her had to succumb to the malice, the number, and the vehemence of his enemies. (ST. LOUIS MARIE DE MONTFORT)

❧ O you who find yourself tossed in the tempests of this world, turn not your eyes from the brightness of this Star if you would not be overwhelmed. If the winds of temptations arise, if you fall among the rocks of tribulation, look up at this Star, call on Mary. If you are tossed by the waves of pride, ambition, detraction, jealousy, or envy, call on Mary. If anger, covetousness, or lust beat on the vessel of your soul, look up to Mary. If you begin to sink in the gulf of melancholy or despair, think of Mary, call on Mary. Let Her not depart from your lips; let Her not depart from your heart; never depart yourself from the example of Her conversation, and you will obtain the suffrage of Her prayers. (ST. BERNARD)

❧ Have no confidence in yourself, but in all your temptations and trials surrender yourself to the Immaculata, and surely you will triumph. (ST. MAXIMILIAN KOLBE)

❧ If you place your trust in Her, the Immaculata will keep you from falling. (ST. MAXIMILIAN KOLBE)

❧ Who would ever dare to snatch these children from the bosom of Mary when they have taken refuge there? What power of hell or what temptation can overcome them if they place their confidence in the patronage of this great Mother, the Mother of God and of them? (ST. ROBERT BELLARMINE)

XV

IMPERFECTIONS

We never offend Him unless we want to offend Him.
(FR. FRANCIS XAVIER LASANCE)

WE OUGHT NOT BE DISCOURAGED
BY OUR IMPERFECTIONS

❧ You may seem to yourself to be full of faults, but don't let that slow you down. God looks more to our good will than to our failings. (ST. CATHERINE OF SIENA)

❧ Let not your imperfections discourage you; your God does not despise you because you are imperfect and infirm; on the contrary, He loves you because you desire to cure your ills. He will come to your assistance and make you more perfect than you would have dared to hope, and, adorned by His own hand, your beauty will be unequaled, like His own goodness. (BL. LOUIS DE BLOIS)

❧ Never let yourself be cast down at the thought of your miseries. The great St. Paul says: *Where sin abounded grace did more abound.* To me it seems that the weakest soul, even if it is the most guilty, is just the one which has the best grounds for hope, and this act by which it forgets itself to throw itself into the arms of God, glorifies Him more and gives Him more joy than all the falling back upon self and all the self-examination which makes it live in its wretchedness, while in its center it possesses a Savior Who comes at every moment to cleanse it. (ST. ELIZABETH OF THE TRINITY)

❧ It is not good to become dejected at the sight of your faults and frailties; the consciousness of our sins and the sight of our shortcomings is a grace of the Lord that saves us from many illusions. Let us leave it up to Christ to see the good, and let us rejoice in our humiliation and in the awareness of our nothingness; let us work in the field where He wants us to be, without being concerned about the harvest that is being reaped, for it is better that we know nothing about it. Be of good cheer. Have confidence in the Lord's goodness! (CARDINAL MERRY DEL VAL)

❧ Our Lord is displeased only when He sees no attempt to get rid of imperfections. But He often purposely does not give the victory over them in order to increase our opportunities of meriting. Make an act of humility and sorrow after failure, and then never a thought more about it. (FR. WILLIAM DOYLE)

❧ "But still," someone may say, "if I know that my multiplied faults have prevented my progress in virtue, and that my negligence is responsible for the persistence of my defects: how can I help being troubled?" In this way: implore forgiveness of God, detest your faults, accept humbly the pain and confusion arising from them; then without losing your time, your peace, and your courage in useless regrets, strive with all diligence to make better progress in the future. But you must preserve your tranquility of heart: trouble is not a remedy for evil, but a new evil in itself. (DOM VITALIS LEHODEY)

❧ Never be discouraged, and no matter what fault you happen to commit, say: Though I should fall twenty times or a hundred times a day, I will arise at every fall and pursue my course. What does it amount to, after all, that you should have met with some accidents on the way, provided you safely reach the journey's end? God will not reproach you after your recovery. Very often those mishaps proceed from the rapidity of our speed and from that ardor which prevents us from taking the necessary precautions. Timid and cautious souls, who always wish to see where they put their feet, who turn aside every moment for fear of making a false step, who cannot bear to have their shoes soiled, never advance so quickly as others who are less punctilious but more daring, and whom death often overtakes in the midst of their course. It is not those who commit the least number of faults that are the most holy but those who have the greatest courage, the greatest generosity, the greatest love, who make the boldest efforts to overcome themselves and are not immoderately apprehensive of tripping or even of falling and being dirtied a little, provided they advance. (ST. FRANCIS DE SALES)

GOD UNDERSTANDS OUR WEAKNESS AND READILY PARDONS US

❧ No one had ever told me before that faults did not pain God; this assurance filled me with joy and made it possible to bear my exile patiently. (ST. THÉRÈSE OF LISIEUX)

❧ One of the great consolations those have who serve God with the fervor they ought is to know that, though they correspond not to His goodness as they should, yet He ceases not to bear with them and to love them, because He is *rich in mercy* (Eph. 2:4); so that all our sins disappear before His infinite mercy like wax that melts before the fire. What sentiments of zeal, gratitude, and cheerfulness ought to be excited in us by the thought that the many faults we daily fall into through weakness do not hinder God from loving us with His wonted goodness, and do not at all diminish His grace in us! (ST. ALPHONSUS RODRIGUEZ)

❧ God does not ask from me perfect prayers or perfect Sacraments. He does not ask me even to overcome my temper or my want of truthfulness. He does not ask these things for He knows He could not get them from me. What, then, does He ask? That I should try to overcome them: only that and nothing more — that I should try day after day, despite failure, repeated and certain, to overcome these obstacles to my union with Him. For goodness consists not in the love of God, but in the attempts to love Him. If, then, I fail, let me not be discouraged, but realizing my own weakness and confident only in God's strength, let me go on striving my best, for my business in life is really little else than to continue to fail without losing courage or lessening effort. The phrase of St. Catherine should ring always in my ear: "God does not ask a perfect work, but infinite desire." (REV. BEDE JARRETT)

❧ Be not troubled if you do not remember all your little faults, for as often as you fall imperceptibly, so you are often raised up imperceptibly. (ST. JOHN CLIMACUS)

❧ Let us try hard, let us trust hard — for you know that His Majesty says that if we are sorry for having offended Him, our faults and evils will not be remembered. O compassion so measureless! (ST. TERESA OF ÁVILA)

❧ It is not being weak if we sometimes fall into venial sins, provided we raise ourselves again immediately by a return of our soul to God, humbling ourselves calmly and gently. We must not think we can live without ever committing some, for no one but Our Lady had that privilege. Certainly, if they delay us a little, they do not, however, turn us out of the way; a single glance at God effaces them. (ST. FRANCIS DE SALES)

❧ Do not grieve at your apparent helplessness. When we begin the day feeling that we have neither the courage nor the strength for the practice of virtue, this is a grace for *now the ax is laid to the root of the tree,* because we rely on Our Lord only. If we fall, we make amends by an act of love, and Jesus smiles once more. He helps us without appearing to do so, and our weak, imperfect love wipes away the tears that wicked men cause Him to shed. (ST. THÉRÈSE OF LISIEUX)

❧ God, being infinite Goodness, knows and has pity on our misery; each time we place ourselves before Him and humbly acknowledge our faults with sincere repentance, He immediately pardons us and cancels all our debts. (FR. GABRIEL OF ST. MARY MAGDALEN)

❧ Whenever you find yourself inclined to diffidence, lift up your heart lovingly to God and be assured that your defects are, in the sight of His infinite goodness, but as a few threads of string cast into a sea of fire. Figure to yourself a burning furnace, as vast as the hemisphere we inhabit: if a piece of string were thrown into it, would it not be so absorbed in the fire as instantly to disappear? *Our God is a consuming fire,* and our imperfections, compared with His goodness, are what a piece of string is to the furnace. When, therefore, we have fallen, let us humble ourselves sorrowfully in His presence, and then with an act of unbounded confidence, let us throw ourselves into the ocean of His goodness where every failing will be canceled, and anxiety will be turned into love. (ST. PAUL OF THE CROSS)

❧ Remember that whatever faults you may commit, your Jesus will never reproach you with bitterness; He will never throw you out into darkness and sorrow; He will hold out His hand with love, and you will learn that your faults, far from driving Him away, will only make Him redouble His tenderness and His care for you. (FR. JOSEPH VARIN)

WHY GOD ALLOWS OUR IMPERFECTIONS

❧ In spite of all our efforts, we fall into faults from time to time. God permits this for two reasons: 1) to keep the soul humble and to make it realize its utter powerlessness when left alone without His fostering hand; and 2) because the act of sorrow after the fault not only washes it completely away, but immensely increases our merit, and being an act of humility bringing us really heartbroken to His feet, delights Him beyond measure. (FR. WILLIAM DOYLE)

❧ I am convinced that perfection, that is, sanctity, is only to be won by repeated failures. If you rise again after a fall, sorry for the pain given to Our Lord, humbled by it since you see better your real weakness, and determined to make another start, far more is gained than if you had gone on without a stumble. The more falls, the better, for every fall means that we have begun again, have made another effort, and so have made progress. (FR. WILLIAM DOYLE)

❧ If it had not been for this small imperfection, you would not have come to Me. Know that as often as you come to Me, humbling yourself and asking My forgiveness, I pour out a superabundance of graces on your soul, and your imperfection vanishes before My eyes, and I see only your love and your humility. You lose nothing but gain much. (OUR LORD TO ST. FAUSTINA)

❧ When you commit a fault which humbles you and for which you are really sorry—it is a gain instead of a loss. (FR. WILLIAM DOYLE)

❧ Our faults are very salutary, inasmuch as they serve to keep us always little and confounded before the Divine Majesty, always distrustful of ourselves, always annihilated in our own eyes. Nothing, indeed, is easier than to avail ourselves of each of our infidelities in order to acquire a new degree of humility and to dig deeper in our hearts, so to speak, the necessary foundation of all true sanctity. Should we not admire and bless the infinite goodness of God Who can thus draw our greatest advantage from our very shortcomings? (FR. JEAN PIERRE DE CAUSSADE)

❧ Perseverance is what God wants. If we get up and start again after each fall, God *will* make saints of us in the end. (FR. WILLIAM DOYLE)

THE FAULTS OF THOSE IN THE WAY OF SPIRITUAL CHILDHOOD

❧ I would like to make you understand by a very simple comparison how much Jesus loves souls, including imperfect ones, who entrust themselves to Him. Imagine that a father has two naughty, disobedient sons, and when he comes to punish them, he sees one of them running away in fear and trembling, while his brother does the opposite: he throws himself into his father's arms, telling him that he is sorry to have hurt him, that he loves him, and that he will prove it by being good from now on. Then, if that child asks his father to punish him with a kiss, I don't think the happy father could harden his heart against his child's filial trust, knowing his sincerity and love. Of course he knows that his son will fall into the same faults again and again, but he is ready to forgive him every time, if his son catches him by the heart every time. (ST. THÉRÈSE OF LISIEUX)

❧ To keep little means not to lose courage at the sight of our faults. Little children often tumble, but they are too small to suffer grievous injury. (ST. THÉRÈSE OF LISIEUX)

❧ If all weak and imperfect souls such as mine felt as I do, none would despair of reaching the summit of the mountain of Love, since Jesus does not look for deeds but only for gratitude and self-surrender. (ST. THÉRÈSE OF LISIEUX)

❧ It is a remark made by the masters of a spiritual life that very often God leaves in the holiest souls some defects which, notwithstanding all their endeavors, they cannot eradicate. He acts thus in order to make them feel their weakness, to show them what they would be without grace, to guard them from the inflation of vanity on account of His favors, to dispose them to receive other benefits with greater humility, to keep a holy self-hatred alive in their breasts, to withdraw them from the snares of self-love, to preserve their fervor and confidence towards Him, and to teach them the necessity of having continual recourse to prayer. The child that tumbles when it wanders a little distance from its mother returns to her with greater tenderness and from experience learns not to quit her in a hurry again. The lesson it has received on its own weakness and its mother's goodness inspires it with a livelier affection for her. (ST. FRANCIS DE SALES)

TURNING TO OUR LADY AFTER WE FALL

❧ If you do fall, submit yourself immediately to Her and implore pardon: Dearest Mother, forgive me, and request

Jesus also to forgive me. Be confident that an act of love will expunge your transgression completely. In your very next confession, acknowledge your sin. But the Immaculata, Jesus, and the Father will have already forgotten it. (ST. MAXIMILIAN KOLBE)

❧ Water, which cleanses everything it touches, is a symbol of Her who purifies every soul that draws near to Her. (ST. MAXIMILIAN KOLBE)

XVI

SORROW

Earth has no sorrow that Heaven cannot heal.
(ST. THOMAS MORE)

SUPERNATURALIZING OUR SORROW

❧ The endurance of sorrow is perhaps the highest and most arduous work we have to do, and it is for the most part God's ordinance that the amount of sorrow to be endured should increase with the amount of holiness enabling us to endure it. (FR. FREDERICK FABER)

❧ God knows everything. There are volumes of comfort in that. God means everything. There is light for every darkness out of that simple truth. Our hearts are full of angels when they are full of sorrows. Let us make them our company and go on our road, smiling all the day, scattering such sweetness round us as mourners only are allowed to scatter, and God will understand us when we go to Him. Who can comfort like those who also mourn? (FR. FREDERICK FABER)

❧ I would like to see you in a gentler spirit of resignation in your genuine sorrow. Do not merely aim at suppressing your grief, but try to sanctify it gently with our Savior. You have a treasure right in your hands enabling you to practice virtue in an eminent degree — do not waste it. Offer everything tenderly to Christ and ask Him to be your comfort. (CARDINAL MERRY DEL VAL)

❧ Remember that a heart torn by thorns is a thousand times closer to Jesus than a heart full of happiness, even holy happiness. (MOTHER AGNES OF JESUS)

❧ Jesus has a special love for the unhappy. (FR. FREDERICK FABER)

❧ There is no sacrifice so pleasing to God as this entire oblation of a crushed and bleeding heart. It is a true holocaust of most sweet savor. The most unctuous and fervent prayers, the most severe of voluntary mortifications have nothing comparable to it, nothing at all approaching its excellence. (FR. JEAN PIERRE DE CASSUADE)

❧ In this world, sorrow is the recompense of sanctity. It is to the elect on earth what the Beatific Vision is to the saints in Heaven. It is God's presence, His manifestation of Himself, His unfailing reward. (FR. FREDERICK FABER)

❧ Sorrow enlightens, sorrow purifies, sorrow detaches one from all that is transitory; it raises the heart on high; it makes one desire the repose of Heaven! Sorrow is the powerful wing which aids us to mount towards God; it is the hand filled with mercy which touches us with compassion. We must kiss this hand which snatches our soul from danger and clothes it with such a radiant beauty! (VEN. MOTHER CATHERINE AURELIA)

❧ Pick up the crucifix and kiss it with real faith because Our Lord invites you to be crucified with Him. Let your will be subject to His, and say over and over: "I desire what Thou desirest, O Lord." Once you are resigned to God's will, be calm and have no fear, for Our Lord certainly does not condemn tears or the cry of a suffering heart. He shed tears Himself and can appreciate the sorrow of your heart. Learn how to be patient and wait things out: He will make you see the inestimable price of this grief of yours that makes you like unto Him and is really a pledge of predestination and a sign of love. (CARDINAL MERRY DEL VAL)

❧ Here is a precious balm to sweeten your sorrows: every day take a drop or two of the Blood which distills from the wounds in the feet of Our Lord and receive It into your soul by meditation; with your imagination, also dip your finger reverently in this Liquor and apply it to your affliction, invoking the sweet Name of Jesus. And you will find your grief diminish. (ST. FRANCIS DE SALES)

SORROW AT THE DEATH
OF OUR LOVED ONES

❧ One never loses those whom one loves in Him Whom we can never lose. (ST. AUGUSTINE)

❧ That death is not to be judged an evil which is the end of a good life. (ST. AUGUSTINE)

❧ Over the departure of him who has accepted death willingly, who has received the efficacious remedies of the Holy Church before dying, there is more occasion to be consoled than afflicted. For, having lived well, he is not dead, but saved from death, since virtuous men do not die, living in Heaven by the magnificent recompense of their merits, and on earth by the glorious memory of their good deeds. (ST. FRANCIS DE SALES)

❧ Oh, if we could hear the sweet and amiable words of some deceased one now happy, he would say to us: "My dearly beloved, I beseech you to consider that I am in the place which I so much desired where I am consoled for all my past labors which have merited for me the glory of immortality. Why do you not console yourself with me? When I was on earth, you made profession of loving me and, sometimes seeing me succeed happily, you rejoiced and congratulated me. Ah! Am I not always the same person? Why then are you afflicted at my departure, since God has given me so much glory? No, I desire everything else from you but sorrow and regret. If you have tears, keep them to weep over the miseries of the world and also over your sins. Do you not know that the evils of the wretched life in which you live are such that you ought rather to praise God than be dejected for His having taken me away from them? The first who leave it only find themselves the more fortunate when they have lived with care for their salvation. No one is esteemed before God for having lived long, but for having lived well." (ST. FRANCIS DE SALES)

❧ I am on my guard against saying, "Do not weep," for it is very just that you should weep a little, as a testimony to the sincere affection you bear towards the dear departed. This will be to imitate Jesus Christ, Who wept a little over Lazarus, His good friend; but it is on condition that those exterior demonstrations should be moderate, and that those sighs and sobs should not to be so much tokens of regret as marks of tenderness.

The imaginary insensibility of those who do not wish us to be men has always appeared to me chimerical; but, at the same time, after we have payed our tribute to the inferior part of the soul, we must do our duty to the superior part, in which is seated, as on a throne, the spirit of faith, which ought to console us in our afflictions and even by our affliction. Blessed are they who rejoice in being afflicted, and who thus transform quassia into honey! God be praised! (ST. FRANCIS DE SALES)

❧ I find that in these moments of great grief, one needs to look up to Heaven; there they are not weeping, but all are joyful because Our Lord has one more among His elect, a new sun brightens the forecourt of Heaven with its rays, all are in the rapture of divine ecstasy; they marvel that we can give the name of *death* to the commencement of life. To them, we are in a narrow tomb, whereas their souls can fly out to the far bounds of "ethereal shores, horizons infinite." When we look upon the death of the just man, we cannot but envy his lot. For him the time of exile is no more; there is now only God, nothing but God. (ST. THÉRÈSE OF LISIEUX)

SORROW AT THE DEATH OF A YOUNG CHILD

❧ What bright and beautiful multitude of glorious souls is this, which forms the outer ring of the stupendous court of the Lamb? It is that portion of the kingdom of grace which the waters of baptism alone have flooded. The little ones have become, as it were, men of thirty-three, like Jesus Himself, and their untried, untempted nature has been washed white as snow in His redeeming Blood. The mightiest scholars upon earth know not so much as they. Earth's highest joys are not so much as a shadow to the Beatific Rapture which possesses their spirits with its pulses of thrilling life. As the pearly whiteness of the dawn of day so is their light in the splendor of that kingdom because their Brother wrought a miracle for them and turned His Blood into water, and washed them clean; and the very Name of the Vision they are gazing on filled them with the grace of adoption and gave them an eternal inheritance that fadeth not away. Is there a lot on earth round which the sunshine of prosperity and joy is shining brightest, which is not purely miserable and undesirable compared with the present glory of the infant members of Jesus whom baptism has saved forever? (FR. FREDERICK FABER)

LET US TURN TO MARY IN OUR SORROW

❧ There was never a heart so broken with sorrow, never anyone so weak that Mary did not help and save and comfort if only they asked Her. (FR. PAUL O'SULLIVAN)

❧ Are you in sorrow? Turn to Mary and She will turn your sorrow into joy and your afflictions into consolations. (ST. LOUIS MARIE DE MONTFORT)

XVII

DESOLATION

*One of the most certain marks that God has great
designs upon a soul is when He sends desolation
upon desolation, suffering upon suffering.*

(ST. VINCENT DE PAUL)

THE STATE OF DESOLATION
IS ONLY TEMPORARY

❧ It is an ordinary thing with those who begin to serve God
and who have not yet had experience of the withdrawal of
grace or of other spiritual vicissitudes, that as soon as they
lose the feeling of sensible devotion and the perception of
that beautiful light which had invited them to run in the ways
of God, they immediately lose breath, as it were, and fall into
very great sadness and pusillanimity. Persons well versed in
the matter give this explanation: they say that a reasonable
being cannot remain for a long time famishing and without
any pleasure, heavenly or earthly; but as souls elevated above
themselves by the taste of superior pleasures easily renounce
all visible objects, so, when, by the divine appointment, this
spiritual joy is taken away from them, they find they are also
deprived of inferior consolations, and, not being yet accustomed to await patiently the return of day, it seems to them
that they are neither in Heaven nor on earth, but that they
are to lie buried in a perpetual night; in such a manner that,
like little children who have just been weaned and who still
seek their mother's breast, they can only weep and languish,
being a trouble to everyone but particularly to themselves.

Not to fall into discouragement, mark. All the seasons of the year are to be found in your soul: sometimes winter with sterility, distractions, torments, disgusts, and weariness; sometimes the roses of May with the sweet scent of holy little flowers; sometimes the heats of desire to please our good God. There only remains autumn, when you do not find much fruit. But it often happens that, in threshing the wheat and pressing the grapes, we find much more than the harvest and the vintage had promised. You would like always to have springtime or summer, but it is necessary to have a change internally as well as externally. In Heaven there will be a perpetual spring as to beauty, a perpetual autumn as to joy, a perpetual summer as to love. There will be no winter there; but here, winter is required for the exercise of self-denial and for the growth of a thousand beautiful virtues which flourish only in sterility. Let us, then, make our little steps forward; if we have a good and resolute affection, we cannot but advance well. (ST. FRANCIS DE SALES)

❧ You should have been prepared to find that the generous spirit which carried you along from sacrifice to sacrifice was not intended to last; it was only meant to strengthen you for your time of trial. To serve God generously when the music of consolation is sounding in our ears is no doubt pleasing to Him, but to be equally faithful when all is black and dark is not only a thousand times more sanctifying, but it is heroic virtue. Hence God, in His eagerness for our perfection, takes away, at times, all sensible consolation, yet is really nearer to us than before. (FR. WILLIAM DOYLE)

❧ If you be for a time cast down with weariness of spirit or afflicted with aridity of heart so that the torrent of devoted love seems to be dried up, will you dare to cry, *"My Lord hath forsaken me* and hath no care for me, since the feelings of joy and devotion I have hitherto known are now gone from me"? Such things must never be uttered by a lover of the gentle Christ Jesus; let them speak thus who know not His ways nor how He is wont to kindle the love of His friends, how for a time He will draw away from you that you may seek Him with greater ardor, and having sought may find Him with greater joy, and having found may hold Him with greater love, and having held may never let Him go. (BL. JORDAN OF SAXONY)

DESOLATION IS OFTEN A MARK OF GOD'S FAVOR

❧ You must not be afraid of what is passing in your soul. Try to remember that what is happening is a mark of love, not of anger. The inner sanctuary of God's love is set round, as it were, with a thick hedge of sharp thorns. No wonder when one tries to force one's way through it, and the thorns pierce to the very heart, human nature should cry out, and, alas, too often weakly turn back from the only road that leads to pure love; no wonder indeed, for this painful struggling, every step of which is, as it were, marked with blood, seems to anger Jesus and drive Him further away. But courage! He is only "pretending" in order to test the valiant lover, and soon the sweets of victory will well repay the hardness of the fight. (FR. WILLIAM DOYLE)

❧ He who is regaled with devotion should not presume, for favor is often a sign of his weakness; and one in desolation should not lose courage, since it is often a sign of strength. (ST. PETER OF ALCANTARA)

❧ We read in the Gospel that the Good Shepherd left the ninety-nine sheep in the desert whilst He sought the one that had strayed. What touching confidence! He can rely on the former; they are held captive by His love and would never try to escape. So the Divine Shepherd of our souls deprives us of the sense of His presence that He may bestow consolations on sinners. (ST. THÉRÈSE OF LISIEUX)

❧ Our Blessed Lord is well pleased with you and will become more so if you walk bravely along the path He has chosen for you in His love: the path of dryness and little sensible consolation. You must be very pleasing in His sight, since He has marked you out for this trial. Mind, it is not a punishment for past infidelity but a special grace reserved for the few. (FR. WILLIAM DOYLE)

DESOLATION PURIFIES OUR LOVE

❧ You seem to be troubled that you cannot love God when trials come, and all is in darkness. But that is just the moment when you love Him most and prove your love the best. If only, when you are in desolation and dryness, you *force* yourself to utter an act of love or an oblation of yourself without a particle of feeling, you make an offering which is of surpassing value in His eyes and most pleasing to His Sacred Heart. A dry act of love is a real act of love, since it is all for Jesus and nothing for self. (FR. WILLIAM DOYLE)

❧ Such desolation and privation of everything should not discourage us; they are not ordered to death, but to life, and even to the fullness of life, which is union with God by love. Therefore, the soul that loves should be neither frightened not alarmed; its ideal is divine union, and it should desire to reach it at any cost; no sacrifice should be too hard, provided it reaches its goal. (FR. GABRIEL OF ST. MARY MAGDALEN)

❧ You must not look upon the deepening of this state of desolation as a punishment but rather as a confirmation of the graces He has given you. He is only plunging your soul deeper into that purifying bath from which it will emerge dripping with choice graces and inebriated with His pure love. Trust Him. He loves you too much to let harm come near you. (FR. WILLIAM DOYLE)

WE MUST BE PATIENT AND PERSEVERE IN THE GOOD

❧ For the honor of God, acquiesce entirely to His will, and do not for a moment suppose that you can serve Him better otherwise; for we can never serve Christ well unless we serve Him in the manner He requires to be served. Now He requires that you serve Him without relish, without feeling, with repugnances and distress of mind. Such service does not give you satisfaction, but it greatly pleases Him; it is not to your taste, but it is in accordance with His good-pleasure. Imagine that you were never to be delivered from your affliction. You would then say to God: "Lord, I am Thine! If my sufferings give Thee satisfaction, increase both their number and their duration." I have confidence in Our Lord that this would be your attitude, and that you would think no more about the matter. At least you would not any longer worry. Adopt the same attitude now. Make friends with your troubles as if you were destined to live always together. And you will find that when you have ceased to think of your deliverance, God will think of it, and He will hasten to help you. (ST. FRANCIS DE SALES)

❧ Think not thyself wholly forsaken, although for a time God has sent thee some tribulation or withdrawn from thee the comfort which thou desirest, for this is the way to the kingdom of Heaven. And without doubt it is more expedient for thee that thou be exercised by adversities than that thou shouldst have all according to thine inclination. Have patience and be of good courage. Comfort will come to thee in its proper season. Wait for Him, and He will come and cure thee. (FR. THOMAS À KEMPIS)

❧ Do not lose heart, dear child; the darkness you feel is not a sign of God's displeasure for every saint has gone through it. You are "minting money" every instant you love, you are helping to save soul after soul each hour you suffer. So you should say with St. Paul, *I exceedingly abound with joy in all our tribulation.* (FR. WILLIAM DOYLE)

❧ It is sad to be compelled to fulfill the most sacred duties with a cold heart and a dissipated mind, to return to them always without zeal or fervor, nay, to have to drag oneself to them as it were by violence; to find oneself before God without any feeling but one of stupid indifference; to pray without recollection; to meditate without affection; to confess one's sins without sorrow; to communicate without relish; to break the Bread of Heaven with less satisfaction than material bread; to suffer externally without interior consolation; to carry heavy crosses without feeling that secret unction which sweetens them. This trial is very mortifying, but it is wisely regulated by the Providence of God Who knows perfectly well His own rights and our necessities. Thou art just, O Lord, and all Thy decrees are dictated by equity itself; and Thy mercy, too, enters largely into all Thy counsels. Souls of good will, it is either in chastisement of your faults God withdraws His consolations, or it is for the purpose of increasing your merits. If it is to punish your faults, why not turn your anger against yourselves? If it is with the view of multiplying your merits, why complain of Him? If He treats you according to your desert, what wrong has He done you? And what thanks do you not owe Him if He designs to make you richer for eternity? (FR. AMBROSIO DE LOMBEZ)

ACTS OF LOVE AND RESIGNATION ARE MORE VALUABLE IN TIMES OF DRYNESS

❧ A single act made in dryness of spirit is of more value than many made with great sweetness, because it is made with a stronger love, though it is not so tender nor agreeable. (ST. FRANCIS DE SALES)

❧ It is one thing to elicit good acts and quite another to feel a sensible impression of them. God demands the works, He does not demand the sentiment. What is more, if we remain faithful to our duties without the support of sensible consolations and sweetness, the good will we manifest shall be only the more pleasing to Him and the more meritorious for ourselves, because it implies more of the spirit of sacrifice. (REV. DOM VITALIS LEHODEY)

❧ You desire to know for certain that God loves you? But at the moment He does not will to impart to you this knowledge. He wills that you should just humble yourself, trust in His goodness, and resign yourself wholly to His good pleasure. Besides, when a person of timorous conscience is in doubt as to whether he has lost the grace of God, it is certain that he has not lost it. For no one can lose God without being fully aware of the fact. Moreover the resolution you have, at least in the depths of your heart, to love God and not to cause Him the slightest displeasure by deliberate purpose, is a manifest sign that you are still in His grace. Abandon yourself, therefore, into the arms of divine mercy, protest that you desire nothing but God alone and His good-pleasure, and banish every fear. Oh, how agreeable to the Lord are the acts of confidence and resignation we make in the midst of this terrifying darkness. (ST. ALPHONSUS DE LIGUORI)

❧ You seem to be a little troubled at finding yourself cold at prayer, as if Our Lord had abandoned you. Yet this is one of the best signs that you are really pleasing to God, since He puts your fidelity to the test by sending desolation. There is no happiness to be compared to the sweetness one tastes at times in prayer; but this, the greatest of all sacrifices, He will ask from you at times. Hence in darkness and dryness, when weariness and disgust come on you, when the thousand petty worries of everyday crowd upon you, *sursum corda*, raise your eyes with a glad smile to the face of Jesus, for all is well—He is sanctifying you. (FR. WILLIAM DOYLE)

❧ Try "basking in the sun of God's love," that is, quietly kneeling before the Tabernacle, as you would sit enjoying the warm sunshine, not trying to do anything except love Him; but realizing that, during all the time you are at His feet, more especially when you are dry and cold, grace is dropping down upon your soul, and you are fast growing in holiness. (FR. WILLIAM DOYLE)

❧ *Nothing* should hinder you from going to Him. Do not attach much importance to whether you are fervent or discouraged; it is the law of our exile to pass from one state to the other; but have faith that He never changes—that in His loving kindness He is ever bending over you to carry you away and establish you in Him. If, despite everything, emptiness and sadness overwhelm you, unite this agony to His in the Garden of Gethsemane when He prayed to His Father: *If it be possible, let this chalice pass from Me.* (ST. ELIZABETH OF THE TRINITY)

✾ After entreating the Father to console you, if it is not His pleasure to do so, muster up all your courage to accomplish the work of your salvation on the cross as if you were never to descend from it. Contemplate our good Master in the Garden of Olives. Having implored consolation of His Father, and knowing it was not the Divine Will to grant it, He thinks no more of it, desires it no more, petitions for it no more, but, as if He had never asked for it, applies Himself valiantly to the work of our Redemption. (ST. FRANCIS DE SALES)

DARKNESS TO ONE IN THE LITTLE WAY OF SPIRITUAL CHILDHOOD

✾ Life is indeed, as you say, hard and wearisome; when Jesus hides Himself, it is difficult to begin the day's work. What has become of our Friend? Does He not see our burden and anguish of heart? Where is He, and why does He not come to comfort us?

Do not fear. He is there beside us. Like a beggar He asks for this grief, these tears, that He may apply them to souls, to our own soul, and He will repay us magnificently. He feels having to hurt us, but He knows that it is the only way to teach us how to know Him as He knows Himself and to become gods. How great is our soul's destiny! Let us remain above this earth and passing things; in those regions we breathe a purer air. If Jesus hides, we guess His Presence! (ST. THÉRÈSE OF LISIEUX)

❧ It is such folly to pass time in fretting instead of resting quietly on the Heart of Jesus. Neither ought the little child to be afraid of the dark, nor complain of not seeing the Beloved Who carries her in His arms. She has only to shut her eyes — that is the one sacrifice God asks of her. If she does this, the dark will lose its terrors because she will not see it, and before long, peace, if not joy, will return once more. (ST. THÉRÈSE OF LISIEUX)

XVIII

SICKNESS

*To endure your sufferings peacefully and gently, in
union with the sufferings of Jesus, is to do much.*
(BL. DOM COLUMBA MARMION)

THE INCOMPARABLE VALUE OF SICKNESS

❧ If we only knew the precious treasure hidden in infirmities, we would receive them with the same joy with which we receive the greatest benefits, and we would bear them without ever complaining or showing signs of weariness. (ST. VINCENT DE PAUL)

❧ In one day of sickness, patiently endured, we shall make more progress in virtue, pay off more of our debt to divine justice for past sins, amass greater treasures of merit, render ourselves more pleasing to God and give Him greater glory, than we could do in a week or a month of health. The time of sickness is a precious time, a time of salvation. (ST. ALPHONSUS DE LIGUORI)

❧ Long sicknesses are among the greatest graces which God gives to those souls He loves the best. (ST. PAUL OF THE CROSS)

❧ There are certain sufferers who become upset and complain more over the trouble they cause and over their inability to do good deeds and pray as they did when they were well, than they do over their sufferings. But they greatly deceive themselves because, as regards the inconvenience caused to others, he who is truly patient wants all that God wants in the manner and with all the inconvenience that He wants. With regards to good works, a day of suffering borne with resignation is worth more than a month of hard work; and, as to prayer, which is better—to be on the cross with Christ or standing at the foot of it contemplating His sufferings? (ST. FRANCIS DE SALES)

❧ What mercy and goodness of God, to make us perform so sweet a penance! Far from complaining, let us adore our Savior's love, which treats us with so much clemency and which deigns, as St. Paul says, to complete that which was wanting to His sufferings. It seems to me an incomparable honor Our Lord does us in using our bodies to suffer again in them for the glory of His Father. Let us then, with the Apostle, glory in our infirmities that the divine power may dwell in us; pay great attention to the sentiments which Our Lord will give you during the holy time of your infirmity, for it is the ordinary method of God to accomplish in sickness that which, if we may so speak, He could not well accomplish in health. (MSGR. JEAN-JACQUES OLIER)

❧ I rejoice with you. What could possibly be more useful to the soul than for the Lord to permit sickness to prevent us from following the normal course of our activities; that is a great grace and privilege He bestows upon us. To live more intimately with God and for the love of God, to increase your spirit of prayer and self-mortification, to renounce from hour to hour external satisfactions and the distractions of your senses is an ineffable joy, a dynamic of peace, an apostolate that will help save souls. (CARDINAL MERRY DEL VAL)

❧ At the hour of your death you will see that you saved more souls by your illness than by all the good works you might have accomplished in health. (ST. JOHN MARIE VIANNEY)

❧ When you do anything with difficulty or which is beyond your strength, I receive it as if I had absolute need of it for My honor; but when you omit anything in order to take due care of your health, referring your act at the same time to My glory, I accept it as if I, being ill Myself, could not do without it. Therefore I will reward you in either case. (OUR LORD TO ST. GERTRUDE THE GREAT)

EMBRACING GOD'S WILL IN TIME OF SICKNESS

❧ We shall be able to suffer well when we understand that suffering is the work of God and the means chosen by God to lead us to Himself. (ST. FRANCIS DE SALES)

❧ One of the greatest areas of impatience is personal illness. So many of us just cannot stand being sick. It seems as though we should simply be able to make an act of the will for the sickness to go away. But it does not work this way. And we have to pamper this human body of ours, give it medicine and better food and especially *rest*. For as soon as we start working again — bam! There goes the body clamoring for attention, clamoring for rest. It is as though we see our bodies as some enemy to our love of God and our service to Him.

But He gave us our bodies. He knows they wear down. He knows they get weak. He knows they sometimes do not work too well. If He made us, our whole being, body and soul, then why should we be impatient with these same bodies? Do we not really indict God and blame Him for a bad job? Are we not in effect saying, "God, if you had done a better job of putting me together, You would get a lot more out of me"? But, you see, He does not want a "lot more out of me." He wants us simply, in all we are doing, to love Him with our body and soul, with our whole human nature to the best of our strength, whatever that may be at any particular moment. And with this love He is satisfied, though sometimes all it may consist of will be a very weak, "I love You." (FR. WALTER CISZEK)

❧ You tell me you are very ill and do not have enough strength to perform your customary pious exercises. But if you live that life in the true spirit of conforming to the will of God, you have within your grasp a wonderful means of sanctification, because then your whole life becomes a continuous act of piety. So, forget all about these apprehensions of yours and go ahead day by day and hour by hour, and leave everything to the good Lord Who is at work within your soul. (CARDINAL MERRY DEL VAL)

❧ Do not refrain when you desire to complain; but I would wish this to be done to God with a filial spirit, as a tender child does to its mother; for, provided it be done lovingly, there is no danger in complaining, or in asking a cure, or in changing place, or in being comforted; only do it with love and resignation into the arms of the most holy will of God. It is foolish to imagine that you do not make acts of virtue well, for they do not cease to be exceedingly good, though preformed languidly, heavily, and as if by force. You cannot give God anything but what you have, and, at this season of affliction, you have no other kind of acts. (ST. FRANCIS DE SALES)

❧ Your life has been entirely consecrated to piety by exercises which are, as it were, the food of your soul; but a sickness breaks the chain of pious practices you had imposed on yourself. Already you can no longer assist at Mass, even on

Sunday; you are deprived of the Sacred Banquet of Communion; very soon, your state of weakness will prohibit you from prayer. Pious soul! Do not complain; you are called to the honor of nourishing your soul by participating with Jesus Christ in *a meat of which*, perhaps, *you did not know*, but the use of which will make your sickness a powerful means of sanctification. *My meat*, He said to His disciples, *is to do the will of Him Who sent Me.* This is the meat that is presented to you, and by it alone can we live to eternal life. Prayer itself is inefficacious if not vivified by this salutary nourishment, according to the words of our Savior in the Holy Gospel: *Not they who say to Me, Lord, Lord, shall enter into the kingdom of Heaven; but he who does the will of My Father shall enter into it.* (PÈRE JEAN-JOSEPH HUGUET)

❧ When God calls us to suffer, He does not require us to act. (ST. FRANCIS DE SALES)

OUR SUFFERING IS THE BEST PRAYER

❧ When some sickness or engagement prevents us from making prayer, we must hope that an hour of suffering will be as agreeable in the eyes of God as an hour of prayer, during which we might, perhaps, seek to gratify ourselves. When we imagine that the multiplicity and perplexity of our exterior occupations hinder us from spending some time with God or thinking often of Him, let us remember that it is not the repose of nature but that of grace which is necessary for the soul in order to attend to God; this repose is found in the cross, in pain, in the love of contempt, better than anywhere else. (PÈRE JEAN-JOSEPH HUGUET)

❧ Let us, when in sickness, utter simply the ejaculation: *Thy will be done.* Let us repeat it with all the fervor we can command, a hundred times, a thousand times, incessantly; and thus we shall please God more than by the practice of all possible mortifications and devotions. (ST. ALPHONSUS DE LIGUORI)

❧ Offering to God one's infirmity, remembering for whom one is suffering and conforming one's will to God's — this is certainly a most excellent prayer. (ST. FRANCIS DE SALES)

❧ So great is My love for souls that it constrains Me to hearken to the desires of the just as often as they are prompted by pure and humanly disinterested zeal. If it is truly in order to serve Me better that the sick desire restoration to health, let them ask it of Me with entire confidence. What is more, if they desire to get strong solely in order to merit a greater reward, I will still allow Myself to be swayed by their importunities, because I so love them as to consider their interests My own. (OUR LORD TO ST. GERTRUDE THE GREAT)

PRACTICING VIRTUE IN TIME OF SICKNESS

❧ If sickness prevents me from observing the regular fasts and abstinence or from assisting *at Mass*, I can sing the praises of God in my heart; I can impose a rigid abstinence on my judgment and will; I can make my eyes fast, and my tongue, and my heart, and all my senses by sincere mortification. What I might have gained by fulfilling the duties proper to those in health, I can make up for by fidelity to those incumbent on the sick, such as patience, renunciation, obedience, and abandonment. (DOM VITALIS LEHODEY)

❧ It is a manifest truth that our souls generally contract, in the inferior part, the qualities and dispositions of our bodies; and I say in the inferior part, because it is that part which is immediately connected with the body and subject to share in the disorders of the body. A delicate body overpowered by the burden of sickness, grieved by many sorrows, cannot permit the heart to be so lively, so active, so prompt in its operations as in health; but all this does not at all interfere with the acts of the soul in the superior part, which are as agreeable to God as if they were made in the midst of the most joyous gaieties of the world, yea, and more agreeable, being made with more pain and difficulty. But they are not so agreeable to the person who makes them because, not entering into the inferior part of the soul, they are not so delectable according to our ideas.

We must not be unjust, nor require from ourselves that which is not in us. When we are inconvenienced in regard to health, we must only require from our spirit some acts of submission, acts of holy union with the good pleasure of God, which are formed in the summit of the soul; and as to exterior actions, we must do the best we can and content ourselves with performing them, though reluctantly, languidly, and heavily. And to improve the languor, heaviness, and dullness of our heart, making them serviceable to divine love, we must embrace a holy abjection; thus will you change the lead of your heaviness into gold, and a gold finer than that of the rarest pleasures of the worldly heart. Have patience then with yourself, that the superior part may balance the ponderousness of the inferior part. (ST. FRANCIS DE SALES)

❧ You are aware that it is God Who has reduced you to your present state; it is He then Who dispenses you from your practices of piety, or rather Who forbids them to you. Hence, be not uneasy, but remember He expects from you in exchange that you will exercise yourself more assiduously in doing His will by renouncing your own, and it is in order that you may make this exercise your principle nourishment that the means of doing so are so frequently provided for you. Indeed, what contradictions, what reverses, what sacrifices does not sickness entail! Projects disarranged, expenses to be incurred, remedies against which you revolt, awkwardness and negligence on the part of those who have care of you; in fine, a multitude of little things that annoy you! How many occasions of saying: God wishes it to be so.... What ought to be your study, then, not to allow a single occasion of this kind to escape, and thus you will deserve to be placed in the rank of those whom Jesus holds most dear; *for whosoever,* He says, *does the will of God, he is My brother, My sister, My mother.* (PÈRE JEAN-JOSEPH HUGUET)

XIX

DEATH

*Tranquility is the all-important thing at the
moment of death, keeping in mind that you are
going from this life to the other as you would
through a door opening up to lead you to God.*

(CARDINAL MERRY DEL VAL)

WE OUGHT NOT FEAR DEATH

❧ The vilest of God's reasonable creatures is never so little
left to himself as when he lies down to die. He is never so
importuned by mercy, so almost cumbered with assistance,
as he is then. (FR. FREDERICK FABER)

❧ Children of men, how long will your hearts be burdened, how long will you seek your sustenance in lies and
shadows? When will you cease imagining death as a curse,
cease regarding it as the abyss of darkness and destruction?
Try today to understand that it is not the obstacle but the
means; it is the paschal transition that leads from the kingdom of shadows to that of reality, from the life of change
to the life of immutability. It is the good sister whose hand
will one day cast off the clouds and idle phantoms to lead
us into the holy of holies of certitude and incomparable
beauty. (FR. CHARLES ARMINJON)

❧ I acknowledge that your life is nothing in comparison
with that of Our Lord Jesus Christ; but, when offered
through love, it is of inestimable value. What does God
care about an alms of two farthings? Yet the poor widow

in the Gospel who gave it deserved to be praised by the Son of God and to be preferred to the scribes and Pharisees who had given much more considerable alms, because, says He, she had given all that she had, and notwithstanding her poverty, had given it with a great heart.

We can say the same of him who gives his life to God: he gives all that he has, without reserving anything, and this is what renders death precious. This is what made the early Christians run with so much eagerness to martyrdom: they all wished to give back to Our Lord the life which they had received from Him, and to compensate by their death for that which He had endured for love of them. We can no longer be martyrs: oh, what an affliction! But still we can die for Jesus Christ! We have a life that we can lose for His love: oh, what a consolation! (ST. FRANCIS DE SALES)

❧ It is by the last grace that death changes its nature for Christians, since, while it seems to divest us of everything, it really begins to clothe us, securing to us the eternal possession of eternal goods. So long as we are detained in this mortal abode, we live subject to change because, if you allow me to use the expression, change is the law of the country in which we dwell, and we possess no good, even in the order of grace, which we may not lose a moment after by the natural mutability of our desires. But as soon as we cease to count the hours and to measure our life by days and years, issuing from figures which pass and shadows which disappear, we arrive at the kingdom of truth where we are set free from the law of change. Then our soul is no more in danger, our resolutions no longer vacillate; death, or rather, the grace of final perseverance, has power to fix them. (BISHOP JACQUES-BÉNIGNE BOSSUET)

❧ Although God is omnipotent and there is nothing impossible to Him, yet in His mercy He has bound Himself not to destroy forever a soul whose will, at its exit from the body, is submissive to His will. As the tree falls, so it lies; and the soul will remain forever in that state in which it is found at the end of life: if submissive to His holy will, its salvation is unquestionable, though a delay may be made. So, by unreservedly abandoning one's self into the arms of God during life and at death, there is nothing to fear. Besides that His will ought to be our satisfaction, and He does not desire that anyone should perish but that all should come to salvation by penance; therefore it is that He will never send a soul submissive to His will into exterior darkness which is prepared only for rebels to His light and to His love. (ST. FRANCIS DE SALES)

❧ O how much of the beauty of God's love is gathered round the dying bed, how much more than we can see, how much more than we believe! We grant that it is unknown ground; but because mercy is so much needed then, because mercy has had so many antecedents with the soul, because it is God's will it should be saved, and finally because God is such a God as we know Him well to be, we boldly claim all that unknown land of Catholic deathbeds for the simple sovereignty of the divine compassion. That hour may explain many inexplicable salvations. The gloomiest mind must admit that it may have shrouded in it endless possibilities of salvation; and with such a God at such an hour, the possibilities grow miraculously into probabilities and forthwith disappear in those sweet sudden certainties with which the dying child of Jesus has fallen asleep upon its Father's bosom. (FR. FREDERICK FABER)

❧ There is nothing dreadful in that which delivers from all that is to be dreaded. (TERTULLIAN)

WE OUGHT TO WELCOME DEATH
WHEN GOD WISHES TO SEND IT

❧ Who can think of what death is and yet doubt that God's wisdom and His love are brought to bear with inexpressible sweetness both in its manner and its time? Men die when it is best for them to die. There are some dangers which they avoid in advance by dying then. They die when they are in the best state for dying. Even the deaths of those who are lost may be mercifully timed. When men die young, it is perhaps because they would have lost themselves if they had lived to be old. When men die late, it is perhaps to give them time to correspond to grace, to do penance for the past, and especially that they may get rid of some evil habit which would else be their perdition, and which the mere infirmity of age will help them to abandon. When men die just as they are coming into the possession of riches, or at the outset of a smiling career of laudable ambition, it is perhaps because God sees in their natural character or in their personal circumstances some seeds of future evil, and so He takes them while all that evil lies innocently undeveloped in their souls.

If God were pleased to tell us, we should probably be amazed at the numbers of convincing reasons that there are why each of us should die when and where and how we do. The very sight of so much legislation and arrangement on the part of God about this one final act of our probation is doubtless pouring into the souls of the blessed at all hours delightful streams of wondering adoration and ecstatic love.
(FR. FREDERICK FABER)

❧ It is vain for those of a sincere faith to say that they do not wish to die so soon in order that they may have time to become better; for they will not advance in virtue unless in proportion as they advance in the disposition which makes one desire death. To desire not to die is not a means to acquire more virtue; it is rather a mark that we have scarcely acquired any. Let those, therefore, who do not desire to die in order that they may be able to become perfect, desire to die, and they will then be perfect. (ST. AUGUSTINE)

❧ Perfection consists in desiring to die that we may no longer be imperfect, that we may wholly cease to offend God, that God may reign perfectly in us, and that this body of sin which we carry about with us until death, may, in punishment of its continual revolts against God, be reduced to dust, fully to satisfy His justice and sanctity, and by this last and most profound humiliation, fully to repair all the injuries which it has committed against the Divine Majesty. We rise towards perfection in proportion as these holy desires of death become more ardent and sincere, and the quickest means of becoming perfect is to desire death with one's whole heart. (ST. FRANCIS DE SALES)

WE MUST NOT LOSE COURAGE AT THE REMEMBRANCE OF OUR INFIDELITIES

❧ Many persons are tormented at death with the remembrance of their crimes, and seeing that they have done no penance, they are tempted to despair. "Oh, if I had fasted! Oh, if I had performed great charities for the poor! Alas! I am no longer in a state to perform them. What will become of me? What shall I do?" You can do something greater than all you have mentioned; namely, accept death and

unite it with that of Jesus Christ. There is no mortification comparable to this: it is the deepest humiliation, the greatest impoverishment, the most terrible penance. And I do not at all doubt but that he who is grieved for having offended God, and who accepts death willingly in satisfaction for his sins, will immediately obtain pardon. What a consolation to be able to perform while dying a greater penance than all the anchorets have been able to perform in deserts, and this at a time when one would seem no longer able to do anything! What a pity to see an innumerable multitude of persons deprive themselves of the fruit of death which of all the pains of life is the one of most merit! Why waste so advantageous an occasion of honoring God, satisfying His justice, discharging one's debts, and purchasing Heaven?
(ST. FRANCIS DE SALES)

❧ You have committed many faults, it is true; but where is the foolish person who would think it in his power to commit more than God could forgive? It is true, indeed, that at the sight of our past sins we ought always to be in fear and in sorrow, but we should not remain thus. We should pass beyond this resting place and call Faith, Hope, and Charity to our assistance: then our most bitter sorrow will be changed into peace, our servile fear will become chaste and filial, and distrust of ourselves, like a piece of exceeding bitter aloes, will be sweetened by the sugar of confidence in God. Against fears that spring from the apprehension of divine judgments we have the buckler of a blessed hope which makes us cast all our confidence, not on our own virtue, but on the mercy of God alone, assuring us that those who trust in His goodness shall never be confounded in their expectations.
(ST. FRANCIS DE SALES)

THE GRACES AND THE JOYS OF THE DYING

❧ Years of merit may be acquired in moments of deathbed temptations. Temptation always accelerates the speed of grace. But this is eminently the case on deathbeds. God may visit His servants with such a death in order to enable them to gain greater glory in Heaven. Or it may be that their spiritual life has been wanting in inward trials, and that the mystical purgation of their souls may not have been complete, and therefore He vouchsafes to perfect their holiness by this manner of death. On this side of the grave, Divine Love has no crucible more delicate than that of a death amidst temptations. Yet it is one which is most painful to the survivors, because it is curtained round with impenetrable gloom, indeed, with anxiety and dismay if the temptations have lasted to the end. But in most cases it is not so. Just at last the cloud lifts and discloses a golden horizon with its outline clear and its edge defined. Could we but bend over, what should we see but the brightness of a blessed eternity and the vicinity of an immediate Heaven, with no deep lake of cleansing fire between? Sad as the first prospect of these curtains of temptation is to the beholder, they cover some operations of grace which for grandeur and sublimity have no equals elsewhere. (FR. FREDERICK FABER)

❧ As we have said of the temptations, so also must we say of the graces of death, that there are others, unknown and unimaginable, peculiar graces out of God's reserved treasury, for such as have believed and have not presumed. At that hour, and in that act, faith gathers exotic graces of stronger, marvelous, many-sided virtues. For what is death to the believer but the falling—and in all falls there is a risk—into the hands of the unknown goodness of our God. (FR. FREDERICK FABER)

❧ There are many joys to the dying which are joys to them because they are dying. As we approach death, if we approach it as Christians should, we begin to enter into the dispositions of the saints. For example, there belongs to our condition a partial inability to sin. There are many sins which we can no longer commit and many which we have no temptation to commit. This is like a faint beginning of Heaven. It is enough to be a joy to us that the mere possibilities of sin are on the move, that any capability of offending God has become dead already. It cheers us on. It melts our hearts. It is a fresh spring of love within us. To be unable to offend God again is part of a saint's desire of Heaven. (FR. FREDERICK FABER)

❧ At the hour of death we do not distinguish among the various blessednesses of Heaven. We see them all in indistinct unity, as contemplative souls see God in contemplation. Heaven is one thing — to be eternally with Jesus. We thought we had already had a great devotion to the Sacred Humanity in our lifetime, but then we find we have hardly known its sweetness, its loveliness, its dearness. Just as, when death beautifies the characters of those we love, we feel as if we had never known them before as they deserved, as if till now we never suspected how much we should have to lose in losing them, so now the beauty of Jesus grows upon us like a glorious dawn; and, though we have desired Him and thirsted for Him all our lives, it is as if we had never known till now how much we were to gain in gaining Him. Words cannot tell the novelty of Jesus to the dying. The joy of that novelty, what less can it be than part of the eternal amazement of our happy souls in Heaven? (FR. FREDERICK FABER)

LET US HOPE IN THE LOVE
AND MERITS OF OUR SAVIOR

❦ It is true, death is hideous; but that life which is beyond the grave, and which the mercy of God will give us, is very desirable. We must by no means fall into diffidence; for, though we are sinners, yet we are far from being as bad as God is merciful to forgive those who repent, who have a will to amend, and who place their hopes in Jesus Christ. Death is no longer ignominious but glorious, since the Son of God has undergone it. We must die! These words are hard, but they are followed by a great happiness: it is in order to be with God that we die. (ST. FRANCIS DE SALES)

❦ I defy you, guilty, desolate, despairing soul, soul overwhelmed by terror, dread, and fear of damnation — I defy you to go before a crucifix or before the holy Tabernacle and say to Jesus, dwelling the more on the words the harder you find it to say them, "My God, I love You with my whole heart because You are infinitely good," and not feel that Jesus is moved by your words, and not hear Jesus reply, "And I, too, love you." Reason not on this. Try it. Could you believe of Jesus Christ that He does not know how to love, or that His Heart is less generous than yours? (FR. WILLIAM DOYLE)

❦ Though one must indeed be pure before appearing in the sight of the All-Holy God, still I know that He is infinitely just, and the very justice which terrifies so many souls is the source of all my confidence and joy. Justice is not only stern severity towards the guilty; it takes account of the good intentions and gives virtue its reward. Indeed, I hope as much from the justice of God as from His mercy. (ST. THÉRÈSE OF LISIEUX)

❧ Jesus has more than once told His saints that He would willingly be crucified over again for each separate soul of man. Where can such love stop? If it be a love short of immense, who has ever exhausted it? Who ever will exhaust it? Look at it in Heaven at this moment — O that we too were there! — it is rolling like boundless silver oceans into countless spirits and unnumbered souls. How Mary's sinless Heart drinks in the shining and abounding waters! How the Sacred Heart of Jesus seems to embrace and appropriate the whole gracious inundation in Itself! A short while and you will be there yourself and still the same vast flood of love. Ages will pass uncounted, and still the fresh tides will roll. Is not this an immensity of love? O beautiful gateway of death! Thou art a very triumphal arch for the souls whom Jesus has redeemed. (FR. FREDERICK FABER)

❧ Let each person who is dying rest on the merits of our Savior Jesus Christ rather than on his own. Let him trust in His goodness and in the prayers of the Blessed Virgin Mary and the Saints and the Elect of God. Let him set before his eyes the most bitter Passion and Death of Christ and remember that ineffable Love which constrained Him to suffer such humiliation; and into those gaping Wounds, and into that fathomless deep of His unbounded pity, let him cast himself and hide himself with all his sins and shortcomings. For the greater glory of God let him offer himself as a living sacrifice to the Lord so as to patiently bear, according to His most acceptable Will and from sincere love for Him, every bitter pain of weakness, and even death itself; yea, and whatever the Lord shall see fit to send upon him in time or eternity. If he shall be able really to do this — if, I say, from pure love he shall have offered himself with a ready mind, and with entire resignation of self to endure every punishment for the honor of the Divine Justice — that man shall neither enter hell nor any place of torment, even if in his single person he shall have committed all the sins of the whole world. (BL. LOUIS DE BLOIS)

❧ It often happens that good and pious souls, and very frequently also souls who are consecrated to Me, wound My Heart to its very depths by some diffident phrase such as, "Who knows whether I will be saved?" Open the Gospel and read there My promises. I promised to My sheep: *I will give them life everlasting; and they shall not perish forever, and no man shall pluck them out of My hand* (Jn. 10:28). Do you understand? No one can take a soul from Me! Why then the insult, "Who knows whether I will be saved"? I have given assurances in the Gospel that no one can pluck a soul from Me, and that I will give that soul eternal life, and so the soul cannot perish. Believe Me, into hell go only those who really wish to go there, for no one can snatch a soul from Me. Oh, if instead of wounding My Heart with such distrust, you would give a little more thought to the Heaven which awaits you! I did not create you for hell but for Heaven, not as a companion for the devil but to enjoy Me in everlasting love. Hell is only for those who wish to go there. (OUR LORD TO VEN. CONSOLATA BETRONE)

❧ How foolish your fear of being damned! After having shed My Blood in order to save your soul, after having surrounded your soul with graces upon graces all through your entire existence, would I permit satan, My worst enemy, to rob Me of that soul at the last moment of her life, just when I am about to gather in the fruit of the Redemption and when, therefore, that soul is on the point of loving Me forever? Would I do that, when in the Holy

Gospel I have promised to give the soul eternal life and that no one can snatch her from My hands? How is it possible to believe such a monstrosity? (OUR LORD TO VEN. CONSOLATA BETRONE)

✤ Final impenitence is found only in a soul who purposely wishes to go to hell and therefore obstinately refuses My mercy, for I never refuse pardon to anyone! I offer the gift of My immense compassion to all, for My Blood was shed for all, for all! No, it is not the multiplicity of sins which condemns a soul, for I forgive everything if she repents; but it is the obstinacy of not wishing to be pardoned, of wishing to be damned! Dismas on the cross had only one single act of faith in Me, but many, many sins; he was pardoned in an instant, however, and on the very day of his repentance, he entered into My kingdom and is a saint! Behold the triumph of My mercy and of faith in Me! No, My Father Who has given Me souls is greater and more powerful than all the demons! No one can snatch souls from the hand of My Father! (OUR LORD TO VEN. CONSOLATA BETRONE)

✤ The celestial King, having guided the soul which He loves even to the end of its life, assists it still in its blessed departure, by which He draws it to the nuptial bed of eternal glory, which is the delightful reward of holy perseverance. And then the soul, all ravished with love for its Beloved, representing to itself the multitude of favors and helps by which He has prevented and assisted it during the days of its pilgrimage, kisses incessantly the sweet succoring hand that led it along the way, and confesses that it is from our Divine Savior alone it holds all its happiness. "O Lord," it then says, "Thou hast been with me and hast kept me in the way by which I have come; Thou hast given me the bread of Thy Sacraments for my nourishment; Thou hast clothed me with the nuptial robe of charity; Thou hast brought me into this abode of glory which is Thy house, O my Eternal Father! What, O Lord, remains, unless for me to declare that Thou art my God forever and ever?" (ST. FRANCIS DE SALES)

THE MASSES WE HAVE HEARD IN LIFE WILL AID US TO DIE IN PEACE

❧ If I were asked upon what a dying man might surely place his trust, I should answer that nowhere could he find more certain ground for confidence than in the Holy Mass, provided that during his lifetime he loved it dearly, heard it devoutly, and offered it with a pure intention. Wherefore, let him say with the Psalmist: *I will sleep the sleep of death in peace,* trusting to the Holy Sacrifice of the Mass, and *I will not fear eternal death, for Thou, O Lord, hast singularly settled me in hope.* I do not believe I shall be lost forever, because I have so many times offered to Thee the acceptable Sacrifice of Justice, thereby causing Thee infinite satisfaction, infinite honor, infinite service, infinite delight, infinite reparation for the offenses my sins have been to Thee. In virtue of this, Thou hast settled me in hope of eternal life. In this steadfast hope I shall fall asleep in the Lord; I shall rest in peace; I shall appear before the judgment seat of Thy justice. (FR. MARTIN VON COCHEM)

❧ If you have been diligent and devout in hearing Mass during life, you will behold at your death a band of fair spirits advance toward you, who will dispel your fears and reassure your heart, saying, "Recognize in us the Masses thou didst hear on earth; we will go with thee into the dread presence of thy Judge; we will speak in thy defense; we will show how deep was thy devotion, how many the sins thou didst expiate and the penalties thou didst cancel. Be of good courage; we will appease the wrath of thy Judge and implore mercy on thy behalf." Oh, what a relief to the poor, afflicted soul to meet such friends to intercede for him! (FR. MARTIN VON COCHEM)

HAVE RECOURSE TO MARY IN THE HOUR OF DEATH

✤ If thou fearest that on account of thy faults, God in His anger will be avenged, what hast thou to do? Go, have recourse to Mary, who is the hope of sinners; and if thou fearest that She may refuse to take thy part, know that She cannot do so, for God Himself has imposed on Her the duty of succoring the miserable. (ST. BONAVENTURE)

✤ *Mother of Mercy!* What words more sweet in the sinner's ear! The past has been a long record of sin and sinfulness, of grace abused and calls neglected. God's inspirations have been despised, His patience abused, His anger defied. In terror the soul looks back on a misspent life; in horror it thinks of a judgment, just and searching, to come. How to face the look of an angry God? How to stand before Him from Whom nothing is hidden? How to answer for the days and years squandered which were given to serve Him alone? Oh! Turn then, poor soul, and look to Mary. Look to Her who is all merciful that She may obtain for you pardon and mercy. She is kind and loving; She has a mother's heart, full of pity for the erring. She will show Herself a Mother of Mercy to the sinner and the fallen. (FR. WILLIAM DOYLE)

❧ O happy confidence! O safe refuge! The Mother of God is my Mother! How firm, then, should be our confidence since our salvation depends on the judgment of a good Brother and a tender Mother. (ST. ANSELM)

❧ One single sigh that Mary offers to the Blessed Trinity is worth far more than all the prayers, desires, and aspirations of all the saints. Many Christians who call upon Her when they are at the hour of death, and who really ought to be damned, are saved by Her intercession. (REVELATION GIVEN TO ST. DOMINIC)

XX

THE END TIMES

The best way to ensure the future is to sanctify the present.
(DOM VITALIS LEHODEY)

KEEPING OUR FOCUS

❧ Happiness and holiness do not depend on external circumstances. Those who truly want to be saints can achieve sanctity anywhere, any time. The worse the circumstances, the greater the challenge and the opportunity. Some martyrs who suffered under the persecutions might not have saved their souls in times of peace. (BR. FRANCIS MALUF)

❧ We must not allow ourselves to be perturbed by the noise of our social strife and the convulsions of our revolutions. All this is but a prelude. It is the chaos that precedes harmony; it is motion seeking rest, twilight on the move towards day. The city of God is being built, invisibly but surely, amidst these shocks and heartbreaking convulsions. Public disasters and great scourges are none other than the sword of the Lord and the harbinger of His justice, separating the chaff from the good seed. Our wars, mortal combats, and civil commotions hasten the day of deliverance when the City of God will be perfect and complete; and, when the turmoil of the ages has passed, there will come a great calm. (FR. CHARLES ARMINJON)

❧ Violent storms encompass me on all sides; yet I am without fear, because I stand upon a rock. Though the sea roar, and the waves rise high, they cannot sink the vessel of Jesus. I fear not death, which is my gain; nor banishment, for the whole earth is the Lord's; nor the loss of goods, for I came naked into the world and must leave it in the same condition. I despise all the terrors of the world, and trample upon its smiles and favor. Christ is with me, whom shall I fear? Though waves rise against me, though the sea, though all the fury of princes threaten me, all these are to me more contemptible than a spider's web. I always say, "O Lord, may Thy will be done; not what this or that creature wills, but what it shall please Thee to appoint, that shall I do and suffer with joy." This is my strong tower, this is my unshaken rock, this is my staff that can never fail. If God be pleased that it be done, let it be so. Whatsoever His will is that I be, I return Him thanks. (ST. JOHN CHRYSOSTOM)

❧ If all the sorrows and calamities of these stormy times, by which the countless multitudes are being sorely tried, are accepted from God's hands with calm submission, they naturally lift souls above the passing things of earth to those of Heaven and arouse a certain secret thirst and intense desire for spiritual things. Thus, urged by the Holy Ghost, men are moved and, as it were, impelled to seek the Kingdom of God with greater diligence, for the more they are detached from the vanities of this world and from inordinate love of temporal things, the more apt they will be to perceive the light of heavenly mysteries. (VEN. POPE PIUS XII)

❧ It is indeed possible that our society may already be virtually beyond redemption. But should the Chastisement come to pass, there are no grounds whatsoever for despair. For God gives each man sufficient grace for his salvation; no one is condemned but for his own fault; and, what is most important of all, we must continually remind ourselves that our Divine Lord has already conquered the prince of this world and all his literally hellish works and pomps. Therefore, let us do what we can — that we *must* do; and what we cannot do, let us leave it to the Almighty with the confidence befitting us as little children of our Heavenly Father. (HAMISH FRASER)

❧ Fear not evil to come upon you from this world; for, perhaps, such evil will never happen, and even if it should happen, God will strengthen you. He commanded St. Peter to walk upon the waves; and St. Peter, seeing the winds and the storm, was afraid, and fear sank him. He sought the assistance of his Master, Who said: *Man of little faith! Why didst thou doubt?* And reaching out His hand, Our Lord helped him. If God requires you to walk on the waves of adversity, fear not, doubt not, God will be with you; have good courage and you shall be delivered. (ST. FRANCIS DE SALES)

VIEWING THE FUTURE FROM THE WAY OF SPIRITUAL CHILDHOOD

❧ It is a great mistake to worry as to what trouble there may be in store for us; it is like meddling with God's work. We who run in the way of Love must never allow ourselves to be disturbed by anything. (ST. THÉRÈSE OF LISIEUX)

❧ The refusal to worry about the future is one of the most important and precious fruits of the spirit of childhood. (MSGR. VERNON JOHNSON)

MARY WILL BE VICTORIOUS

❧ Truly we are passing through disastrous times, when we may well make our own the lamentation of the prophet: *There is no truth, and there is no mercy, and there is no knowledge of God in the land* (Osee 4:1). Yet in the midst of this tide of evil, the Virgin Most Merciful rises before our eyes like a rainbow, as the arbiter of peace between God and man. (ST. PIUS X)

❧ The righteous will suffer greatly. Their prayers, their penances, and their tears will rise up to Heaven, and all God's people will beg for forgiveness and mercy and will plead for my help and intercession. And then Jesus Christ, in an act of His justice and His great mercy, will command His angels to have all His enemies put to death. Suddenly, the persecutors of the Church of Jesus Christ and all those given over to sin will perish, and the earth will become desert-like. And then peace will be made, and man will be reconciled with God. Jesus Christ will be served, worshiped, and glorified. Charity will flourish everywhere. The new kings will be the right arm of the Holy Church, which will be strong, humble, and pious in its poor but fervent imitation of the virtues of Jesus Christ. The Gospel will be preached everywhere, and mankind will make great progress in its faith, for there will be unity among the workers of Jesus Christ, and man will live in fear of God. (OUR LADY OF LA SALETTE)

❧ During the first three centuries, the Church was persecuted. The blood of martyrs watered the seeds of Christianity. Later, when the persecutions ceased, one of the Fathers of the Church deplored the lukewarmness of Christians. He rejoiced when persecution returned. In the same way, we must rejoice in what will happen, for in the midst of trials, our zeal will become more ardent. Besides, are we not in the hands of the Blessed Virgin? Is not our most ardently desired ideal to give our lives for Her? We live only once. We die only once. Therefore, let it be according to Her good pleasure. (ST. MAXIMILIAN KOLBE)

In the end, my Immaculate Heart will triumph. The Holy Father will consecrate Russia to me, and she will be converted, and a period of peace will be granted to the world. (OUR LADY OF FATIMA)

PART THREE

Saved by Hope

Let us hold fast the confession of our hope without
wavering.... For we are saved by hope.

(ST. PAUL)

XXI

HOPE

The virtue most needed in the spiritual life is hope.
(FR. FREDERICK FABER)

OUR HOPE IS IN GOD'S GOODNESS

❧ Were our salvation in our own hands, we would indeed have reason to fear. But it is in God's hands. Let us then trust in God: let us hope in Him. (ST. GABRIEL POSSENTI)

❧ I hope because I possess infinite merits, infinite treasures; I hope because I have in my hand the key of Heaven; I have the key to the Heart of my Heavenly Father—I have the Blood of His Divine Son! I hope because the Gate of Heaven is Mary, my Mother! My hope is as infinite as the God upon Whom it rests. I hope against all hope—and I shall not be confounded. (VEN. MOTHER CATHERINE AURELIA)

❧ Great indeed was the confidence of the good thief. Conscious to himself of every sort of guilt and sin, without a single redeeming good work, he had passed his lawless life in taking the goods and even the lives of men; yet, at the end of his days, at the very gates of death, he conceived a hope of the life to come, which he had so grievously forfeited, or rather, which he had never done anything to deserve. If the thief had cause to hope, who shall henceforth despair? (ST. BERNARD)

❧ My hope is in Christ Who strengthens the weakest by His divine help. I can do all in Him Who strengthens me.

His power is infinite, and if I lean on Him, it will be mine. His wisdom is infinite, and if I look to Him for counsel, I shall not be deceived. His goodness is infinite, and if my trust is fixed in Him, I shall not be abandoned. (ST. PIUS X)

❧ The weakest, even the most sinful person has the greatest right to hope. By forgetting self and casting herself into the arms of God, she glorifies Him more than by any self-examination and self-reproach, which keep her attention fixed on her own defects rather than on the Savior within her Who is always willing to purify her. (ST. ELIZABETH OF THE TRINITY)

❧ Wait upon the Lord; be faithful to His commandments; He will elevate your hope and put you in possession of His Kingdom. Wait upon Him patiently; wait upon Him by avoiding all sin. He will come, doubt it not; and in the approaching day of His visitation, which will be that of your death and judgment, He will Himself crown your holy hope. Place all your hope in the Heart of Jesus; it is a safe asylum; for he who trusts in God is sheltered and protected by His mercy. To this firm hope, join the practice of virtue, and even in this life you will begin to taste the ineffable joys of Paradise. (ST. BERNARD)

❧ Clothe me, O God, with the green garment of hope. A living hope in You gives the soul such ardor, so much courage and longing for the things of eternal life that, by comparison with what it hopes for, all things of the world seem to it to be, as they are, dry, faded, dead, and without value. Grant that I may set my eyes on naught but You alone. Then You will be pleased with me, and I shall be able to say in all truth that I received from You as much as I hoped for. (ST. JOHN OF THE CROSS)

FOCUSING ON HEAVEN PUTS
ALL ELSE IN PERSPECTIVE
❧

❧ We must often draw the comparison of time and eternity. That is the remedy for all our troubles. How small will the present moment appear when we enter that great ocean! How much will we then wish we had doubled our penances and sufferings while that moment lasted. (ST. ELIZABETH ANN SETON)

❧ A day will come when we, like Jesus, shall rise bright and glorious, when all the pains and trials of this life will give place to peace and happiness unspeakable. On earth they will plan great enterprises; buildings will rise and other works begin, but we shall have no part in them. Our labor will be over, and our rest will have commenced. We are but pilgrims in this world, and pilgrimages do not last forever. But remember, it is not by satisfying nature we can gain Heaven, not by shaking off whatever troubles us. It is by courageously doing all that God asks of us in the circumstances in which we are placed. Take all God sends you to suffer; Heaven will repay you for all. (SR. LOUISE VANDERSCHRIEK)

MARY AS OUR HOPE
❧

❧ It is not without reason that Holy Church, in the words of Ecclesiasticus, calls Mary *the Mother of holy hope* (Ecclus. 24:24). She is the Mother who gives birth to holy hope in our hearts, not of the vain and transitory goods of this life, but of the eternal rewards of Heaven. (ST. ALPHONSUS DE LIGUORI)

❧ All power is given to Mary in Heaven and on earth, and nothing is impossible to Her. She can raise even those who are in despair to the hope of salvation. (ST. PETER DAMIAN)

❧ Who, O Lady, can be without confidence in thee, since thou assistest even those who are in despair? And I doubt not that whenever we have recourse to thee, we shall obtain all that we desire. Let him, then, who is without hope, hope in thee. (ST. BERNARD)

❧ Efforts to increase devotion to the Blessed Virgin are, to me, among the most encouraging signs that God has not forgotten us, that there are still faith and love on earth, and that there is still a recuperative principle in Christian society. I thank God, for society itself, that there are still those who delight to call themselves children of Mary and to keep alive in our cold, heartless world the memory of Her virtues. While She is loved and reverenced, there is hope for society. (ORESTES BROWNSON)

XXII

CONFIDENCE

Our confidence is due to the omnipotence of God.
The devil is powerful, but not omnipotent.
(BR. FRANCIS MALUF)

THE NATURE OF CONFIDENCE

❧ Christian confidence consists in perfect abandonment to God over and above every provision of human prudence. Oh, what joy it is to walk in this perfect dependence on Providence, to be always under this divine protection! (ST. JANE FRANCES DE CHANTAL)

❧ Confidence must live and work in the dark as briskly as in the light. It must be gay, playing blithely with difficulties, for difficulties are the stones out of which all God's houses are built. Of a truth, our whole generosity with God is nothing more than the measure of our confidence in Him. To sum it up in one word—in the pursuit of sanctity, confidence is progress. (FR. FREDERICK FABER)

❧ Confidence is the manliness of a humble soul. It is also the strength of love—not its effort or its impulse, but its abiding, constitutional strength. It is love chastised and therefore equable and steadfast. It is so eminently its nature to be practical that it can never remain only a sentiment or a pathos or an inward smoothing of the soul. It breaks out into action, as if it could not be kept in; and, like the bodily vigor of youth, it is often scarcely conscious of its own exertions. Moreover, it is the happiness of religion, that sunshine in which perseverance is comparatively easy, that light in which all the virtues combine properly and have ample room and fair play, the atmosphere in which delusion, discouragement, and indiscretion are, to our relief, least at their ease. (FR. FREDERICK FABER)

❧ Confidence is the only true worship. (FR. FREDERICK FABER)

❧ St. Paul writes: *We are confident of this very thing, that God, Who has begun the good work, will perfect the same to the day of Jesus Christ.* Carry away with you this lesson of confidence in God. Confidence means hope resting on His goodness; trust reposing on His love. Cast your whole weight upon it: throw the whole burden of your soul upon God. He loves you, He created you. He redeemed you, He has chosen you, He has called you to His grace, He has been working in you from your Baptism to this hour. If you wish to know why you may confide in God's love to you not only in the general sense of confidence, because He has mercy upon all, but why you may confide in God's love to you personally and by name, and one by one — lay to heart these motives of trust and gratitude.

Remember what you were once. How many who hear me can recollect the time when, through sin, they were dead before God; when they were *like the leper white as snow*; when they were walking for years in darkness, without the knowledge of God, turning their back upon His light, in bondage to manifold sins. Remember who and what it was that brought you back to life. Your resurrection from that state of spiritual death was as much a miracle of God's supernatural power as the raising of Lazarus from the grave. God offered mercy and love to you. He raised you from death and loosed you from your winding sheet of habitual sin. Confide in Him, therefore, for the future. You did not then know what He was doing for you. You know it now. It is the pledge of what He will do for you hereafter. He Who has begun that good work, if you do not thwart it, will make it perfect.

Again, see what you are at this moment. I trust that you who hear me are living the life of grace, in union with God, in prayer, in self-knowledge, in habitual confession, and in communion in the Body and Blood of Jesus Christ. I will not doubt that you are in full friendship with the Sacred Heart of our Divine Lord through the working of His grace in your hearts. If so, what brought you to this state? Who brought on the spring after the winter, and the summer after the spring? Who made you to be what you are now? It was not yourselves. It was the love and the grace of the Holy Spirit working in you; chiefly when you knew it not.

Think also what you may be hereafter. You may be saints. You may persevere to the end. Yow may grow in the light of faith all the days of your life, until upon your death bed you will perhaps see the first rays of the presence of God. You may grow in the confidence of hope, until the calmness, and the sweetness, and the brightness shed abroad in your soul shall be a foretaste of the eternal bliss of God. All this is within your reach: God has begun it in you. He will accomplish it, if you will work together with Him to the end. (CARDINAL HENRY EDWARD MANNING)

OUR CONFIDENCE IN THE FATHER'S LOVE

❧ When the prodigal son said to himself, "I will arise and will go to my Father," we might have asked him what he trusted to for his pardon. Upon what had he grounded his confidence? Upon what hope or assurance did he presume to appear in the presence of him whom he had so heinously offended? His answer would have been, "This is the assured grounds of my confidence — that he is my father. I have forfeited all title to the name or rank of his son; but he hath not lost the quality or affection of a parent. I need no stranger to intercede with a father. The tender affection of his own breast pleads powerfully within him and is sure to incline him in my favor. His paternal heart is moved and yearns to restore to a son by pardon that life which he formerly gave him by birth." (ST. PETER CHRYSOLOGUS)

❧ Happy we, if we know how to trust God as He should be trusted! A child with his mother is full of innocent, respectful liberties. He never doubts of gaining his end. He never anticipates a refusal till it actually comes, no matter how often it has come before. He was refused yesterday; so he feels sure today. If refused, he persists with the persuasions of a not disobedient love, and argues with a playful smile. When he is definitely refused, he goes up to her and kisses her and runs away as happy with his mother's affectionate will as if he had got what he wanted. So must we venture to be with our Eternal Father. (FR. FREDERICK FABER)

❧ Full of confidence in that vast extensive Providence which embraces all causes and all effects in its designs, the Christian is replenished with joy and learns to turn all things to good. If God sends him prosperity, he accepts with submission the present from Heaven and honors that mercy which delights in bestowing favors on the miserable. If adversity, he remembers that *trial produces hope*, that war is made to secure peace, and that if his virtue conquers, it will one day be crowned. Never does he despair because he is never without resource. Can he despair of his fortunes to whom there still remains an entire kingdom, and a kingdom no other than that of God? What power can cast him down who is supported by so sweet a hope? (BISHOP JACQUES-BÉNIGNE BOSSUET)

❧ After we have placed ourselves entirely in God's hands with complete confidence in Him, we must not fear adversity; for if some misfortune should befall us, God will know how to turn it to our good through ways which we do not know now, but will know some day. (ST. VINCENT DE PAUL)

❧ We never glorify God more than when, despite the sight of our sins and unworthiness, we are so filled with confidence in His mercy and in the infinite merits of Jesus Christ, that we throw ourselves on His bosom full of confidence and love, sure that He cannot repel us. (BL. DOM COLUMBA MARMION)

OUR CONFIDENCE IN CHRIST'S LOVE

❧ Do not fear. Jesus is more powerful than all hell. At the invocation of His Name, every knee in Heaven, on earth, and in hell must bend. This is the consolation of the good and the terror of the wicked. (ST. PIO OF PIETRELCINA)

❧ I am here, fear not. I am thine Advocate Who has made thy cause Mine own. I am thy Surety Who is come to pay thy debts. I am thy Lord Who has redeemed thee with My Blood, not in order to abandon thee, but to enrich thee, having bought thee at a great price. (OUR LORD TO ST. ALPHONSUS DE LIGUORI)

❧ Do you want proof that whatever happens is for our good? This is it: God has said, "I will never abandon you; I will be with you always." If a gentleman should promise you this, you would trust him. But God makes this promise to you, and do you doubt it? Do you want a stronger foundation for belief than the word of God, which is infallible? Yes, He promised it, He wrote it, He has given His word — so rest assured. (ST. AUGUSTINE)

❧ The Christ of the Gospels is one yearning over humanity, longing to find men and women whose faith and confidence in Him would enable Him to lift them out of their miseries and work wonders for them and in them and through them beyond all human understanding. (MSGR. VERNON JOHNSON)

❧ It is not sufficient to say, "My God, I have confidence in You." You must make the interior act of freeing yourself from all anxiety and rest on My Heart like St. John, the Beloved Apostle. I await this confidence from every soul. (OUR LORD TO SR. MARY OF THE TRINITY)

THE GREATER OUR NEED, THE GREATER SHOULD BE OUR TRUST

❧ Confidence in God ought to be greater in proportion to the pressing nature of the necessity in which we are placed. When Jesus cried in the anguish of His Passion, *My God, My God, why hast Thou forsaken Me?* He was at that time exhibiting a pattern of the highest perfection in the exact fulfillment of the obedience required from Him by His Eternal Father with Whom He was wholly united. He gives utterance to His perfect confidence in God in order to teach us, His children, that the more afflicted

we are, the more we ought to rely on aid from above.
(ST. CATHERINE OF BOLOGNA)

❧ When we find ourselves in some danger, we must not lose courage but confide much in the Lord; for where danger is great, great also is the assistance of Him Who is called our Helper in tribulation. (ST. AMBROSE)

❧ When one thinks only of God, and confides entirely in Him, trying to serve Him faithfully, God takes care of him. The greater the confidence placed in Him, the greater His care. Nor is there any danger of His care failing, since He has an infinite love for those who trust in Him. (ST. FRANCIS DE SALES)

CONFIDENCE IN THE WAY
OF SPIRITUAL CHILDHOOD

❧ Jesus deigns to point out to me the only way which leads to Love's divine furnace, and that way is self-surrender: it is the confidence of the little child who sleeps without fear in its Father's arms. (ST. THÉRÈSE OF LISIEUX)

❧ What is required from us? Humility and confidence: *Whosoever is a little one, let him come to Me!* "To be wholly little," that is to say, to know and love our helplessness, and for that reason, "to go to Him," that is, to Infinite Love, this is how we enter the lift of St. Thérèse's Little Way. And then He carries us up. All we have to do is not interfere, to yield ourselves to His upward movement. He will lift us up above ourselves, above our wretchedness and our shortcomings, and, little by little, will free us from ourselves, from our egoism! That is His work, His essential work. He will do this divine work if, while desiring its realization in us, we rely in no way on ourselves, but rather, fearlessly, unhesitatingly, and unreservedly on Him, on His gratuitous and all-powerful love. The desire to love, humility, and confidence; that is all. (PÈRE LOUIS LIAGRE)

❧ It seems to me that these two dispositions of humility and confidence are the line of demarcation between the purely ascetical spiritual life and the beginnings of the mystical life; the life, that is to say, where the divine action definitely begins to outweigh the human. If the soul resolutely lays aside self, surrenders itself to the Spirit of God, it begins the true divine life; it enters the way of sanctity. (PÈRE LOUIS LIAGRE)

❧ The chief originality of the Little Way of Childhood consists in putting ourselves into the hands of God and by force of confidence, love, and abandonment, being carried by Him to the highest summits of Charity. Thus it is God Who does all. As for the soul, she shall do nothing but be docile to the interior movements which her Divine Bearer will impress upon her, and her sole occupation will be to love Him whilst He carries her. (REV. GABRIEL MARTIN)

❧ I know that many saints have passed their lives in the practice of amazing penance for the sake of expiating their sins. But what of that? In My Father's house there are many mansions. These are the words of Jesus, and therefore I follow the path He marks out for me; I try to be nowise concerned about myself, and to abandon unreservedly to Him the work He deigns to accomplish in my soul. (ST. THÉRÈSE OF LISIEUX)

❧ When we keep little, we recognize our own nothingness and expect everything from the goodness of God, exactly as a little child expects everything from its father. Nothing worries us, not even the amassing of spiritual riches. (ST. THÉRÈSE OF LISIEUX)

🏵 Personally, I find perfection quite easy to practice because I have realized that all one has to do is take Jesus by the heart. Consider a small child who has displeased his mother by flying into a rage or perhaps by disobeying her; if he sulks in a corner and screams in fear of punishment, his mother will certainly not forgive his fault; but if he comes to her with his little arms outstretched, smiling and saying, "Kiss me, I won't do it again," his mother will immediately press him tenderly to her heart, forgetting all that he has done. Of course she knows quite well that her dear little boy will do it again at the first opportunity, but that does not matter—if he takes her by the heart, he will never be punished. (ST. THÉRÈSE OF LISIEUX)

OUR CONFIDENCE IN MARY
SHOULD BE BOUNDLESS

🏵 Follow Christ's example and trust in His Mother. Have confidence—She is all powerful. Has He not made Her the Distributrix of all graces? Is She not able to give all She wishes, to whom She wishes, and at any time She wishes? Have confidence: She is goodness itself. Since He has made Her all-powerful, could He have failed to make Her at the same time all-merciful? Have confidence: you are Her child. Does a mother ever refuse her child anything she can give to it? Have confidence: in giving to you, it is to Christ that She gives, for She knows that He lives in you, and that whatever is done to the least of His brothers is done to Him. When you invoke Her, you give Her the joy of continuing to take care of Him: to nourish, carry, shield, and rear Him. Have confidence: She desires to give you more than you desire to receive, because She loves you more, and loves Jesus in you more than you can ever love yourself. (FR. EMILE NEUBERT)

❧ Be of good heart, then, all you who are children of Mary. Remember that She accepts as Her children all those who choose to be so. Rejoice! Why do you fear to be lost when such a Mother defends and protects you? (ST. ALPHONSUS DE LIGUORI)

❧ If Mary is for us, who can be against us? (ST. ANTONINUS)

❧ If I love Mary, I am certain of perseverance and shall obtain whatever I wish from God. (ST. JOHN BERCHMANS)

❧ Shall a man who has an army of a hundred thousand soldiers about him fear his enemies? A faithful servant of Mary, surrounded by Her protection and Her imperial power, has still less to fear. (ST. LOUIS MARIE DE MONTFORT)

❧ Read, and read again, as often as you please, all that is said of Mary in the Gospels, and if you can find the least trace of severity recorded of Her, then fear to approach Her. But no, this you can never find; and, therefore, go to Her with a joyful heart, and She will save you by Her intercession. (ST. BERNARD)

❧ O poor lost sinners, despair not! Raise up your eyes and cast them on this beautiful Star and breathe again with confidence. (ST. BONAVENTURE)

❧ You ought to have confidence not because *you* are good, but because *She* is good. Does She cease to be good when you are bad? (FR. EMILE NEUBERT)

❧ There is not one single heroic act that we are unable to perform with the help of the Immaculata. (ST. MAXIMILIAN KOLBE)

❧ We can reach any height of perfection if our confidence in the Mother of God is strong enough. (VEN. TERESA QUE-VEDO)

❧ When nothing else remains, there is still Our Lady! (FR. LOUIS COLIN)

XXIII

GOOD WILL

*Courage! God asks only of us our good
will. His grace does the rest.*

(ST. THEOPHANE VÉNARD)

THE VALUE OF GOOD WILL

❧ Free will makes us our own; an evil will makes us the
devil's; a good will, God's. (FR. JEREMIAS DREXEL)

❧ In all things and above all things, hold on to your
good will, for this disposition alone will impart to your
soul the splendor and the special merit of all the virtues.
He who possesses this good will, this sincere desire to
advance My glory, to thank Me and to compassionate
My suffering, to love and to serve Me as much as all creatures combined, will, without any doubt, receive a reward
compatible with My infinite goodness. (OUR LORD TO ST.
GERTRUDE THE GREAT)

GOOD WILL ENSURES OUR
CONTINUAL ADVANCEMENT

❧ There is no creature of good will, no matter how weak
and insignificant, who, in the Name of Jesus, cannot aspire
to sanctity. (FR. GABRIEL OF ST. MARY MAGDALEN)

❧ So long as our wills remain loyal to Him, He is very
near us, lovingly occupied with the work of curing us and
making us better. Whilst He detaches and humbles us, He

is all the time supporting us with His invisible grace; He will continue to assist us to the end, if we only have the good will to pray and to struggle. (DOM VITALIS LEHODEY)

❧ He does much in the sight of God who does his best, be it ever so little. (ST. PETER OF ALCANTARA)

❧ It is impossible that we should not be continually advancing, even without our being conscious of the fact, so long as we do all that depends upon ourselves, that is to say, so long as we have the good will to make progress and prove this good will by serious efforts. (REV. DOM VITALIS LEHODEY)

❧ Peace, the gift which the Divine Child brought with Him from above, will not be bestowed on those individuals who are endowed with a good understanding or a good memory; it will not be granted to those who excel in bodily strength, who are remarkable for their personal beauty or for their noble birth; it will be given solely and exclusively to men of good will, no matter if all else be lacking to them—intellectual superiority, distinguished beauty, a splendid physique, high position. And who is the man of good will? He who desires and asks and strives after nothing else but solely and wholly what God wills. (FR. FRANCIS XAVIER LASANCE)

❧ Jesus will never allow a soul of good will to finish a holy life by an unhappy death. (REV. DOM VITALIS LEHODEY)

XXIV

HOLY DESIRES

*The more God wishes to bestow on us,
the more does He make us desire.*

(ST. JOHN OF THE CROSS)

GOD SEES AND WILL
SATISFY OUR DESIRES

❧ Why should he who has God for the object of his intentions and who does what he can, torment himself? Why should he trouble himself? What has he to fear? No, no, God is not so terrible to those who love Him; He is content with a little, for He knows that we have not much. (ST. FRANCIS DE SALES)

❧ Desire what you need, desire what God wants, desire what is right, desire Heaven and the means of reaching Heaven, which is grace. The promise of having only these desires: your desires will always be fulfilled. (FR. JOHN HARDON)

❧ I am not a despiser, but the Fulfiller of holy desires. (GOD THE FATHER TO ST. CATHERINE OF SIENA)

❧ Our Lord regards what you desire sincerely to become, rather than what you are. (VEN. CORNELIA CONNELLY)

❧ Blessed are they who ardently crave sanctity, for their desire shall be fulfilled. (ST. VINCENT PALLOTTI)

❧ The desire to love God, when it is sincere, is so pleasing to Our Lord that He never fails to satisfy it, and that beyond all our aspirations. (BL. DOM COLUMBA MARMION)

❧ I have found from long experience that God never fills a soul with an ardent and lasting desire for anything—love, holiness, etc.—without in the end gratifying it. (VEN. FRANCIS LIBERMANN)

❧ We must all have the desire of attaining the height of virtue, but we must not lose courage when we do not attain immediately the essence of virtue, nor should we be dissatisfied, provided that we do our best. (ST. FRANCIS DE SALES)

❧ It is very necessary for us not to contract our desires but put our trust in God; for if we do violence to ourselves, by little and little, we shall, though not all at once, reach that height which many saints, by His grace, have reached. If they had never resolved to desire, and had never, by little and little, acted upon that resolve, they never could have ascended to so high a state. (ST. TERESA OF ÁVILA)

❧ I assure you that Supreme Goodness has prepared the times and the ways for us to do great deeds for Him. Be eager, then, to increase your holy desires, and be not satisfied with little things because God wants great things! (ST. CATHERINE OF SIENA)

❧ God does not fail to repay, even in this life, every good desire. (ST. TERESA OF ÁVILA)

❧ Have a little patience, and you will see that all will go well; for the dear Savior of our souls has not given us those inflamed desires of serving Him, without intending to provide some opportunity for doing so. He postpones the hour of the accomplishment of your holy desires only to make you find it happier; for the loving heart of our Redeemer arranges and adjusts the events of this world to the greater good of those who unreservedly devote themselves to His love. It will come, then, the happy hour you desire, the day which Providence has named in the secret of Its mercy. (ST. FRANCIS DE SALES)

THE POWER OF HOLY DESIRES

❧ I can well understand the pain of longing to love Him intensely and at the same time being powerless to prove that love. But, child, you have a powerful weapon in your hand—desires. Desires please Him immensely. Often repeat your desire to love. (FR. WILLIAM DOYLE)

❧ If in a soul there is nothing else but the longing to love its God, everything else is there already, because God is not present where there is no desire of His love. Say to God: "Do You want greater love from me? I have no more. Give me more, therefore, and I will offer it to You." Don't doubt that God will accept this offer. (ST. PIO OF PIETRELCINA)

❧ The soul that desires Me possess Me in very truth. (GOD THE FATHER TO ST. CATHERINE OF SIENA)

❧ In the measure you desire Him, you will find Him. He so esteems our turning to look at Him that no diligence will be lacking on His part. (ST. TERESA OF ÁVILA)

❧ Desire never ceases to pray even though the tongue be silent. If ever desiring then ever praying. (ST. AUGUSTINE)

HOLY DESIRES IN THE WAY OF SPIRITUAL CHILDHOOD

❧ He sees what a tiny little child you are, and how useless even your greatest efforts are to accomplish the gigantic work of becoming a saint. But this longing, this stretching out of baby hands for His love, pleases Him beyond measure; and one day He will stoop down and catch you up with infinite tenderness in His divine arms and raise you to heights of sanctity you little dream of now. (FR. WILLIAM DOYLE)

XXV

SANCTITY

You will become a saint if you really want to.
(ST. MARIE OF THE INCARNATION)

GOD WISHES US TO BE SAINTS

❧ We can, if we will, become a saint, for God will never refuse us the help to do so. (ST. JOHN MARIE VIANNEY)

❧ I have long had the feeling that, since the world is growing so rapidly worse and God has lost His hold, as it were, upon the hearts of men, He is looking all the more earnestly and anxiously for big things from those who are faithful to Him still. He cannot, perhaps, gather a large army around His standard but He wants everyone in it to be a *hero*, absolutely and lovingly devoted to Him. If only we could get inside that magic circle of generous souls, I believe there is no grace He would not give us to help on the work He has so much at heart—our personal sanctification. (FR. WILLIAM DOYLE)

❧ If only you are faithful to Him and exact in following His inspirations, He will raise you to a height of sanctity you do not dare to dream of now. (FR. WILLIAM DOYLE)

WE MUST DESIRE SANCTITY
AND STRIVE FOR IT

❧ When we study the lives of the saints, we seem to find that apparently they were all "great" souls. They either

222

followed God from their youth and, like the Little Flower, never refused Him anything; or else, even in their sins, they showed a "greatness" and thoroughness which after their conversion, seems at first to have been the cause of their heroic sanctity. Once converted, they never looked back. Such greatness of soul, we know is not ours; we have not even the grit to be great in sin. Their determination, their thoroughness, their whole-heartedness, have little in common with our faint-hearted futility. Even in our sins, we are merely mean and treacherous; we try to have it both ways; we have no generosity in doing good, or even in doing bad; we are inconstant and inconsequent; we are failures. The counselors of despair are quick to remind us what Our Lord said of those who were neither hot nor cold — that He would begin to vomit them out of His mouth because they were lukewarm — and we get the impression that there is no conversion, no hope of advance, for the tepid.

That is just where we must stir up our faith and glory in our infirmities. Even if our sanctification is difficult — and there is no reason to admit that it is, for such a soul has a proximate disposition for a very high degree of humility — we must not forget that our sanctification is to be more the work of God than our own work, that God's plan is to glorify Himself by His mercy, and that mercy is most glorified when it is exercised towards great misery. The more difficult the work and the less claim we have on God's help for it — the more will His mercy be glorified in making us saints. Therefore, our very hopelessness is a reason for hoping without limit! (DOM EUGENE BOYLAN)

❧ Why is it that pusillanimous souls are to be found who say that holiness is not for them, that perfection is something beyond their power? Do you know what makes them speak thus? It is their lack of faith in the efficacy of Christ's merits. By dying for us Christ has given us free and confident access to the Father, and through Him there is no grace for which we cannot hope. (BL. DOM COLUMBA MARMION)

❧ The constant will to advance and the steady pursuit of perfection are accounted perfection. (ST. BERNARD)

❧ It depends on myself whether I become a saint or not. If I wish and will to be one, half the battle is over. Certainly God's help is secured. Every fresh effort to become holy gets fresh grace, and grace is what makes us holy and pleasing to God. (FR. WILLIAM DOYLE)

❧ We must have the care which God wishes us to have of perfecting ourselves and, nevertheless, leave to Him the care of our perfection. God wishes us to have a peaceful and tranquil care, such as will make us perform what is judged proper by those who guide us, and that we go faithfully forward in the way marked out by the rules and directions given us; as for the rest, to repose on His paternal bosom, endeavoring, as far as possible, to keep our soul at peace, for the abode of God is in Himself and in the peaceful heart. (ST. FRANCIS DE SALES)

❧ Our possibilities of holiness are greater than we like to suppose. We estimate them below the truth because it is painful to our self-love to contemplate such a gulf as really exists between what we actually attain and what we might attain. For the same reason, we underestimate the amount of grace we receive. A detailed correspondence to grace in things quite within our compass, would lead us almost unawares to the heights of sanctity. (FR. FREDERICK FABER)

❧ If only everyone could grasp this fact: Every tiny thing (aspirations, self-denial, etc.) makes us holier than we were. Just think of the thousands of tiny things done each day for God: every one of them has added to our merit, making us more pleasing in His sight and each moment holier. (FR. WILLIAM DOYLE)

❧ We must do everything in our power, give without counting the cost, practice virtue at every opportunity, deny ourselves constantly, prove our love by all kinds of attentions and marks of affection; in a word, do all the good deeds in our power for love of God. But since all this is really very little, it is important to place all our trust in Him Who alone sanctifies all deeds, and can sanctify without them. (ST. THÉRÈSE OF LISIEUX)

❧ This firm resolution to become a saint is extremely pleasing to Me. I bless your efforts and will give you opportunities to sanctify yourself. If you do not succeed in taking advantage of an opportunity, do not lose your peace, but humble yourself profoundly before Me and, with great trust, immerse yourself completely in My mercy. In this way, you gain more than you have lost, because more fervor is granted to a humble soul than the soul itself asks for. (OUR LORD TO ST. FAUSTINA)

WE MUST NOT LOSE COURAGE

❧ We must all have the desire of attaining the height of virtue, but we must not lose courage when we do not attain immediately the essence of virtue, nor should we be dissatisfied, provided that we do our best. (ST. FRANCIS DE SALES)

❧ As long as the desire of pleasing God remains in your

heart, and there is a steady, constant effort towards perfection, you need not be uneasy about your state of soul. Everything else, small imperfections and even deliberate faults, coldness in prayer, are mere details in a life which is very pleasing to God. Do not expect to see much progress, but rest assured that the advance is certain and steady. (FR. WILLIAM DOYLE)

❧ Every day sanctifying grace is increasing in your soul in spite of faults and failings; therefore every day you are more pleasing to God even though you pain Him by infidelities. You can say each day, "I am holier than I was yesterday." (FR. WILLIAM DOYLE)

❧ Never fear that your past faults and infidelities will prevent you from reaching the degree of union that God intends for you; in an instant He can repair all that. (BL. DOM COLUMBA MARMION)

❧ If you do what lies in your power, Our Lord will make you so strong that you will astonish men. And how easy this is for His Majesty since He made us from nothing. (ST. TERESA OF ÁVILA)

❧ Holiness depends less upon what we do than upon why and how we do it. (FR. FREDERICK FABER)

❧ Even if we conceive of His plan as setting a certain height of holiness for each man, we should also remember that He can lead us to that height from any point we may reach in our wanderings. If we lose our way and leave the path He has marked out for us, He can still bring us to the goal by another route. It is not unreasonable to suppose that this alternative way will be more difficult; its very difficulty, however, is an assurance of the height to which it can lead us, for it affords us a new opportunity of gaining merit and showing our love. (DOM EUGENE BOYLAN)

THE LOVE OF GOD AS
THE ESSENCE OF PERFECTION

❦ I know of only one means to attain perfection: *love*. Let us love since our hearts were made for nothing else. (ST. THÉRÈSE OF LISIEUX)

❦ Some make the sanctification of man to consist in austerity, others in giving to charity, others in frequenting the sacraments, others in prayer. But for my part, I know of no other perfection than loving God with all one's heart. Without this love, all the virtues are only a heap of stones. (ST. FRANCIS DE SALES)

❦ If you want to know how to grow in holiness, grow in lifting your heart to the true love of God, to the relish of the things that belong to God. When that is there, all the other virtues flourish. (BR. FRANCIS MALUF)

CONFORMITY TO GOD'S WILL
AS THE HEIGHT OF PERFECTION

❦ It happens sometimes — too often — that we go very far in search of perfection, whereas we have it continually within our reach. After all, holiness is nothing else practically than the union of conformity between man's will and God's will. The more perfect this conformity is — that is to say, the more real it is and based on love — the more it unites the creature to the Creator, so that to become a saint it would suffice to practice perfectly holy abandonment; for in its perfect degree this abandonment supposes the soul to be altogether absorbed and completely transformed into the will of God. (REV. GABRIEL MARTIN)

❧ The height of perfection does not consist either in interior consolations, or sublime raptures, or in visions, or in the gift of prophecy; but rather in rendering our wills so conformed and submissive to God's will that we embrace with our whole heart whatsoever He ordains, and accept the bitter as gladly as the sweet the moment we perceive it to be His good pleasure. (ST. TERESA OF ÁVILA)

❧ The more joyfully souls do His will, the greater is their perfection. (ST. THÉRÈSE OF LISIEUX)

❧ Be assured that in this conformity of man's will with God's consists the highest perfection we can attain, and those who practice it with the greatest care will be favored by God's greatest gifts and will make the quickest progress in the interior life. Do not imagine there are other secrets. All our good consists in this. (ST. TERESA OF ÁVILA)

❧ He who wishes to become holy easily has not to choose the things which do not please him. He has only to love God, giving witness to his love by looking to follow His will; that is where perfection exists. He who follows the will of God with all his heart is a saint. And even if, in this conformity to the will of God, he does not encounter sorrow, nor difficult things, nor suffering, he is, nevertheless, a saint. Holiness is found in God, and God conveys it to us when we allow Him to act freely with us. (BR. MARCEL VAN)

❧ Entrust yourself completely to My will, saying, "Not as I want; according to Your will, O God, let it be done unto me." These words, spoken from the depths of one's heart, can raise a soul to the summit of sanctity in a short time. In such a soul I delight. (OUR LORD TO ST. FAUSTINA)

❧ O dear souls, let me repeat to you: do what you are doing; suffer what you are suffering: sanctity will cost you no more. It is only your heart that need be changed. By the heart we mean the will. This change, then, consists in willing what comes to us by the order of God. Yes, holiness of heart is a simple *fiat*, a simple disposition of conformity to the will of God. And what is easier? For who could not love so adorable and merciful a will? Let us love it, then, and through this love alone all within us will become divine. (FR. FRANCIS XAVIER LASANCE)

PRAYER AS A MEANS OF SANCTITY

❧ The contemplation of Our Lord is not only holy, it is sanctifying; just thinking of Him, looking at Him with faith and love, sanctifies us. (BL. DOM COLUMBA MARMION)

❧ I assert fearlessly that if only we all prayed enough, and I mean by that a constant, steady, unflagging stream of aspirations, petitions, etc., from the heart, there is no one, no matter how imperfect, careless, or even sinful, who would not become a saint and a big one. (FR. WILLIAM DOYLE)

SUFFERING AS A MEANS OF SANCTITY

❧ Holiness is not a matter of fine words, not even a matter of just thinking or feeling them; it consists in being truly willing to suffer. (ST. THÉRÈSE OF LISIEUX)

❧ You must bear in mind that, if God has marked you out for great graces and possibly a holiness of which you do not even dream, you must be ready to suffer; and the more this comes to you, the happier it ought to make you. (FR. WILLIAM DOYLE)

❧ If you are trying to be a saint, the world is a happy conspiracy working for your benefit. Even the things that would be disastrous for those who are not trying to be saints are, to you, blessings. Yes, even crosses, whatever they might be and no matter how heavy they are. For you, they are working unto good, playing their part in preparing a place of everlasting glory for you in the life to come. This is, in truth, the heart of wisdom. (BR. FRANCIS MALUF)

SPIRITUAL CHILDHOOD AS A FORM OF SANCTITY

❧ "Holy spiritual childhood is a more perfect state than the love of suffering, for nothing immolates a man to such a degree as to be sincerely and peacefully lowly. The childlike spirit kills pride far more surely than the spirit of penance," according to Msgr. Gay. The apparent contradiction disappears if we remember that the fundamental reason both for suffering and for humility is to give ourselves to God and to be transformed into Him. Whatever achieves that best is the more perfect. And one cannot improve on the will of God as a means of sanctification whether He sends us joy or sorrow. It is His will — and that is all that really matters. (DOM EUGENE BOYLAN)

❧ You remind me of a tiny child beginning to stand upright, but unable as yet to walk. Longing to reach her mother at the top of the stairs, she keeps on lifting her little foot to mount the first step; it is a fruitless task. She falls over again and again, unable to make any progress. By the practice of every virtue, keep on lifting your little foot to scale the stair of perfection, but do not imagine that you will be able to scale even the first step! No, but God does not ask more than your good will. From the top of the stairs, He is lovingly watching you. Soon, won by your fruitless efforts, He Himself will come down, and taking you in His arms, will bear you away forever to His kingdom — which you will never leave again. (ST. THÉRÈSE OF LISIEUX)

❧ When I read certain treatises where perfection is set forth as encompassed by a thousand obstacles, my poor little head grows weary very quickly. I close the learned book which puzzles my brain and dries up my heart, and in its stead I open the Holy Scriptures. Then all appears clear, luminous. One single word discloses to my soul infinite horizons; perfection seems easy; I see that it is sufficient to recognize our nothingness and to leave oneself like a child in the arms of the good God. Let great souls and sublime intellects enjoy the beautiful books which I cannot understand still less put into practice. I rejoice in being little. (ST. THÉRÈSE OF LISIEUX)

OUR LADY AS THE SUREST MEANS TO SANCTITY

❧ Of all the means to possess Jesus Christ, Mary is the sweetest, the easiest, the shortest way, and the holiest. (ST. LOUIS MARIE DE MONTFORT)

❧ We never advance more rapidly in love of the Son than when we travel by the Mother. There is no time lost in seeking Him if we go at once to Mary; for He is always there, always at home. She is the short road to Him. (FR. FREDERICK FABER)

❧ When the Holy Ghost has found Mary in a soul, He flies there. He enters there in His fullness; He communicates Himself to that soul abundantly, and to the full extent to which it makes room for His Spouse. Nay, one of the greatest reasons why the Holy Ghost does not now do startling wonders in our souls is because He does not find there a sufficiently great union with His faithful and inseparable Spouse. (ST. LOUIS MARIE DE MONTFORT)

❧ The more the Holy Ghost finds Mary, His dear and inseparable spouse, in any soul, the more active and mighty He becomes in producing Jesus Christ in that soul and that soul in Jesus Christ. (ST. LOUIS MARIE DE MONTFORT)

❧ Mary is like a holy magnet attracting Eternal Wisdom to Herself with such power that He cannot resist. This magnet drew Him down to earth to save mankind and continues to draw Him every day into every person who possesses it. Once we possess Mary we shall, through Her intercession, easily and in a short time possess Divine Wisdom. (ST. LOUIS MARIE DE MONTFORT)

❧ He who gives himself without limits to the Immaculata will in a short time attain a very high degree of perfection and procure for God very great glory. (ST. MAXIMILIAN KOLBE)

❧ Holiness increases in proportion to the devotion that one professes for Mary. (FR. FREDERICK FABER)

❧ There will be a direct proportion between the number of souls entirely devoted to the service of the Immaculata and the number of truly heroic saints. (ST. MAXIMILIAN KOLBE)

XXVI

GRACE AND THE DIVINE INDWELLING

God only asks to overwhelm us with graces.
We grieve Him in not believing this sufficiently.
(MOTHER AGNES OF JESUS)

WHAT GRACE IS

❧ What is grace? Who shall be able to worthily define it? It is a free gift, an undeserved bounty, a light for the darkness of our spirit, something which touches and changes the heart with exquisite charm and irresistible power; in a word, it is a divine influence, which, doing away with the perverse and corrupt inclinations of the old man, puts in their stead the noble thoughts and longings of the new, so that from the sinner that he was, he becomes a penitent, a just man, and a saint. Such is grace. (MSGR. JEAN-JOSEPH GUAME)

❧ Grace is not a different thing than glory. It is only glory in exile, while glory is but grace at home. Grace is the solid treasure; glory is only its exaltation and success. (FR. FREDERICK FABER)

❧ Each augmentation of grace is a mission of a Divine Person, a contact with God, a more intimate and exquisite union with Him. (FR. FREDERICK FABER)

THE POWER OF GRACE

❧ Consider what wonders grace works in the soul. It invests her with surpassing loveliness, rendering her so fair and attractive that the beauty of the sun, the stars, the flowers cannot compare with hers. God Himself takes pleasure in it and would rather that Heaven and earth should pass away than that the beauty of such a soul should be marred or destroyed by mortal sin. Even the least degree of grace is productive of this beauty, but it is enhanced and increased by each added grace. (FR. MARTIN VON COCHEM)

❧ Grace is all-powerful. By its help, we can break all our bad habits, overcome all temptations, and gain all the virtues we need. (MOTHER MARY LOYOLA)

❧ We live in an ocean of grace, as fishes live in the deep sea. It is above, beneath, around us, everywhere and overwhelmingly. Surely if it is not hard for a man to live in the pure bright air of heaven, and some shock of disease or outward accident must supervene to cut short the thread of his existence, so it cannot be hard in this fresh, buoyant, bracing atmosphere of grace for a man to save his soul, and it must be some danger which he himself has sought, or some poison which he has willfully imbibed — and after that pertinaciously refused the antidote, which can destroy his soul — and even then with difficulty. A man must struggle to be out of grace, when grace is so around him. We believe that in all things man's will is free, but that in nothing is he less free than to be lost eternally. (FR. FREDERICK FABER)

WE ARE CONSTANTLY
BEING OFFERED GRACE
❧

❧ God has more desire to give us graces than we have to receive them from Him. (ST. AUGUSTINE)

❧ Everything is a grace! (ST. THÉRÈSE OF LISIEUX)

❧ If we could but have hearts to feel, and eyes in our souls to see, where we really are! There are good angels around us, and graces are raining down upon us, great and small, all our lives long; inspirations are falling upon us, thick as snowflakes, and almost as softly and as silently; we are fastened with a thousand fastenings to great unknown eternal purposes, and we feel them no more than a strong man feels the cobwebs and the gossamer on the autumnal grass. And all the while we are closed all round, and walled in, not so much with the sun and moon and stars, with the air and the floor of our own planet, as with the living and inevitable Presence of the All-Holy, Who will not spare us one moment from His sight, and Who even while we sleep expects us to do our work of glorifying Him, and Whose love of us, and therefore His jealousy of us, is as everlasting as Himself. (FR. FREDERICK FABER)

❧ We underestimate the amount of grace we receive. A detailed correspondence to grace in things quite within our compass would lead us almost unawares to the heights of sanctity. (FR. FREDERICK FABER)

❧ Be it known that a pious Christian, by every good work he performs, increases God's grace within him, and this not merely by great works, but by every good work however insignificant, even by every holy thought and pious aspiration. Now, seeing that God's grace is so easily won, and that he who corresponds to it obtains so great a reward, who will not strive to do what is good and to serve God with all his heart? (FR. MARTIN VON COCHEM)

❧ Every fresh effort to become holy gets fresh grace, and grace is what makes us holy and pleasing to God. (FR. WILLIAM DOYLE)

❧ Every instant, we can grow in grace and, consequently, acquire a new degree of eternal glory. In the course of a few years we can therefore accumulate hundreds of thousands, perhaps millions of degrees. That is to say, it is in our power to enlarge a thousand-fold, a million-fold, our capacity for seeing, loving, and possessing God. What a magnificent increase of glory for Him, of happiness for us, and throughout all eternity! (REV. DOM VITALIS LEHODEY)

❧ No action is excluded from the domain of grace, of charity, of merit. There is no action which may not serve to increase the life of grace in us. (BL. DOM COLUMBA MARMION)

❧ Alas! If we would but let each day's grace lead us whither it wills with its gentle step, its kind allurement, and its easy sacrifice, in what a sweetly incredible nearness to the world of the saints should we not find ourselves before many years were gone by! (FR. FREDERICK FABER)

❧ Do not be over-anxious about the abuse of grace. Fear is good, without doubt, but it is necessary that it be a loving fear, peaceful and calm — like that of a child who fears he has not embraced his father with enough tenderness. (VEN. MOTHER CATHERINE AURELIA)

GRACE PURSUES EVEN SOULS
ESTRANGED FROM GOD

❧ Of the thousands of souls in the world today unhappily immersed in the gulfs of mortal sin, is there one whom a whole multitude of beautiful actual graces is not soliciting to return to God? O such pathetic invitations to come back to Him; such fair lights of God's tender compassion riding over the dark soul like the white sunbeams over a stormy landscape; such sweet remorses, sharp, but very, very sweet; such cold sobering thoughts of future punishment; such wise artful alternations of crosses and consolations; such lifelike speakings of dead books; such barbed words of preachers; such solemn eloquence of the deaths of those we love; such a nameless sensible thraldom of God and grace and heavenly presences, which we never can shake off—all these, now with a very clamor of assaulting armies, now with low, soft, and songlike pleadings, are the forces of actual grace, which have never been drawn off from before the gates of the heart, however long they may have been obstinately barred against God by a countless garrison of mortal sins. (FR. FREDERICK FABER)

THE GRACE OF THE PRESENT MOMENT

❧ Of all the many kindnesses of God to man, is there any kindness greater than the permission to live each day as a life apart, to make of each day a perfect thing, unspoiled by what may have been, still more by what may not be? And yet is there any kindness of God more commonly neglected, more recklessly thrown away?

It is what I am now, not what I have been or shall be; what I do now, not what I have done or shall do, that here and now matters most to me, and to God, and to all the world besides.

Those who face that which is actually before them, unburdened by the past, undistracted by the future, these are they who live, who make the best use of their lives; these are those who have found the secret of contentment. (REV. ALBAN GOODIER)

❧ The surest method of arriving at a knowledge of God's eternal purposes about us is to be found in the right use of the present moment. We must esteem our present grace, and rest in it, and with tranquil assiduity correspond to it. Our present grace is the most infallible will of God. It is a revelation from God, which almost always brings its own authoritative interpretation along with it. What we want for our sanctification is not merely grace, but the right grace, the right grace at the right time and in the right place. God's will does not come to us in the whole but in fragments, and generally in small fragments. It is our business to piece it together and to *live* it into one orderly vocation. Like a lantern in the night, grace gives light around our feet, a circle of light just wide enough to prevent our stumbling. But then we must look at our feet. If we strain our eyes into the gloom ahead of us, we shall stumble in spite of the lantern; nay, sometimes we shall even stumble because of it, its shadows move so suddenly and with such unwieldy strides.

Our present grace is also the one least beset with delusions, and we can act safely upon it, although perhaps not comfortably, even when we do not see how it matches with what has just gone before, or how it can fit into any conceivable future which our circumstances will allow. The hours are like slaves which follow each other, bringing fuel to the furnace. Each hour comes with some little kindling of God's will fastened upon its back. If we thus esteem our present grace, we shall begin to understand God's purposes. For safety and for swiftness, for clear light and successful labor, there is nothing like the present. (FR. FREDERICK FABER)

APPRECIATING THE PRESENCE OF GOD WITHIN US

❧ To reach the ideal life of the soul, we must live in the supernatural, must realize that God dwells within the depths of our soul and do all things with Him; then nothing can be trivial, however commonplace in itself, for we do not live in but above such things. A supernatural soul does not deal with secondary causes but solely with God. How this simplifies our view of life! It resembles the existence of the blessed spirits, and the soul is freed from self and from all else. (ST. ELIZABETH OF THE TRINITY)

❧ O thou soul, most beautiful of creatures, who so earnestly longest to know the place where thy Beloved is, that thou mightest seek Him and be united to Him! Thou art thyself that very tabernacle where He dwells, the secret chamber of His retreat where He is hidden. Rejoice, therefore, and exult, because thy Good and all thy Hope is so near thee as to be within thee; yea, rather, rejoice that thou canst not be without it, for, lo, *the kingdom of God is within you.* (ST. JOHN OF THE CROSS)

❧ God is not only our God, but our own God. He is really ours in a way in which He is no one else's, through His special love of us separately. He is not distant. He is not common property between all His creatures, though He is most truly so. His arms are not round all men, and round us among them, though verily His arms are so round us. But His arms are round our own selves. We have Him all to ourselves, in secret caresses, in private embraces, in a privileged exclusiveness. He is the God of our own souls — simply, sweetly, truly, our own private God. (FR. FREDERICK FABER)

❧ The soul which loves God is made a Heaven which He inhabits, and in which she converses with Him in the midst of her own substance. Though He is infinite, He invites us to converse with Him and declares that it is His delight to be with us. Shall we not look upon it as our greatest happiness and comfort to be with Him and to enjoy the unspeakable sweetness of His presence? Oh! What ravishing delights does a soul taste which is accustomed by a familiar habit to converse in the Heaven of her own interior with the Three Persons of the adorable Trinity! Dissipated worldlings wonder how holy solitaries can pass their whole time buried in the most profound solitude and silence of creatures. But those who have had any experience of this solitude are surprised, with far greater reason, how it is possible that any souls which are created to converse eternally with God, should here live in constant dissipation, seldom entertaining a devout thought of Him Whose charms and sweet conversation eternally ravish all the blessed. (FR. ALBAN BUTLER)

❧ While your body is resting, think how He is rest to your soul, and how, just as a child loves to be in its mother's arms, so you also may find your repose in the arms of this God Who is all around you. We cannot depart from Him, but alas, at times we forget His holy presence and leave Him all alone, while we concern ourselves with things apart from Him. It is so easy, this intimacy with God; it is restful rather than tiring, like a child resting under its mother's eye. (ST. ELIZABETH OF THE TRINITY)

❧ If for one year we have faithfully walked in God's presence, at the end of that time we shall have reached the heights of perfection without having noticed it. (ST. TERESA OF ÁVILA)

XXVII

THE SALVATION OF SOULS

The whole world is not worth as much as one single soul, for the world passes away, but the soul is immortal and eternal.

(ST. JOHN CLIMACUS)

OUR FAITH OBLIGES US TO LABOR FOR SOULS

❧ To save our souls, of course, is the first work we have to look to, but we shall do that in saving others. (VEN. MOTHER MARY POTTER)

❧ Thou art saved by God; do thou then save others. Thou art thyself snatched by Christ from death, so thou, therefore, snatch others from the dangers that lead to death. This is the great office confided by God to thee and to those who have the strength for it, an office that excels all the works of the most virtuous of mortal men: to be the companion and fellow-laborer of Jesus Christ, and by thy zeal, thy cares, thy ardor, thy love, and thy prayers to seek the lost sheep, to lead it to penance, and to present it before God as a pure sacrifice. No gift is more agreeable to Him than to lead a saved soul before His throne. (ST. JOHN CLIMACUS)

❧ Certain souls will become especially dear to us, either because we have special charge of them, or for some other particular reason. We must give God to them, and we must give them, all of them and absolutely, to God. The

Heavenly Father sacrificed His only-begotten Son, the eternal object of His complacency, so that they might not perish but have life everlasting. Our Lord immolated Himself for them on the Cross, offers Himself for them every instant on our altars, nourishes them with His own Substance, has given them the Church, the priesthood, the Sacraments, and constantly favors them with a super-abundance of interior and exterior graces. By His Holy Spirit, moreover, He enlightens, attracts, urges, circumvents them; He conquers and sustains them; He pursues, recalls, and pardons them. In short, He loves them, loves them infinitely in spite of their many miseries. However ardent may be our zeal for souls, can it ever compare with the zeal God exhibits? (REV. DOM VITALIS LEHODEY)

❧ Behold this outstanding feature of Our Lord's own strategy: the transformation of society by means of chosen souls. The little flock of disciples chosen and formed by Christ Himself, and afterwards set on fire by the Holy Ghost, was enough to begin the regeneration of the world. (DOM JEAN-BAPTISTE CHAUTARD)

❧ The sacrifices exacted from us by active works draw so much supernatural value from the glory they give to God, and from their effects in the sanctification of souls, and acquire from these sources such great wealth of merits, that a man vowed to the active life can, if he wills, rise each day a further degree in charity and union with God, that is to say, in sanctity. (DOM JEAN-BAPTISTE CHAUTARD)

NOTHING GREAT IS REQUIRED
IN WORKING FOR SOULS

❧ God wills that humble souls, who love Him and invoke His help, should govern the world with divine goodness and power. God wills that His servants should save and sanctify souls and inaugurate in them the reign of Divine Love. Our position in the natural order depends on our work, abilities, circumstances, etc., but in the supernatural order, we can exercise an immeasurable influence. (ST. MAXIMILIAN KOLBE)

❧ Every soul can be instrumental in this great work of saving souls. Nothing great is required, the smallest acts suffice: a step taken, a straw picked up, a glance restrained, a service rendered, a cordial smile. All these offered to Love are in reality of great profit to souls and draw down floods of grace on them. (OUR LORD TO SR. JOSEFA MENÉNDEZ)

❧ You may say that you are unable to lead souls to God and have no means of doing so; that you would gladly do this, but, being unable to teach and preach like the Apostles, you do not know how. The devil sometimes puts ambitious desires into our hearts, so that, instead of setting our hand to the work which lies nearest to us, and thus serving Our Lord in ways within our power, we may rest content with having desired the impossible. Apart from praying for people, by which you can do a great deal for them, do not try to help everybody, but limit yourself to your own companions; your work will then be more effective because you have the greater obligation to do it. Do you imagine it is a small advantage that you should have so much humility and mortification, and should be the servant of all and show such great charity towards all and such fervent love for the Lord that it resembles a fire kindling all their souls, while you constantly awaken their zeal by your other virtues? This would indeed be a great service to the Lord and one very pleasing to Him. By your doing things which you really can do, His Majesty will know that you would like to do many more, and thus He will reward you exactly as if you had won many souls for Him. (ST. TERESA OF ÁVILA)

SUFFERING AS A MEANS
TO WIN GRACE FOR OTHERS

❧ Since souls are so very dear to God, no sacrifice should be too much to save them. Every little victory over self helps. (FR. WILLIAM DOYLE)

❧ Very pleasing to Me is the willing desire to bear every pain and fatigue, even unto death, for the salvation of souls; for the more the soul endures, the more she shows that she loves Me. (OUR LORD TO ST. CATHERINE OF SIENA)

❧ The apostle does indeed suffer. But he knows that all redemption, be it merely that of a single soul, is a great work, accomplished above all by suffering. He is certain that generosity in supporting trials increases his progress in virtue and procures greater glory for God; and this certainly is enough to sustain him. (DOM JEAN-BAPTISTE CHAUTARD)

❧ Soul-pain is the price of conversions. If you want to win souls for Christ, you must be willing to endure the anguish for sin that sinners do not experience in order to win, at least ultimately, the grace of repentance for them. You may have to go through the agonies of delayed hopes, and even seeming failure at the end, for someone whose soul has been your deep concern. But your sincere devotion to bring a soul to Christ will not be in vain. God alone knows the secret workings of His grace in souls. (FR. LAWRENCE LOVASIK)

ᴥ When you come right down to it, it is not *how* we physically accept pain — bodily or mental pain — but what we do with it when we have it. How we *use* it is the big question. We are not masochists; we do not accept pain because we like it. Nor do we accept it just to be better and stronger people. Nor do we accept it as the Stoics did because there is nothing else to do about it. Christ accepted pain and suffering in order to *use* it for our redemption, to be our Redeemer. This is the only reason, finally, why we should accept pain: that through this suffering — a suffering we neither asked for nor desired, a suffering we would have totally rejected had we been able — through this suffering God will redeem many souls. (FR. WALTER CISZEK)

ᴥ When, in the Mystical Body of Christ, a member voluntarily suffers through love, another infirm member is healed. When the servants of God immolate their bodies and hearts, the Lord spares the body of an unfortunate person whose strength is spent, or cures a sick heart which had not the courage to break its chains. When, in the Mystical Body, a generous soul sacrifices its own will, in another, the Lord revives a dead will and grants it the grace of conversion. (FR. REGINALD GARRIGOU-LAGRANGE)

ᴥ And He will ultimately comfort us; He will send us His angels to minister to us. When the pain and the heartache have run their course, when the souls that needed saving have been saved through our humiliation or rejection or hurt, through our temptations or worrying, then will the comfort of God overwhelm us. When we have cried out in our own abandonment, in our own inability to raise our hearts or our minds or even our eyes to God in prayer, then, somehow, peace will come; somehow, we will be able to say: *Father, into Thy hands I commend my spirit.* (FR. WALTER CISZEK)

WHEN OUR EFFORTS SEEM UNSUCCESSFUL

✤ Howsoever bitter may be our lack of success in our apostolate, we must recognize in it the permission of God, accept it with peaceful abandonment, and turn it to account for our own spiritual progress. It is one of the very best occasions for entrenching ourselves more securely in humility, detaching ourselves from vainglory and human consolations, purifying our intentions, and resolving for the future to seek God alone in our spiritual ministrations. (DOM VITALIS LEHODEY)

THE NEED FOR CHARITY

✤ We expect to vanquish the enemy and to extend the kingdom of God not by brutal carnage but by deeds of love and mercy. (ST. MAXIMILIAN KOLBE)

✤ Kindness has convinced more sinners than zeal, eloquence, or learning, and these three things have never converted anybody without kindness having something to do with it. (FR. FREDERICK FABER)

✤ Remember that a loving glance and a sweet smile have a greater influence on a soul than the loveliest sermon. Is not it true that feeling yourself loved and understood in a holy manner can make the way of perfection seem a lighter one to travel? (OUR LORD TO VEN. CONSOLATA BETRONE)

THE NEED FOR PRAYER

❧ Our first weapon is prayer. Some, not as well instructed as others in the battle for souls, often neglect or underestimate this weapon. They believe work and action to be the chief instruments for success in our battle, but it is not so. Prayer, and again I emphasize prayer, is the most effective weapon in the battle to liberate souls. Why? Because only supernatural means can result in a supernatural accomplishment. It is grace and grace alone which illuminates the mind and strengthens the will, leads to conversion and to the soul's liberation from the fetters of sin. (ST. MAXIMILIAN KOLBE)

❧ There is no more powerful means for converting souls than prayer — intimate, familiar, burning prayer, which moves and bends God's mercy towards the sinner for whose return you are asking. Interior souls, souls of prayer, save their brothers of disorder even without suspecting it. A word prepared during prayer enters, penetrates, and gains a soul. (PÈRE GUSTAVE DE RAVIGNAN)

❧ How many souls we may convert by our prayers! There are some among them for whom one *Pater* and *Ave* would be enough to tip the scale. (ST. JOHN MARIE VIANNEY)

❧ Get all the prayers you can. Even an aspiration may save a soul. (FR. WILLIAM DOYLE)

❧ Pray! The faint murmur of supplication from a holy soul has more power to raise up legions of apostles than the eloquent voice of a recruiter of vocations who has less of the spirit of God. The spirit of prayer, then, which goes hand-in-hand in the true apostle with zeal, will be the chief reason for the fruitfulness of your work. (DOM JEAN-BAPTISTE CHAUTARD)

❧ A man of prayer is capable of everything. Hence it is very important that missionaries dedicate themselves to this practice with great affection, because without it they will accomplish little or nothing, whereas through it, more than by letters or persuasive speech, they will be capable of touching hearts and winning souls. (ST. VINCENT DE PAUL)

❧ A short but fervent prayer will usually do more to bring about a conversion than long discourses or fine speeches. He who prays is in touch with the First Cause. He acts directly upon It. And by that very fact, he has his hand upon all the secondary causes, since they only receive their efficacy from this Superior Principle. And so, the desired effect is obtained both more surely and more promptly. (DOM JEAN-BAPTISTE CHAUTARD)

❧ Prayer is the most efficacious means of giving peace to souls, filling them with happiness, and bringing them closer to God's love. Prayer renews the world. Prayer is the indispensable condition for the rebirth and life of each person. Through prayer, St. Thérèse, having never left her cloister, became the patroness of all the missions and not only in a nominal sense, as experience proves. Let us pray, pray well and much, vocally and mentally, and we will experience how the Immaculata will more and more possess our souls and how in every way we will become more like Her. (ST. MAXIMILIAN)

❧ I say to you, every prayer that is offered for anyone augments his eternal happiness; no sincere prayer ever fails of its effect, although the eye of man may not be able to perceive in what way or manner. (OUR LORD TO ST. GERTRUDE THE GREAT)

WITH MARY WE CAN ACCOMPLISH WONDERS

❖

❧ Sometimes, as you think over how weak you are and how difficult the task confided to you is, you start to ask yourself, "What can I really do?" What can you do? By yourself, nothing. With Mary, wonderful things. Was it not because He Who is mighty looked upon the nothingness of His handmaid that He accomplished great things in Her? Have you never read that *the foolish things of the world hath God chosen, that He may confound the wise; and the weak things of the world hath God chose, that He may confound the strong*? (FR. EMILE NEUBERT)

❧ Remember that your apostolate is Her apostolate, and that your interests are Hers. It was to Her, not to you, that God confided the mission of crushing the serpent's head and of establishing the Kingdom of Her Son in this world; you only participate in Her mission. She is the commandress-in-chief of the army of Christ; you are Her soldier. It is Her children, not yours, who must be saved. Does not a mother desire the salvation of her children much more ardently than a stranger would? Does not the general wish for victory much more intensely than the mere private does? Are not the interests of Jesus infinitely more precious to Her than to you? Now, She is all powerful through the omnipotence of God, and She can confer this omnipotence on all those who act in Her name. (FR. EMILE NEUBERT)

❧ The soul of Mary is a pure capacity for Jesus. If the soul of Jesus passed into Mary, and if the soul of Mary passed into Her children of predilection, these children would also be possessed entirely by Jesus. (FR. EMILE NEUBERT)

❧ Since the Immaculata is the *Mother of all grace*, since She is the dispenser of the gifts of God and the official delegate of His mercy, it suffices to surrender oneself unconditionally to Her gentle guidance in order that, having become Her docile instruments, we may accomplish wonders. (ST. MAXIMILIAN KOLBE)

❧ Never will a true son of Mary run out of arguments, of means, or even of expedients when it becomes necessary, in almost hopeless cases, to strengthen the helpless and give consolation to those who cannot be consoled. (DOM JEAN-BAPTISTE CHAUTARD)

❧ The most efficacious apostolate is to make Mary directly known, loved, and served. As soon as we have introduced the Blessed Virgin into another's life, She will assume the responsibility of forming him to the likeness of Jesus and of inspiring him with Her own passion for the salvation and sanctification of Her other children. Making someone a convinced apostle of Mary is more than making a hundred ordinary Christians, for the influence of such an apostle extends indefinitely. (FR. EMILE NEUBERT)

❧ Stir up love and confidence toward Mary Immaculate everywhere. You will soon see tears flowing from the eyes of the most hardened sinners, prisons will be emptied, the ranks of earnest workers will increase, and the family hearths will give the pleasant odor of virtue. Peace and happiness will destroy pain and discord because then it will be a new era. (ST. MAXIMILIAN KOLBE)

❧ Innumerable are the souls I have saved from the infernal dragon because of their devotion to me, even though they recited only one *Ave* or said one word in my honor and invocation. (OUR LADY TO VEN. MARY OF AGREDA)

❧ When will Her medal be found on every breast, and when will every heart in the world beat for Her? I believe there is no better means of accelerating the arrival of this grace-filled moment than for each of us to deepen his dedication to the Immaculata. The more committed we are to Her, the more She can direct us. (ST. MAXIMILIAN KOLBE)

❧ Let everyone strive not so much to change his environment, as to perfect himself and personally to come closer to the Immaculata. In this way all who draw near to Her will be reciprocally drawn nearer to one another. (ST. MAXIMILIAN KOLBE)

❧ Sanctification, zeal for the apostolate, success in our missionary ministry depend not on wisdom, wit, talent, numerous prayers or penances, but on the perfection of holy obedience only. Why is this? Because God's will and the Immaculata's will are infallibly revealed in holy obedience. By obedience we become instruments in the hands of the Immaculata. As Her will is perfectly united with God's will, by holy obedience our will is united with Hers, and so we become infinitely wise, powerful, and good in our mission. What an infinite exaltation of a creature! How can the most admired geniuses compete with this status? (ST. MAXIMILIAN KOLBE)

❧ When Mary is living in the heart of Her apostle, he will be guaranteed the use of the persuasive eloquence of our Blessed Mother Herself, speaking in him and moving souls with whom all else has failed. (DOM JEAN-BAPTISTE CHAUTARD)

❧ The man with true devotion to Mary becomes all-powerful over the Heart of his Mother. And so, what apostle can doubt the efficacy of his apostolate when, by his devotions, he can control the all-powerful mediation of Mary in the distribution of the merits of the Precious Blood? (DOM JEAN-BAPTISTE CHAUTARD)

❧ The more that you gain the favor of that august Princess and faithful Virgin, the more you will act by pure faith; a pure faith which will make you care hardly at all about sensible consolations and extraordinary favors; a lively faith animated by charity, which will enable you to perform all your actions from the motive of pure love; a faith firm and immovable as a rock, through which you will rest quiet and constant in the midst of storms and hurricanes; a faith active and piercing, which like a mysterious pass-key, will give you entrance into all the mysteries of Jesus, into the last ends of man, and into the Heart of God Himself; a courageous faith, which will enable you to undertake and carry out without hesitation great things for the glory of God and for the salvation of souls; lastly, a faith which will be your hidden treasure of divine wisdom and your omnipotent arm, which you will use to enlighten those who are in the darkness of the shadow of death, to inflame those who are lukewarm and who have need of the heated gold of charity, to give life to those who are dead in sin, to touch and overthrow, by your meek and powerful words, the hearts of marble and the cedars of Lebanon, and finally, to resist the devil and all the enemies of salvation. (ST. LOUIS MARIE DE MONTFORT)

XXVIII

THE CHURCH & THE FAITH

*In this wicked world, in these evil days when the
Church measures her future loftiness by her present
humility, and is exercised by goading fears, tormenting
sorrows, disquieting labors, and dangerous temptations,
she soberly rejoices, rejoicing only in hope.*

(ST. AUGUSTINE)

THE GREATNESS OF
THE CATHOLIC CHURCH

❧ And thus it is, O Church, that being founded on Christ
thy Spouse, thou givest us a share in thine own divine
immutability! Established as we are in thee, there is not a
truth which the eye of our faith cannot see; there is not a
blessing which, despite our weakness, we may not make our
own; there is no object shown us by hope, which we may
not attain. Thou holdest us in thine arms; and from the
height whereto thou raisest us, we see the mysteries of time
and the secrets of eternity. Our eye admiringly follows thee,
whether we consider thee as militant on earth, suffering in
thy dear ones who are in the temporary state of expiation,
or triumphant in Heaven. Thou art with us in our exile, and
already art thou, in millions of thy children, heiress of the
eternal kingdom. Keep us near thee, nay, within thee, O
thou our Mother, who art the beloved Spouse of Our Lord.
To whom shall we go but to thee? Is it not to thee, and
to thee alone, that He has entrusted the words of eternal
life? (DOM PROSPER GUÉRANGER)

❧ Nothing can be compared with the Church. The walls decay and fall to pieces; the Church does not grow old. The walls are overthrown by barbarians; the Church cannot be conquered even by the spirits of evil; the facts themselves prove that these words are not an empty boast. How many have fought against the Church, and these her enemies have perished; but she has risen above the heavens. Such is the greatness of the Church. When she is attacked, she triumphs, and when she is outraged, she only appears the more glorious for it. (ST. JOHN CHRYSOSTOM)

THE CHURCH WILL TRIUMPH
OVER ALL ADVERSITIES

❧ The Mystical Body of Christ can no more live without suffering than our eyes without the light of the sun. Until the end of the world, Christ will agonize in His members, and it is by this agony that the Church, His Spouse, will bring forth saints. For souls that have received everything from the Church, is it not a noble vocation to live and immolate themselves for their Mother? (MERE FRANÇOISE DE JESUS)

❧ With us in the Church Militant there are those who are unaware of the magnitude and seriousness of the battle, of the weakness in our ranks, and of the hidden forces behind the enemy; but there are also those who know enough about these things to be discouraged. The latter are worse than the first because to be discouraged is a practical denial of God. The shout of our God proclaiming: "I have conquered the world," still echoes in the land. (BR. FRANCIS MALUF)

❧ Amongst the illusions entertained by a certain class of Catholics, there is none more pitiable than the notion that the Truth requires a great number of defenders and friends.

To these people, numbers seem a synonym for force. Now true force — real power, in the physical as in the moral order — consists in intensity rather than in extension. The millions of Xerxes' army constituted a force of tremendous extension, but a single platoon of well-armed soldiers — knowing what they are defending, against whom they fight in order to defend the Truth — is preferable a thousand times over. Faith possesses a power of its own, which it communicates to its friends and defenders. It is not they who give the Truth power, but Truth which charges them with its own vigor. This is the kind of soldiers we need. This is the kind who have always and will yet do something more for the glory of His Name. They go into the deadly, imminent breach and never flinch. No compromising, no minimizing with them. They plant their banner on the topmost height and form a solid, invincible phalanx around it that not all the legions of earth and hell combined can budge a single inch. (DON FELIX SARDA Y SALVANY)

❧ In all ages, the Catholic Church has been attacked by the sword and the written word, but she has always emerged triumphant. The Church has seen kingdoms, republics, and empires crumble to ruin. She alone is firm and unshaken. Nineteen centuries have passed since her foundation, and she is still in full vigor. Others shall come after us and shall still see her vigorous. Guided by God, the Church shall overcome all earthly vicissitudes; she shall conquer all her enemies; she shall advance with steady pace through the centuries, through all human upheavals until the end of time. Then she will gather all her children in one kingdom in the realm of the blessed. (ST. JOHN BOSCO)

❧ O holy Roman Church! Thou hast forever put thy trust in the Lord; and He, faithful to His promise, has humbled before thee the haughty ones that defied thee. Where now are the caesars who boasted they had drowned thee in thine own blood? Where the emperors who would ravish the inviolate virginity of thy faith? Where the heretics who, during the past centuries of thine existence, have assailed every article of thy teaching and denied what they listed? Where the ungrateful princes who would fain make a slave of thee, who hadst made them what they were? Where that empire of Mohamet which has so many times raged against thee, for that thou, the defenseless State, didst arrest the pride of its conquests? Where the reformers who were bent on giving the world a Christianity in which thou hadst no part? Where the modern sophists in whose philosophy thou wast set down as a system that had been tried, and was a failure, and is now a ruin? And those kings who were acting the tyrant over thee, and those people who will have liberty independently and at the risk of truth; where will they be in another hundred years? Gone and forgotten as the noisy anger of a torrent; whilst thou, O Holy Church of Rome, built on the immovable rock, wilt be as calm, as young as ever. Whence this thy stability, but from Him Who is very truth and justice? Glory be to Him in thee! (DOM PROSPER GUÉRANGER)

❧ All the clocks that strike the hours on earth mark some new victory of the Mystical Body of Christ over the rebel spirit. Each grace given is a blow struck. Each Sacrament administered is a fortress taken. Each mercy granted is a gain for Heaven. (FR. FREDERICK FABER)

❧ Do not lose heart, children, for as the Lord has been angry, so later He will bring healing. And the Church shall quickly regain her own beauty and shine as before. And you shall see the persecuted restored and impiety retiring to its own hiding places, and the True Faith in all places speaking openly with all freedom. (ST. ANTHONY OF THE DESERT)

THE CHURCH AND CIVIL SOCIETY

❧ At the time when the Church is most persecuted, God raises up in the world the greatest number of saints. (FR. PAUL OF MOLL)

❧ The triumph of the Catholic cause is secure, even from a human point of view. The human soul is naturally Christian; everything great and good gravitates towards the Gospel. Human society is drawn instinctively in the direction of Jesus Christ whenever it obeys the laws of self-preservation. The spirit of evil may do its worst; it will but precipitate events and hasten the day when humanity will have choice only between Catholic civilization and revolutionary anarchy. And then the choice will soon be made. (GODFREY KURTH)

❧ As long as God lives we will never believe in the permanent triumph of evil or in the impossibility of repairing the greatest wrongs that may have been committed. We by no means despair of the future; we by no means despair of seeing religion again recovering its hold on men's hearts and on men's consciences; we by no means despair of seeing again peoples and nations, sovereign princes and states recognizing the authority of Peter and acknowledging the supremacy of the spiritual over the temporal. Political atheism is a falsehood, and no falsehood can live. Its triumph can be but temporary and last no longer than the heated passions which have given it birth. (ORESTES BROWNSON)

❧ The Church has two offices: the one is to convert and to save individuals, and the other is to sanctify and to uphold the civil order of mankind. But when the civil society of man refuses any longer to be guided and upheld by the sanctifying grace and the sovereignty of God, the Church shakes off the dust from her feet and goes back to her apostolic work of saving men one by one. She is at this time doing that work and will do it, and in doing it the Church becomes more free, more independent, more separated from all contacts and embarrassments of this world. She may indeed be persecuted; perhaps she may become less in numbers because nations and races go out from her. But she becomes once more what she was in the beginning, a society of individuals, vigorous, pure, living, and life-giving. For the Church, then, we have no fear. (CARDINAL HENRY EDWARD MANNING)

❧ It is the glorious privilege of the Catholic Church that she needs naught but the common right in order that she may conquer the universe. (GODFREY KURTH)

DEVOTION TO MARY IS MOST NECESSARY IN MODERN TIMES

❧ It is to devotion to the Virgin Mother of God, as a powerful means of reconverting and repurifying Christian nations, that we must have recourse. The enemy of man to be overcome is the same old enemy of God. Man would be God, not in God's way, but in his own; he would stand on himself and suffice for himself. In the pride of his strength and the light of his own intellect, he refuses to bend to the Highest and to learn of the Wisest, and his strength turns to weakness, his light to darkness, and his manhood disappears. He loses heart, and likens himself to a worm, and crouches and grovels. What can restore him? Not today need we fear an excess of faith, an excess of devotion. The enemy is a cold, freezing rationalism which, pretending to be reason, becomes lifeless materialism. Nothing can overcome him but devotion to Her who, as the Mother of God, was to crush the serpent's head. We must call on Mary to call on God with us and for us, to help us as He did the first Christians. (ORESTES BROWNSON)

❧ During the first three centuries, the Church was persecuted. The blood of martyrs watered the seeds of Christianity. Later, when the persecutions ceased, one of the Fathers of the Church deplored the lukewarmness of Christians. He rejoiced when persecution returned. In the same way, we must rejoice in what will happen, for in the midst of trials, our zeal will become more ardent. Besides, are we not in the hands of the Blessed Virgin? Is not our most ardently desired ideal to give our lives for Her? We live only once. We die only once. Therefore, let it be according to Her good pleasure. (ST. MAXIMILIAN KOLBE)

Addendum

THE VIRTUE OF HOPE

*The God of hope fill you with all joy and peace
in believing, that you may abound in hope
and in the power of the Holy Ghost.*

(ST. PAUL)

Now in these words to the Romans, Saint Paul says that God is the God of hope. Hope is so great a grace that he gives the name and title of Hope to God Himself, and that because He is the object of our hope. God is our hope because He is our bliss. It is bliss that we hope for. Again, God is the giver of our hope because hope also is a gift of the Holy Ghost. Moreover, God is the support of our hope, because it is by His love and His strength and His grace that the hope which He inspires into us is nourished and sustained. God is also the motive of our hope because of His infinite love. Therefore he says, *The God of hope fill you with all joy and peace in believing*— for peace and joy are the fruits of hope, as hope is the fruit of faith — *that you may abound in hope*, that you may be filled and pervaded and penetrated with hope, *and in the power of the Holy Ghost.*

Now hope is the second of the three theological virtues or powers infused into the soul. It is a virtue which bestows on us a confidence of attaining, by the grace of God, to future bliss, and of receiving from God all the helps that are necessary to attain that future bliss. The object of hope, then, is the goodness and grace of God.

We will look a little more closely, first of all, into what hope is; next, consider what are its fruits; and then, what are the contraries or opposites of hope.

HOPE AS A DESIRE FOR GOD

Hope, then, is a gift of the Holy Ghost which produces in the soul two things. The one is a desire after God, and the other is a trust in God. And hope itself is produced in this manner: the light of faith illuminates the whole reason, and thence the whole soul, with the knowledge of God, of His existence, of His perfections, of His glory, of His beauty, and of His sweetness. It reveals to the reason, and through the reason to the whole soul, that God created us for Himself, that He made us that we might know Him, love Him, serve Him, and worship Him in this world and in eternity, and that thereby we may become beatified or blessed in Him.

Faith therefore illuminates us to know that God is the end for which we were made, and that if we live for anything below God or out of God, we fail of the end of our creation. And faith shows us not this only, but that God alone is the adequate end of the human soul; that money, wealth, pleasure, friendship, the whole world, is too small to fill the capacity of the soul; that the soul of man, made in the image of God, has a likeness of the immensity of God Himself, and that nothing is adequate to fill it — to fill his intellect, and his heart, and his mind — but God only Who made him; and that unless he corresponds with the Original to the likeness of which he was made, he can never be satisfied. There will be a hunger and thirst which nothing can satiate or slake in time or in eternity. And as

God is the only adequate end of man, He is the only end for which man can live without being degraded. If a man lives for this world, or for pleasure, or for money, or for honor, or for the science of this world, whatsoever end below God he live for, the soul in that proportion is lowered and debased. It is changed into the likeness of creatures, and thereby deprived of the likeness of the Creator.

But the soul that is united with God, and lives for God, is elevated and conformed to the perfect Original of which it is the image. And, further, God is the only end that can beatify or satisfy the soul with bliss. Everything below God is mutable, imperfect, full of change and of vicissitude. God, and God alone, is immutable in His bliss, and He beatifies immutably all those who are united with Him. All other things, sweet as they may be, precious as we count them, happy as we may be in them for a time, all must change and pass away. God alone is changeless, because God alone is eternal; and if we live for any end that is not changeless and eternal, we shall be disappointed of our hope.

When the soul is once illuminated with these truths, there springs up a hunger and a thirst to which neither the hunger nor the thirst of the body is for its intensity to be compared. The body hungers and thirsts for its natural food; the soul after God, Who is the breath of its life, its sole and only sustenance. Its desire becomes more and more intense as God is more and more known and appreciated. We hope, therefore, to attain our chief good, and we hope for all the means and helps whereby we may attain to the love, and the knowledge, and the worship, and the joy, and the peace of God hereafter. Both the end and the means, therefore, are the objects of hope.

HOPE AS A TRUST IN GOD

The other motive of hope is a trust in God springing from experience. As we come to know Him, we come to appreciate His character. In the measure in which we know by experience that God is charity, and sanctity, and pity, and goodness, and fidelity, we grow to trust Him with a personal confidence, as of heart with heart. Saint Augustine says that it is out of our own heart that we believe in the heart of a friend, for it is by faith that we love one another. It is not by looking on the countenance of a friend, for the countenance may beam upon us, and we may trust it, but the heart may be false and far off. That which we trust, and on which we rest our hope, is the heart which we have never seen. We know it only by a sort of intuition of faith, by which we penetrate beyond that which we do see. So it is with God. Though He is invisible, yet this hunger and thirst of the soul, illuminated by faith, reaches to the heart of God and trusts in it. We rest upon the goodness and upon the love of God, not only as the great Ruler of the universe, but upon His personal goodness to ourselves, one by one, as a Friend and a Father.

And still more than this. From this trust in God springs up an experience of His goodness. Just as with a friend you may be thoroughly persuaded of his love for you before you have ever made trial of it by experience, nevertheless, as year after year goes on, you come to know by his unvarying conduct that what he says he is, and that what he does for you springs from his unchanging love; from this you gain an experience of his character higher and surer than all intellectual conviction. It is this that Saint Paul means when he says, speaking of our Divine Lord, *I know Whom I have believed.* I know His character, His conduct, His heart; I have made trial of Him, *and I am sure that He is able to keep that which I have committed unto Him,* that is, myself and my salvation, *unto that day*—the day of His coming.

All our lives then, we are making trial by experience of the goodness of God. You have known it from your childhood. You have known it by the manifold and multiplied indications of His love to you in every period of your life, by the care with which He has watched over you, by all the operations of grace whereby He has guided you, all the absolutions He has bestowed upon you, by the peace He has shed abroad in your heart, by the help He has given you in temptation, by the consolations that have come down upon you like showers in the time of your sorrow and desolation of heart. All this has taught you to know Him, and to say out of the depth of your own experience what the Psalmist said, *I believe that I shall see the good things of the Lord in the land of the living,* and again when he said, *Taste and see that the Lord is sweet. Blessed is the man that hopeth in Him; How great is the multitude of Thy sweetness, which Thou hast hidden for them that fear Thee.* Such, then, is the nature of hope.

THE FRUITS OF HOPE

Now what are its fruits? Just as faith bears hope and charity like two fruitful branches, so both hope and charity bear again a multitude of fruits. The first fruit of hope is an appreciation of God. You know that we are all bound, if we would enter into life eternal, to love God above all things. But that love of God does not mean the love of our emotions, or the sensible love which we feel towards human friends—it does not mean this, because this cannot be commanded. But the love of appreciation means the love of the reason, the conscience, and the will. We know by the light of faith, and we have made trial by the experience of hope, that God is good and sweet above all things, and that it were better for us to lay down our lives than to lose God. When Judas appraised our Lord at thirty pieces of silver, he was but an example of what all men do who do not love God above all things. They sell God for the world, for a little gold or for baubles. They are continually showing that they set small price on the Eternal God. But those who learn by hope and by trust to know what God is, prize Him as they know Him and as they have found Him by experience, and therefore above all other things.

And, next, where there is this appreciation, there is a great fear of losing God, a holy fear lest we should come short of our union with God in eternity. Just in proportion as we hope for the bliss of God, in that proportion also we have the fear of losing God, which, like a shadow following the substance, is inseparable. The more truly we prize anything, the more we fear to lose it; and the fear we have of losing anything may be taken as the measure of the price we set upon it. If we love a friend greatly, in that measure we fear to lose him. We may take that fear as the measure of the love we bear him. And therefore the holy fear of losing God springs up straightway from our appreciation of God. What is the pain of loss — which is a pain more keen than the pain of sense even in souls that are lost eternally — but the appreciation of God which comes too late, when salvation is lost for ever, and when union with God can no more be attained? From this holy fear springs humility; that is, the consciousness of what we are. It shows us our entire dependence upon God. In ourselves we are nothing and can do nothing. Unless He sustain us we cannot stand, and unless we stand we can never persevere. We are as unstable as the perpetual shifting of the wind and the restless undulation of the water. We are never in one stay. Saint Paul says, *I know that in me,* that is, in my flesh, *there dwelleth no good thing, for that which I would I do not, and that I would not, that I do.*

Then, from humility comes strength, which can spring from nothing but hope. We never attempt things that we know to be impossible. If we come face to face with a perpendicular cliff, no man who has not lost his reason would try to scale it; but if we come to the foot of a mountain, howsoever high and steep it may be, we know that we can scale it, if only we will to put out our strength and persevere. Our salvation is not barred by any cliff, because the Precious Blood of Jesus has made our way plain; but it is like the mountain which is both precipitous and steep. To scale it needs patient effort and strong perseverance. And where there is hope, which springs from the consciousness that all things are possible, there will come strength at all hours to accomplish our task. In warfare, men will fight as long as there is hope of victory, in the instant in which they fail of hope their weapons drop from their hands; and even when in flight before the enemy, men have strength to fly as long as there is hope of escape, but, when the hope of escape is lost, they cast themselves upon the ground; and as a man swimming for life will strike out strongly so long as there is hope to reach the shore, but will cast up his arms and sink when that hope is gone — so it is in working out our salvation. When Saint Paul says, *Work out your salvation with fear and trembling,* he adds also the motive of unfailing confidence and strength. The hope and the confidence that our salvation is possible is this, *for it is God that worketh in you to will and to do.*

THE OPPOSITES OF HOPE

Lastly, let us see what are the opposites of hope.

The first is presumption. As I have said, hope is a sure confidence founded on the goodness and grace of God. Presumption is a confidence founded upon ourselves. When we trust in anything out of and below God, it is a presumptuous confidence. When our Divine Lord was carried to the pinnacle of the temple, and was bid to cast Himself down to prove His Godhead, Satan tempted Him to an act of presumption. He knew the will of His Heavenly Father, and He would not pass beyond the limits of that will. So is it with us. So long as we are in the ways of God we are safe, because so long we are strong. When we pass over the bounds of that way, both safety and strength depart from us.

And the signs of this presumption are many. First of all, if men venture into the occasions of sin, whether it be moral or intellectual danger, it is clear they are trusting to themselves, for they know that the help of God will keep them so long only as they avoid temptation; but if they run into temptation, having no warrant to believe that the help of God will follow them, they are guilty of presumption. When men say, "I can take care of myself; what matter where I go, or what I do, or what I read, or with whom I live?"—men that so speak and act are trusting in themselves, and are deliberately and formally putting from them the help of God. Men who say, "I will repent one day, but not yet. I hope I shall be a better man before I die. I will go on for a while, but I always hope that the day of conversion and repentance will come to me"— such men are presumptuous. They have no warrant so to hope for salvation. And they also who neglect the means of salvation, prayer, and the holy Sacraments, with the other helps that are around us, have no warrant whatever to expect that God will work miracles of grace to save them. If they will not take the way which God has shown them, they can have no other hope to arrive at the end. Those who neglect the holy Sacraments, who turn their backs upon confession and communion and think that their salvation may be otherwise obtained, have no warrant whatever to expect that God will fulfill their confidence.

I will give another example, and it is an answer to a question often put to Catholics: "Why do you ask the prayers of the saints? May you not pray to God yourself? May you not go straight to Him?" Certainly we may. But the man who says, "I do not ask for the prayers of others, because I can confide in my own prayers," is self-convicted of presumption. No, let us ask the prayers of all the friends of God upon earth, and of all the saints of God in Heaven. They intercede for us. Let us indeed pray for ourselves day by day, and that earnestly; but the more prayers that are offered up for me, the more I thank God for it; and if all the prayers of the servants of God on earth and in Heaven can be obtained by asking them, I will ask them till I die. They who despise these helps are neither humble nor have they the grace of confidence in hope. Such, then, is the first opposite.

The other opposite of hope is despair, which grows into desperation. We have already seen that the direct antagonist which destroys faith is infidelity: because infidelity is the proper opposite of faith. Charity and the sanctifying grace of God are lost by any mortal sin whatsoever, whether it be of the flesh or the spirit. But faith and hope can only be lost by their own proper opposites; and as the proper opposite of faith is infidelity, so the proper opposite of hope is desperation. What, then, is desperation?

I said before that hope and fear always go together, and that as the one rises the other falls. Now there are four kinds of fear. There is the holy filial fear of losing God, of which I have spoken before. This sanctifies the soul. It is called a filial fear of God because it is the fear of sons. It was perfect in our Divine Lord and Savior Jesus Christ. But there is a fear which is called a servile fear, which is the fear of servants, and this, too, is compatible with the love of God and with salvation, because there is a just and legitimate fear of sons, and a just and legitimate fear of servants. But there is a third kind of fear, which is called the fear of slaves — a servile slavish fear of the terrors of hell, a fear of the judgment without hatred of sin, without love of God, without hunger and thirst after Him as our bliss and as our eternal end. It is the fear of which Saint Augustine speaks when he says that those who fear hell more than they fear sin show that they neither love God nor hate sin. And then, lastly, there is the fear of devils — the fear of those who believe and tremble — and that diabolical fear is the fear that generates despair. It is the fear that enters when hope is lost, a fear, accompanied by a sickness and a weariness of God, and this is akin to the seventh deadly sin, called Sloth. From this state of the heart and soul springs enmity against God. When the hope of seeing Him in eternity is lost, there comes a foretaste of the pain of loss, in which men turn against God with the enmity of despair. It is of such we read in the Apocalypse, where

Saint John says that those on whom the wrath of God was poured gnawed their tongues for pain, and blasphemed the God of Heaven. These, then, are the two opposites of hope — presumption and despair.

ABOUNDING IN HOPE

Now let us turn back to the words of Saint Paul: *The God of hope fill you with all peace and joy in believing, that you may abound in hope and the power of the Holy Ghost.* The light of Heaven and the waters that come down to moisten the earth are not more abundant than is the grace of God in the hearts of those who are ready to receive it. Open your hearts wide, and they shall be filled. Lift up the empty vessels, and they shall overflow with the presence of the Holy Ghost.

Therefore, dear brethren in Jesus Christ, let our first resolution be this: to hope for God's greatest gifts. Do not be deceived by the false humility of those who say, "It is not for me to hope to be a saint." You are all called to be saints; you are therefore bound to be saints. Now or hereafter, if you are saved, saints you must be. If you are to be perfect in eternity before the Throne, you must be saints in part and in some measure now on earth. Ask, then, for the greatest gifts of grace. Ask that your hearts may be dilated with the love of God; that so you may love God above all things, that you may love Him with your whole heart, your whole mind, and your whole soul, and your whole strength. Be contented with nothing less. *Seek ye first the kingdom of God and His justice.* It is His command. Can you seek for more than this? There is neither humility nor obedience in seeking less. The kingdom of God is God

Himself. He is His kingdom, and if you have the kingdom of God you have God Himself. In the Lord's Prayer every day we say *Hallowed be Thy name,* that is, may Thy name be sanctified throughout the whole world; *Thy kingdom come, Thy will be done on earth as it is in Heaven.* As the angels and saints do Thy will, so may we. May sinful, corrupt, rebellious men, as we are, be converted by Thy grace, and do Thy will on earth as saints and angels. They who have the mock humility of asking little things of God, Who is the giver of all great and perfect gifts, show a want of faith in the greatness of His generosity. He has already given His only-begotten Son, He has given the Holy Ghost. What greater gifts are there beyond these?

Then let us ask for the greatest blessings. Let us ask for them in their perfect fullness. Let us ask for them because Jesus Christ has purchased them for us with His Precious Blood; and if He has paid the price of His Precious Blood to make them ours, will He refuse you when you ask Him for them? Ask for them because He has promised to give them. He has passed His word, He has pledged His fidelity. *Ask, and you shall receive; seek, and you shall find; knock, and it shall be opened unto you. Whatsoever you shall ask in prayer believing, you shall receive.* Ask the greatest gifts of God, because in asking them you honor Him. If a son should come to his father and should ask him some paltry trifling gift, the father would suspect that the heart of the son was mistrustful, and that he did not confide in his paternal love. If we treat friends in this niggardly and ungenerous manner, they resent at once the misconception that we show of their true character by the little things that we can trust them to do for us; but when we ask a friend to do great things for us, he takes it as a proof that we confide in the largeness of his heart. So it is with God. You will remember the servant who, being indolent, folded his talent in a napkin and buried his pound in the earth; and when his master came, what was his excuse? *I knew that thou wert an austere man;* that is, he added insult to the wrong he had done — he had a mean, unworthy, ungenerous conception of his master's character. There was the real root of his sin. His lord would not have laid to heart the loss of the talent; but he deeply laid to heart this mean conception of his own generosity.

Therefore we should hope for the noblest, highest, and largest gifts; hope to be saints; hope for every sort of good; hope that we may see God speedily after departing hence. You know that Purgatory and expiation are before us all. Nevertheless, hope that that expiation may be speedy, and that your entrance into the vision of God may be hastened. And while you hope for the greatest things, avoid the least occasions of sin. The man that goes into the occasions of sin shows at once that he does not appreciate God. He puts a mean price upon God; he values God less than a fleeting pleasure or a worthless profit. It shows, too, that he has no hatred of sin; and a heart that does not hate sin is an unfilial and a servile heart. It is far on the way to be an evil heart. Men do not willingly go into the infection of plague, or fever, or pestilence; yet they go boldly into the occasions of sin. *He that loves danger will perish in it.* The heart that does not hate sin is a heart that does not hunger and thirst after God. The love of God is not in it. It is an ungenerous heart. If the sins we have committed caused our Divine Redeemer His mental sorrows, His agony in the garden, His passion upon Calvary, and if, after all these, we are willing to venture into the occasions of sin, if we are not willing to choose His life of the Cross in preference to the fair and bright life of the world, our hearts must be unlike to His. He chose these things for us, and we make Him ill returns.

KNOW YOURSELF

Besides this, learn to know the worst of yourselves. Do not paint your face and attire your heads when you go before God. Learn to know yourselves as you are in the sight of God. Learn to know that you are His creatures, and therefore that you are but a little dust. The breath of God, and the steadfast exercise of His benevolent will, keep you what you are. You are His creatures. Learn, then, your own unworthiness; your unprofitableness before Him. You are servants of God. The stars shine, for God made them to that end, and the trees drop their fruit, for to that they were created, and the seed that we sow in the field springs into its harvest.

But man, created to the image of God, with a reason like the Eternal Son, and having in it the seven gifts of the Holy Ghost, wastes his great gifts, and perishes. The barren fig-tree is our type. But there is a deeper lesson still. Learn to know what we are as sinners in the sight of our Redeemer and our Sanctifier. Remember, dear brethren, the mortal sins which perhaps stained and blotted your life in boyhood, manhood, middle life, and even in the drawing on of old age. You know what they are. Remember the crowd and the multitude of venial sins which every day are committed, so numerous, so subtle, so stealthy, that when you kneel down at night to examine your conscience you cannot fix upon a tenth part of them. Remember the sins of omission you have committed all your life. How you have broken the First Commandment, which commands you to have no other god but God alone; and yet you have made idols of the world, and of pleasures, and of vanities, and of friends, and of yourselves. You worship and serve yourselves more than God; and yet that commandment obliges you to know and to love God above all. What else shall I say? Take the sum of the graces that God has bestowed upon you on the one side, and the multitude of sins that you have committed against God on the other, multiply them together, and you will know your debt before God.

And when you have come to know your state so as to be perhaps almost tempted to despair, and to say that it must be impossible for you to be saved, cast yourselves with your whole weight upon the eternal and changeless goodness of God in Jesus Christ. When your sins are upon you as black clouds, or glaring as crimson, so that you are almost driven from your hope, cast yourself into the fountain of the most Precious Blood of Jesus Christ. When your temptations, and your miseries, and the remnants of your past sins, and of your spiritual maladies, cling to you with the tenacity of a shadow, so that you are never at rest, cast yourself into the furnace of the Sacred Heart of Jesus. The fire of that Divine Heart will consume them as the dross. They will disappear before Him, and they will have no power to harm.

CAST YOUR CARE UPON HIM

Hear the words of the Holy Ghost, and hope in Him: *Casting all your care upon Him, for He hath care of you. When thou passest through the waters, I will be with thee, and the rivers shall not overflow. When thou walkest through the fire, thou shalt not be burnt, and the flames shall not burn in thee.* In the midst of all temptations, remember the words of our Divine Master when the Apostle thrice besought Him to deliver him from the minister of satan who buffeted him; the answer came, *My grace is sufficient for thee, for My strength is perfected in weakness.* Put, therefore, your trust in the Sacred Heart which was pierced for us, and say to our Divine Lord in your prayers every day, *Thou wilt keep peace, because we have hoped in Thee. Lord, I trust in Thee that Thou wilt keep me, that Thou wilt be round about me. Like the mountains round about Jerusalem, so is the Lord round about His people.* Thou wilt keep me in perfect peace — not only in peace, but in perfect peace — peace with God, peace with men, peace with myself, peace in time, peace for eternity — perfect peace — in *the peace that passeth all understanding.* But our minds must be *stayed on Thee;* that is, our whole intellect by the light of faith, and our whole heart by the grace of hope, must rest on Thee. Our mind is stayed on Thee, because it trusteth in Thee; it trusts because it loves, and it loves because it knows. We stay ourselves on Thee because we have had experience and trial of Thy love.

Therefore, *be nothing solicitous, but in all things, in supplication and thanksgiving, let your requests be made known to God.* Say to Him, "Lord, I have hoped in Thee, and I know that neither in life, nor in death, nor in eternity, shall I ever be confounded."

CARDINAL HENRY EDWARD MANNING
❧ FROM HIS BOOK, *THE INTERNAL MISSION OF THE HOLY GHOST* ❧

Appendices

APPENDIX I

ENCOURAGING POEMS

The Church herself is the most sacred and august of poets. Poetry is a method of relieving the overburdened mind; it is a channel through which emotion finds expression, and that a safe, regulated expression. Now what is the Catholic Church, viewed in her human aspect, but a discipline of the affections and passions? What are her ordinances and practices but the regulated expression of keen, or deep, or turbid feeling, and thus a "cleansing," as Aristotle would word it, of the sick soul? She is the poet of her children; full of music to soothe the sad and control the wayward—wonderful story for the imagination of the romantic; rich in symbol and imagery, so that gentle and delicate feelings, which will not bear words, may in silence intimate their presence or commune with themselves. Her very being is poetry.

(ST. JOHN HENRY NEWMAN)

THE KINGS
(LOUISE IMOGEN GUINEY)

A man said unto his Angel:
"My spirits are fallen low,
And I cannot carry this battle:
O brother! Where might I go?

"The terrible Kings are upon me
With spears that are deadly bright;
Against me so from the cradle
Do fate and my fathers fight."

Then said to the man his Angel:
"Thou wavering, witless soul,
Back to the ranks! What matter
To win or to lose the whole,

"As judged by the little judges
Who hearken not well, nor see?
Not thus, by the outer issue,
The Wise shall interpret thee.

"Thy will is the sovereign measure
And only events of things:
The puniest heart, defying,
Were stronger than all these Kings.

"Though out of the past they gather,
Mind's Doubt, and Bodily Pain,
And pallid Thirst of the Spirit
That is kin to the other twain,

"And Grief, in a cloud of banners,
And ringletted Vain Desires,
And Vice, with the spoils upon him
Of thee and thy beaten sires —

"While Kings of eternal evil
Yet darken the hills about,
Thy part is with broken saber
To rise on the last redoubt;

"To fear not sensible failure,
Nor covet the game at all,
But fighting, fighting, fighting,
Die, driven against the wall."

REMEMBER THE HOLY CROSS
(ST. BONAVENTURE)

Would'st thou dwell in joy abounding,
All thy life with light surrounding,
Make the Cross thy constant care;
On the Rood of thy Redeemer
Be thy soul an ardent dreamer,
Bear it with thee everywhere.

Be thou toiling, be thou sleeping,
Be thou smiling, be thou weeping,
Deep in grief or ecstacy;
Be thou coming, be thou going,
Pale with pain, with pleasure glowing,
Let the Cross thy comrade be.

Every sin and every sorrow,
Every ill that life can borrow,
In the Cross will gain surcease;
In the Cross, though sore and grieving,
He that humbly seeks relieving,
Findeth refuge, findeth peace.

LINES FOR A DRAWING
OF OUR LADY OF THE NIGHT
(FRANCIS THOMPSON)

This, could I paint my inward sight,
This were Our Lady of the Night:

She bears on Her front's lucency
The starlight of Her purity:

For as the white rays of that star
The union of all colors are,

She sums all virtues that may be
In Her sweet light of purity.

The mantle which She holds on high
Is the great mantle of the sky.

Think, O sick toiler, when the night
Comes on thee, sad and infinite,

Think, sometimes, 'tis our own Lady
Spreads Her blue mantle over thee,

And folds the earth, a wearied thing,
Beneath its gentle shadowing;

Then rest a little; and in sleep
Forget to weep, forget to weep!

THE WILL OF GOD
(FR. FREDERICK FABER)

I worship Thee, sweet Will of God,
  and all Thy ways adore;
And every day I live, I seem
  to love Thee more and more.

Thou wert the end, the blessed rule
  of our Savior's toils and tears;
Thou wert the passion of His Heart
  those three and thirty years.

And He hath breathed into my soul
  a special love of Thee,
A love to lose my will in His,
  and by that loss be free.

I love to see Thee bring to naught
  the plans of wily men;
When simple hearts outwit the wise,
  O Thou art loveliest then.

The headstrong world, it presses hard
  upon the Church full oft,
And then how easily Thou turn'st
  the hard ways into soft.

I love to kiss each print where Thou
  hast set Thine unseen feet;
I cannot fear Thee, blessed Will,
  Thine empire is so sweet.

When obstacles and trials seem
  like prison walls to be,

I do the little I can do,
and leave the rest to Thee.

I know not what it is to doubt,
my heart is ever gay;
I run no risk, for, come what will,
Thou always hast Thy way.

I have no cares, O blessed Will!
For all my cares are Thine:
I live in triumph, Lord, for Thou
hast made Thy triumphs mine.

And when it seems no chance or change
from grief can set me free,
Hope finds its strength in helplessness,
and gaily waits on Thee.

Man's weakness, waiting upon God,
its end can never miss,
For men on earth no work can do
more angel-like than this.

Ride on, ride on, triumphantly,
Thou glorious Will, ride on!
Faith's pilgrim sons behind Thee take
the road that Thou hast gone.

He always wins who sides with God,
to him no chance is lost;
God's Will is sweetest to him, when
it triumphs at his cost.

Ill that He blesses is our good,
and unblessed good is ill;
And all is right that seems most wrong,
if it be His sweet Will.

AN EVENING VISIT
(SR. MARY ANGELITA)

I come before Thee, Lord, at close of day,
My soul with fears and sad misgivings stirred;
Too tired to pray, I kneel before Thy face
And lay my burden down without a word.

I gaze in silence on the little door
That keeps love's patient Prisoner in thrall,
Nor ask for more; my troubled heart has room
For naught save this one thought—"Thou knowest all."

Tired! It seems as if I could not bear
Another day the cross that is my share,
The hidden cross that frets my spirit more
Than all life's ceaseless toil and anxious care;

The daily cross that others never see,
Or, seeing, smile, perchance, that weight so slight
Could make me falter. (Ah, no heart but Thine
Its weary pain to me can gauge aright!)

Faint-hearted! For the way seems long and hard,
And everywhere the cruel thorns are strown,
And it would seem as if Thy chastening love
Had bid me tread that bitter path alone.

Faithless! The task committed to my charge
Is marred with imperfections in Thy sight,
And many a fault and infidelity
Thine eye hath marked, since dawned the morning light.

Discouraged! Yes, for never feeble will
Was half so frail and full of change as mine;

Yet do I gather strength to try anew
Beneath the pity of Thy glance divine.

No lesser love could ever understand
How I could mean so well and do so ill,
Or find the cause of many a humbling fall
In wayward impulse, not in traitor will.

The pain of perseverance, the fatigue
Augmented by each toiling step and slow,
Till 'neath a straw's light weight my soul seems crushed,
All these, dear Lord, Thy Sacred Heart doth know.

Thou art the only Friend Who, reading deep
The inner self, from careless eyes concealed,
Dost draw not back with lessened love before
The waywardness and weakness there revealed.

And who save Thee could pardon thus each fault,
Reading the effort none beside would see,
Bearing as tenderly the thousandth time
As if Thou ne'er before hadst pardoned me?

Kind hearts and true I sometimes find, to give
The alms of cheering word and helping hand,
To counsel, to encourage, sympathize,
But only Thou, dear Christ, dost understand.

I rise to go. I've breathed no word of prayer,
Yet is my spirit tranquil with the peace
Of Thy sweet pardon, like a mother's kiss
That soothes our fears and bids our grieving cease.

And courage new is mine, my cross to bear
As long as Thou dost will, along life's way,
Although I thought, but one short hour ago,
I could not brook its weight another day.

One parting gift, sweet Jesus, I would ask;
  Not granted heart's desire, surcease from fear,
    Nor lifted cross. This only is my plea:
  Give me, dear Lord, the grace to persevere!

Draw me to Thee, though it should need the scourge
  Of bitter grief to bring me to Thy feet;
    And teach me, when life's path is full of pain,
  To find my solace in Thy Presence sweet.

LIFE AND DEATH
(SR. MARY CHRISTINA)

"If this be life," said a spirit,
As it bent beneath its load,
"Oh, what must the future Death be
To which *this* is but the road?
If this battlefield strewn with corpses
That all unburied lie
Be the dwelling place of the living,
What is there for them that die?

"Of an infinite evil impending,
To stand in an infinite dread —
If this be the lot of the living,
Say what is the doom of the dead?
If 'tis Life that my soul doth sever
From its dear and sole Delight,
Do they call that 'Death' which forever
Doth me and me Love unite?"

No. The devil has changed — the liar! —
The names of Life and Death,
Lest men should to Life aspire,
And leave him alone beneath.
This is Death, poor burdened spirit,
Then be patient beneath thy load,
[For] that which thou shalt inherit
is Life — and the Life of God.

PEACE SHALL COME AT LAST
(SR. MARY CHRISTINA)

Awake, arise, O soul, from sleep,
From those wide fields where no winds blow
Thou canst not now those visions keep
That so delight thee, they must go
Into the dreamy past.

Awake, O senses, to the wear
Of life, the caution and the strain;
There is much yet to do and bear
Ere death shall be the end of pain,
And peace shall come at last.

Return, weak heart, take up thy weight,
And bear it through another day;
The joy that seemed so real of late
Like other joys must sink away
Into the dreamy past.

Return to labor and to pain;
Forget not grief, nor seek for rest;
Sigh not for death, 'tis worse than pain;
Death will end all when God sees best,
And peace shall come at last.

CONFIDO ET CONQUIESCO
(ADELAIDE ANNE PROCTER)

Fret not, poor soul: while doubt and fear
　　Disturb thy breast,
The pitying angels, who can see
How vain thy wild regret must be,
　　Say, Trust and Rest.

Plan not, nor scheme, — but calmly wait;
　　His choice is best.
While blind and erring is thy sight,
His wisdom sees and judges right,
　　So Trust and Rest.

Strive not, nor struggle: thy poor might
　　Can never wrest
The meanest thing to serve thy will;
All power is His alone: Be still,
　　And Trust and Rest.

Desire not: self-love is strong
　　Within thy breast;
And yet He loves thee better still,
So let Him do His loving will,
　　And Trust and Rest.

What dost thou fear? His wisdom reigns
　　Supreme confessed;
His power is infinite; His love
Thy deepest, fondest dreams above;
　　So Trust and Rest.

APPENDIX II

ENCOURAGING PRAYERS

When we kneel down and make the Sign of the Cross
reverently, God at once turns to us and gives us all His
attention as fully as if there was no one else in existence.
(FR. PAUL O'SULLIVAN)

ACT OF HOPE AND CONFIDENCE IN GOD
(ST. CLAUDE DE LA COLOMBIÈRE)

✠ My God, I believe most firmly that Thou watchest over all who hope in Thee, and that we can want for nothing when we rely upon Thee in all things; therefore, I am resolved for the future to have no anxieties, and to cast all my cares upon Thee. In peace in the selfsame I will sleep and I will rest, for Thou, O Lord, singularly hast settled me in hope.

Men may deprive me of worldly goods and of honors; sickness may take from me my strength and the means of serving Thee; I may even lose Thy grace by sin; but my trust shall never leave me. I will preserve it to the last moment of my life, and the powers of hell shall seek in vain to wrest it from me. In peace in the selfsame I will sleep and I will rest.

Let others seek happiness in their wealth, in their talents; let them trust to the purity of their lives, the severity of their mortifications, to the number of their good works, the fervor of their prayers; as for me, O my God, in my very confidence lies all my hope: For Thou, O Lord, singularly hast settled me in hope. This confidence can never be in vain, for no one has hoped in the Lord and has been confounded.

I am assured, therefore, of my eternal happiness, for I firmly hope for it, and all my hope is in Thee. In Thee, O Lord, have I hoped. Let me never be confounded.

I know, alas! I know but too well that I am frail and changeable; I know the power of temptation against the strongest virtue. I have seen stars fall from Heaven, and pillars of the firmament totter; but these things alarm me not. While I hope in Thee, I am sheltered from all misfortune, and I am sure that my trust shall endure, for I rely upon Thee to sustain this unfailing hope.

Finally, I know that my confidence can not exceed Thy bounty, and that I shall never receive less than I have hoped for from Thee. Therefore I hope that Thou wilt sustain me against my evil inclinations; that Thou wilt protect me against the most furious assaults of the evil one, and that Thou wilt cause my weakness to triumph over my most powerful enemies. I hope that Thou wilt never cease to love me, and that I shall love Thee unceasingly. In Thee, O Lord, have I hoped. Let me never be confounded.

PRAYER TO MARY
(ST. LOUIS MARIE DE MONTFORT)

❧ Hail Mary, beloved Daughter of the Eternal Father! Hail Mary, admirable Mother of the Son! Hail Mary, faithful spouse of the Holy Ghost! Hail Mary, my dear Mother, my loving Mistress, my powerful sovereign! Hail my joy, my glory, my heart and my soul! Thou art all mine by mercy, and I am all thine by justice. But I am not yet sufficiently thine. I now give myself wholly to thee without keeping anything back for myself or others. If thou still seest in me anything which does not belong to thee, I beseech thee to take it and to make thyself the absolute Mistress of all that is mine. Destroy in me all that may be displeasing to God, root it up and bring it to naught; place and cultivate in me everything that is pleasing to thee.

May the light of thy faith dispel the darkness of my mind; may thy profound humility take the place of my pride; may thy sublime contemplation check the distractions of my wandering imagination; may thy continuous sight of God fill my memory with His presence; may the burning love of thy heart inflame the lukewarmness of mine; may thy virtues take the place of my sins; may thy merits be my only adornment in the sight of God and make up for all that is wanting in me.

PRAYER TO THE ARCHANGEL GABRIEL
(ST. JOHN EUDES)

❧ I revere and honor the blessed Archangel St. Michael as the Angel of holy humility, signified by his very name: *Quis Ut Deus? Who Is Like God?* and because he has overthrown the proud prince of rebellion, together with all other apostate angels; but thee, O glorious St. Gabriel, *I revere* as the Angel of holy love, because thou didst announce the Mystery of Love, and thou art the Angel of the Mother of beautiful love. Enkindle this divine fire in the hearts where it is extinct. Inflame the hearts of those in whom it already burns. Consume the hearts of those already inflamed with this sacred fire, particularly those who have a sincere and perfect devotion to this divine Mary.

For, being the guardian of the Mother, thou art the Angel protector of all Her children, especially of those who make profession of serving, honoring, and loving Her, as children well reared and trained should honor and love the best and most amiable Mother that ever was or ever will be. Thou hast for such an extraordinary care and solicitude; thou art more frequently with them; thou hast a singular desire to converse with them; thou dost enlighten, conduct, and guard them in perils; thou dost defend them against the enemies of their salvation and fortify them in their afflictions; thou dost love them more tenderly and protect them more powerfully; thou dost pray for them more ardently and procure for them more often the occasions and means to exercise the zeal they have for the honor and service of their Queen; thou dost treat them in all things and everywhere more favorably, and assist them more especially at the hour of death. Finally, thou dost bestow upon them a thousand favors which they will never understand until that beautiful and blessed day of eternity, when they will render thee unceasing thanks.

PRAYER TO OBTAIN COURAGE IN COMBAT
(ST. THÉRÈSE OF LISIEUX)

✣ O Lord God of Hosts, Who hast said in Thy Gospel, *I am not come to bring peace but a sword,* arm me for the fight. I burn to do battle for Thy glory, but I pray Thee to strengthen my courage. Then with holy David I shall be able to exclaim: *Thou alone art my shield; it is Thou, O Lord, Who teachest my hands to war.* O my Beloved, I know the warfare to which Thou hast destined me; it is not on the field of battle that I shall fight. I am the prisoner of Thy love, I have freely riveted the chain which binds me to Thee and cuts me off forever from the world. My sword is *Love!* With it, like Joan of Arc, "I shall drive out the strangers from the land, and have Thee proclaimed King"— over the kingdom of souls. In truth, O Lord, Thou hast no need of so weak an instrument as I; but Joan, Thy chaste and valiant bride, has said: "We must do battle before God gives us the victory." O my Jesus, I shall do battle for Thee, then, until the evening of my life. As

Thou didst not will to enjoy rest upon earth, I would follow Thine example, then this promise which fell from Thy divine lips will be fulfilled in me: *If any man will follow Me, where I am there also shall My servant be, and My Father will honor him.* To be with Thee, to be in Thee — that is my one desire. The assurance Thou givest me that it shall be realized sustains me in my exile, while I await the joyous day when I shall behold Thee face to face everlastingly.

PRAYER OF THE ENAMORED SOUL
(ST. JOHN OF THE CROSS)

✠ Thou wilt not take away from me, O my God, what Thou hast once given me in Thine Only-Begotten Son, Jesus Christ, in Whom Thou dost give me all I desire. I will therefore rejoice; Thou wilt not tarry if I wait for Thee. Wait in hope, then, O my soul, for from henceforth thou mayest love God in thy heart.

Mine are the heavens and mine is the earth; mine are the people, the righteous are mine, and mine are the sinners; the angels are mine, and the Mother of God, and all things are mine; God Himself is mine and for me, because Christ is mine, and all for me. What dost thou, then, ask for, what dost thou seek, O my soul? All is thine, all is for thee. Do not take less, nor rest with the crumbs which fall from the table of thy Father. Go forth and exult in thy glory, hide thyself in it, and rejoice, and thou shalt obtain all the desires of thy heart.

RELISHING GOD'S PRESENCE IN THE SOUL
(ST. JOHN OF THE CROSS)

✠ O my God, make me understand that I am Thy dwelling-place, the hiding place where Thou dost conceal Thyself.

Have courage and rejoice, my soul, knowing that the object of thy hope is so near to thee that He dwells in thee, and thou canst not exist without Him. What more could I desire, and what do I seek outside of myself, O my Lord and my God, when Thou hast deigned to put Thy kingdom, Thy dwelling-place, in my very soul? Here, then, in the innermost sanctuary of my heart, I wish to love, desire, and adore Thee; no, I shall no longer go to seek Thee outside myself.

EMBRACING INTERIOR DESOLATION
(ST. ALPHONSUS DE LIGUORI)

✣ Jesus, my hope, my love, the only love of my soul! I do not deserve that Thou shouldst impart to me Thy consolations and sweetness. Reserve them for the sinless souls who have always loved Thee. As for me, who have so often offended Thee, I am unworthy of them and do not ask them of Thee. There is only one thing I desire of Thee, and it is this: Grant that I may love Thee, O my God! Grant that I may accomplish Thy will during my whole life, and then dispose of me in the manner that pleases Thee best. I consecrate to Thee my body, my soul, my will, my liberty. I no longer desire to live for myself, but only for Thee. Afflict me as it pleases Thee; give me only Thy grace and Thy love, and I shall be content to be deprived of everything else.

PRAYER FOR INTERIOR PEACE
(ST. ELIZABETH OF THE TRINITY)

✣ O my God, Trinity Whom I adore, help me to become entirely forgetful of self, that I may establish myself in Thee, as changeless and as calm as though my soul were already in eternity! May nothing disturb my peace nor draw me forth from Thee, O my immutable Lord, but may I penetrate more deeply every moment into the depths of Thy mystery. Give peace to my soul, make it Thy Heaven, Thy cherished dwelling-place, Thy home of rest. Let me never leave Thee alone, but keep me ever there, all absorbed in Thee, in living faith, adoring Thee, and wholly yielded up to Thy creative action!

PRAYER TO BECOME LOVE'S PREY
(ST. THÉRÈSE OF LISIEUX)

❧ O Eternal Word! O my Savior! Thou art the Divine Eagle Whom I love and Who allurest me. Thou Who, descending to this land of exile, didst will to suffer and to die, in order to bear away each single soul and plunge it into the very heart of the Blessed Trinity—Love's eternal home! Thou Who, returning to Thy realm of light, dost still remain hidden here in our vale of tears under the appearance of the white Host, to nourish me with Thine own substance. Forgive me, O Jesus, if I tell Thee that Thy love reacheth even unto folly, and at the sight of such folly what wilt Thou but that my own heart should leap up to Thee? How could there be any limit to my trust?

I know well that for Thy sake the saints have made themselves foolish—being *eagles* they have done great things. Too little for such mighty deeds, my folly lies in the hope that Thy love accepts me as a victim, and in my confidence that the angels and saints will help me to fly unto Thee with Thine own wings, O my Divine Eagle! As long as Thou willest I shall remain with my gaze fixed upon Thee, for I long to be fascinated by Thy divine eyes, I long to become Love's prey.

PRAYER IN PRAISE OF THE HOLY NAME
(ST. BERNADINE OF SIENA)

✠ O glorious Name! Gracious Name! Name full of love and virtue! Through Thee, sins are forgiven, enemies overcome, the sick healed, the suffering strengthened in adversity! You are the honor of believers, the master of preachers, support of the weak. Holy desires are nourished by the ardor of Thy fire; and by it, necessary suffrages are obtained, contemplative souls are inebriated, and the triumphant are glorified in heavenly glory! By Thy most Holy Name, O sweet Jesus, Thou makest us reign with the blessed, Thou, their glory, Thou Who triumph gloriously with the Father and the Holy Spirit in perfect Unity and Trinity, forever and ever.

O Name of Jesus, exalted above every other name! O triumphant Name! O joy of angels! O terror of hell! All hope of pardon, of grace, and of glory is found in Thee! O sweetest Name, Thou pardonest the guilty, Thou reformest evil habits, Thou fillest the timid with divine sweetness and drive away terrifying vision! O glorious Name! By Thee, the mysteries of eternal life are revealed, souls are inflamed with divine love, strengthened in time of struggle, and freed from all dangers. O desirable Name! Delightful Name! Admirable Name! Venerable Name! Little by little Thou dost raise the souls of the faithful by Thy gifts and graces to the heights of Heaven. All to whom Thou dost communicate Thine ineffable grandeur, by Thy power attain to salvation and glory!

APPENDIX III

RECOMMENDED READING

*Why do you not use the time when you have
nothing to do for reading or for prayer?
Why do you not go and visit Christ our Lord
and speak with Him and listen to Him?
For when we pray we speak with God,
and when we read, we listen to God.*

(ST. AMBROSE)

THE SPIRITUAL LIFE

The Challenge of Faith by Br. Francis Maluf
Christ and His Mysteries by Bl. Dom Columba Marmion
Christ the Life of the Soul by Bl. Dom Columba Marmion
Consoling the Heart of Jesus by Fr. Michael Gaitley
Consoling Thoughts of St. Francis de Sales arranged by Père Huguet
Creator and Creature by Fr. Frederick Faber
The Dialogue of St. Catherine of Siena by St. Catherine of Siena
Heliotropium: Conformity of the Human Will to the Divine by Fr. Jeremias Drexel
The Hidden Power of Kindness by Fr. Lawrence G. Lovasik
Holy Abandonment by Rev. Dom Vitalis Lehodey
The Imitation of Christ by Thomas à Kempis
Jesus Appeals to the World: from the Writings of Sister Consolata Betrone by Fr. Lorenzo Sales
Little Catechism of the Act of Oblation of St. Thérèse of the Child Jesus by the Sisters of Carmel
The Little Way of Spiritual Childhood by Rev. Gabriel Martin
A Retreat with St. Thérèse by Père Louis Liagre
The Soul of the Apostolate by Dom Jean-Baptiste Chautard
Spiritual Childhood by Msgr. Vernon Johnson
Spiritual Conferences by Fr. Frederick William Faber

The Spiritual Conferences of St. Francis de Sales by Rev. H.B. Mackey
This Tremendous Lover by Dom Mary Eugene Boylan
Trustful Surrender to Divine Providence: The Secret of Peace and Happiness
    by Fr. Jean Baptist Saint-Jure and St. Claude de la Colombière
*Words of Love: Spoken by Our Lord to Three Twentieth-Century Victim
    Souls* compiled by Fr. Bartholomew Gottenmoller

MARIAN LITERATURE

The Glories of Mary by St. Alphonsus de Liguori
Life of Union with Mary by Fr. Emile Neubert
My Ideal: Jesus Son of Mary by Fr. Emile Neubert
True Devotion to Mary by St. Louis Marie de Montfort
Union with Our Lady by Ven. Marie Petyt

HAGIOGRAPHIES
(LIVES OF THE SAINTS)

Bernadette Speaks: A Life of St. Bernadette in Her Own Words by Fr.
    Rene Laurentin
The Biographical Memoirs of St. John Bosco: Volume I by Giovanni
    Battista Lemoyne
He is My Heaven: The Life of St. Elizabeth of the Trinity by Jennifer
    Moorcroft
The Life of St. Catherine of Siena by Bl. Raymond of Capua
The Life of St. Margaret Mary Alacoque by the Most Rev. Emile Bou-
    gaud
Marie of the Incarnation: Mystic and Mother by Mother Denis Mahoney
Martyrs of the Coliseum by Fr. A.J. O'Reilly
Mary's Knight: The Life of St. Maximilian Kolbe by Claude R. Foster
Mercy My Mission: Life of Sister Faustina Kowalska by Sr. Sophia
    Michalenko
Pax Tecum Filumena: The Life of St. Philomena by William Thomas
    Walsh
Perfect Friend: The Life of Blessed Claude de la Colombière by Georges
    Guitton

Portrait of St. Gemma: A Stigmatic by Sr. Saint Michael
St. Francis of Assisi by St. Bonaventure
St. Madeleine Sophie: Her Life and Letters by Mother Margaret Williams
St. Teresa of Ávila by William Thomas Walsh

AUTOBIOGRAPHIES
✿

Autobiography of Marcel Van
Autobiography of St. Teresa of Ávila
Memoirs of Josef Cardinal Mindzenty
The Story of a Soul by St. Thérèse of Lisieux

BIOGRAPHIES
✿

Abbot Columba Marmion: A Master of the Spiritual Life by Dom Raymond Thibant
Father William Doyle, SJ: A Spiritual Study by Professor Alfred O'Rahilly
The Life of Cornelia Connelly: Foundress of the Society of the Holy Child Jesus by a Religious of the Society
The Life of Fr. De Smet, SJ: Apostle of the Rocky Mountains by Fr. E. Laveille
The Life and Work of Mother Louise Margaret by Fr. Patrick O'Connell
Mary Was Her Life: The Story of Sister Maria Teresa Quevedo by Sr. Mary Pierre
Merry in God: A Life of Father William Doyle by a Jesuit
The Spiritual Life of Cardinal Merry del Val by Rev. Jerome Dal-Gal
Sr. Louise: American Foundress of the Sisters of Notre Dame de Namur by Sr. Helen Louise
Sister Miriam Teresa by a Sister of Charity

HISTORY
✿

The Church at the Turning Points of History by Godfrey Kurth
The Continuity of Religion by Bishop Jacques-Bénigne Bossuet
The Whole Truth About Fatima by Frère Michel de la Sainte Trinite

SOCIAL ISSUES

Fatal Star by Hamish Fraser
The Fourfold Sovereignty of God by Henry Edward Manning
Liberalism Is a Sin by Don Felix Sarda y Salvany

DEVOTION

The Foot of the Cross by Fr. Frederick William Faber
The Blessed Sacrament by Fr. Frederick William Faber
Creator and Creature by Fr. Frederick William Faber
Devotion for the Dying by Mother Mary Potter
The Four Last Things: Death, Judgment, Hell, and Heaven by Fr. Martin von Cochem
The Hidden Treasure: Holy Mass by St. Leonard of Port Maurice
The Incredible Catholic Mass by Fr. Martin von Cochem
Introduction to the Devout Life by St. Francis de Sales
The Little Catechism of the Act of Oblation of St. Thérèse of the Child Jesus by the Sisters of Carmel
The Secret of the Rosary by St. Louis Marie de Montfort
St. Thérèse: Messenger of Mary by Rev. Albert H. Dolan

INDEX OF AUTHORS

Not to fall into discouragement, mark: it is a sovereign remedy to discover our trouble to some wise friend who can solace us.
(ST. FRANCIS DE SALES)

SAINTS

ISAIAS THE PROPHET: Born circa 750 BC in the Kingdom of Juda. Old Testament prophet and author of the Scriptural book of Isaias. Martyred by being sawed in half.

Introduction

ST. ALPHONSUS DE LIGUORI: Born in Naples, Italy, on September 27, 1696; died in Pagani, Italy, on August 1, 1787. Bishop, Founder of the Congregation of the Most Holy Redeemer (Redemptorists), and Doctor of the Church. Patron saint of moralists, confessors, lawyers, and those suffering from arthritis.

Introduction; The Blessed Virgin Mary; Love {2}; Mercy {2}; The Holy Will of God {2}; The Holy Mass; The Holy Eucharist {2}; Prayer {4}; Suffering; Temptations {2}; Desolation; Sickness {2}; Hope; Confidence {2}; Encouraging Prayers

ST. ALPHONSUS RODRIGUEZ: Born in Segovia, Spain, on July 25, 1532; died in Palma, Spain, on October 31, 1617. Jesuit lay-brother. Patron saint of Majorca.

Prayer; Imperfections

ST. AMBROSE: Born in Trier, Germany, in 340; died in Milan, Italy, on April 4, 397. Theologian, bishop of Milan, and Doctor of the Church. Baptized St. Augustine. Patron saint of beekeepers and candlemakers.

Love; Confidence; Recommended Reading

❧ **ST. ANDRÉ BESSETTE:** Born in Quebec, Canada, on August 9, 1845; died in Montreal, Canada, on January 6, 1937. Lay-brother in the Congregation of the Holy Cross. Famous for miracles and devotion to Saint Joseph.

Trials

❧ **ST. ANGELA OF FOLIGNO:** Born in Foligno, Italy, in 1248; died there on January 3, 1309. Third Order Franciscan visionary. Patroness of widows and those afflicted by temptations against holy purity.

Suffering

❧ **ST. ANSELM:** Born in Aosta, Italy, in 1033; died in England on April 21, 1109. Benedictine monk, theologian, bishop, and Doctor of the Church; known for his ontological proof for the existence of God.

The Blessed Virgin Mary; Mercy; Death

❧ **ST. ANTHONY OF THE DESERT:** Born in Heracleopolis Magna, Egypt, on January 12, 251; died in Egypt on January 17, 356. Anchorite. Invoked against skin diseases.

Prayer; Temptations; The Church and the Faith

❧ **ST. ANTHONY OF PADUA:** Born in Lisbon, Portugal, on August 15, 1195; died in Padua, Italy, on June 13, 1231. Franciscan priest, Doctor of the Church, and Wonder-worker. Canonized less than one year after his death. Patron saint of finding lost things.

Mercy

❧ **ST. ANTONINUS:** Born in Florence, Italy, on March 1, 1389; died there on May 2, 1459. Dominican friar and archbishop of Florence.

Confidence

❧ **ST. AUGUSTINE:** Born in Tagaste in present-day Algeria on November 13, 354; died in Hippo (present-day Annaba) in Algeria on August 28, 430. Bishop and Doctor of the Church. Famous for his autobiography *The Confessions*. Patron saint of brewers because of the immorality of his youth.

Prayer {4}; Suffering {2}; Sorrow; Death {2}; Confidence; Holy Desires; Grace and the Divine Indwelling; The Church and the Faith

⊱ ST. BENEDICT JOSEPH LABRE: Born in Amettes, France, on March 25, 1748; died in Rome on April 16, 1860. Franciscan tertiary and pilgrim. Patron saint of bachelors and homeless people.

Prayer

⊱ ST. BERNARD: Born in Fontaine-lès-Dijon, France, in 1090; died at the Clairvaux Abbey in France on August 20, 1153. Cistercian monk, founder and abbot of the abbey of Clairvaux, and Doctor of the Church. Known for the persuasive power of his eloquence. Patron saint of beekeepers and candlemakers.

The Blessed Virgin Mary; Love; Mercy {3}; Suffering; Trials; Temptations; Hope {3}; Confidence; Sanctity

⊱ ST. BERNADETTE: Born in Lourdes, France, on January 7, 1844; died in Nevers, France, on April 16, 1879. Visionary who saw Our Lady as the Immaculate Conception eighteen times between February 11 and July 16, 1858. Later became a religious with the Sisters of Charity. Patron saint of those ridiculed for their faith.

The Holy Rosary

⊱ ST. BONAVENTURE: Born in Bagnoregio, Italy, in 1221; died in Lyon, France, on July 15, 1275. Franciscan theologian, philosopher, cardinal, bishop, and friend of St. Thomas Aquinas.

The Blessed Virgin Mary; Death; Confidence; Encouraging Poems

⊱ ST. BRIDGET OF SWEDEN: Born c. 1303 in Uppland, Sweden; died July 23, 1373, in Rome. Mystic, mother of eight children (including St. Catherine of Sweden) and foundress of the Order of the Most Holy Savior (the Bridgittines). Patron saint of Sweden.

The Blessed Virgin Mary {2}; Mercy {3}; Prayer

⊱ ST. CAMILLUS DE LELLIS: Born in Bucchianico (now Abruzzo), Italy, on May 25, 1550; died in Rome on July 14, 1614. Priest and founder of the Ministers of Sick (the Camellians). Patron saint of the sick, doctors, nurses, hospitals, and those addicted to gambling.

Sacrifice

❧ **ST. CATHERINE OF BOLOGNA:** Born in Bologna, Italy, on September 8, 1413; died there on March 9, 1463. Poor Clare nun, mystic, and spiritual writer. Patron saint of artists.

Confidence

❧ **ST. CATHERINE OF SIENA:** Born in Siena, Italy, on March 25, 1347; died in Rome on April 29, 1380. Dominican tertiary, mystic, and Doctor of the Church. Patron saint of Italy.

Love; Divine Providence {2}; The Passion; Imperfections; Holy Desires {3}; The Salvation of Souls

❧ **ST. CHARLES OF SEZZE:** Born in Sezze, Italy, on October 19, 1613; died in Rome on January 6, 1670. Franciscan friar.

Love

❧ **ST. CLAUDE DE LA COLOMBIÈRE:** Born in Saint-Symphorien-d'Ozon, France, on February 2, 1641; died in Paray-le-Monial, France, February 15, 1682. Jesuit priest, missionary, and confessor to St. Margaret Mary Alacoque.

The Holy Will of God {2}; Divine Providence {2}; Prayer {7}; Suffering {4}; Trials {2}; Encouraging Prayers

❧ **ST. DOMINIC:** Born in Caleruega, Spain, on August 8, 1170; died in Bologna (now Emilia-Romagna), Italy, August 6, 1221. Priest and founder of the Order of Friars Preachers (the Dominicans). Patron saint of astronomers.

Death

❧ **ST. ELIZABETH ANN SETON:** Born in New York City, USA, on August 28, 1774; died in Emmitsburg, Maryland, on January 4, 1821. Convert, wife and mother of four children, foundress of the Sisters of Charity, and the first native-born American to be canonized.

Hope

☙ ST. ELIZABETH OF THE TRINITY: Born in Avor, France, on July 18, 1880; died in Dijon, France, on November 9, 1906. Carmelite.

Love; Trials; Imperfections; Desolation; Hope; Grace and the Divine Indwelling {2}; Encouraging Prayers

☙ ST. EPHREM: Born in Nisbis, Mesopotamia (now Nusaybin, Turkey), c. 306; died in Edessa (now Şanlıurfa, Turkey) on June 9, 373. Theologian, poet, hymnographer, and Doctor of the Church. Patron saint of spiritual directors.

Trials

☙ ST. FAUSTINA: Born in Glogweic, Poland, on August 25, 1905; died in Krakow, Poland, on October 5, 1938. Religious of the Sisters of Our Lady of Mercy, mystic, and recipient of the Divine Mercy revelations.

Love {3}; Mercy {5}; The Holy Will of God; The Passion {2}; Prayer {2}; Suffering {3}; Imperfections; Sanctity {2}

☙ ST. FRANCIS DE SALES: Born in the Kingdom of Savoy in Switzerland, August 21, 1567; died in Lyons, France, on December 28, 1622. Bishop, missionary, spiritual writer, Doctor of the Church, and co-founder with St. Jane Frances de Chantal of the Order of the Visitation of Holy Mary (the Visitation Sisters). Patron saint of Catholic writers and journalists.

Love {5}; Mercy {4}; The Holy Will of God; Divine Providence {5}; The Holy Eucharist; Prayer {3}; Suffering {5}; Trials {2}; Temptations {7}; Imperfections {3}; Sorrow {4}; Desolation {4}; Sickness {6}; Death {7}; The End Times; Confidence; Holy Desires {3}; Sanctity {3}; Index of Authors

☙ ST. GABRIEL POSSENTI: Born in Assisi, Italy, on March 1, 1838; died in Abruzzi, Italy, on February 27, 1862. Passionist novice. Patron saint of handgunners and sharpshooters.

Hope

☙ ST. GEMMA GALGANI: Born in Camigliano, Italy, on March 12, 1878; died in Lucca, Italy, on April 11, 1903. Passionist tertiary and mystic. Patron saint of pharmacists and those struggling with temptations against purity.

Love; Suffering; Temptations

❧ **ST. GERTRUDE:** Born in Eisleben, Thuringia (now Germany), on January 6, 1256; died in Saxony, Germany, on November 17, 1302. Benedictine abbess and mystic. Patron saint of cats, gardeners, and the dead.

The Passion {2}; The Holy Mass; The Holy Eucharist; Sickness {2}; Good Will; The Salvation of Souls

❧ **ST. HILARY OF POITIERS:** Born in Poitiers, France, c. 315; died there in 367. Bishop and Doctor of the Church. Patron saint of academically struggling students.

Mercy

❧ **ST. IGNATIUS OF LOYOLA:** Born in the Basque region of Spain on October 23, 1491; died in Rome on July 31, 1556. Priest, missionary, and founder of the Society of Jesus (the Jesuits). Patron saint of retreatants and retreat masters.

The Holy Eucharist; Suffering

❧ **ST. JOHN OF ÁVILA:** Born in Almodóvar del Campo, Spain, on January 6, 1499; died in Montilla, Spain, on May 10, 1569. Priest, reformer, spiritual director, and Doctor of the Church. Patron saint of Spanish secular priests.

Suffering

❧ **ST. JOHN BERCHMANS:** Born in Diest, Belgium, on March 13, 1599; died in Rome on August 13, 1621. Jesuit seminarian. Patron saint of altar boys.

Confidence

❧ **ST. JOHN BOSCO:** Born in Becchi, Italy, on August 16, 1815; died in Turin, Italy, on January 31, 1888. Priest and founder of the Society of Saint Frances de Sales (the Salesians) and co-founder with St. Maria Domenica Mazzarello of the Institute of the Daughters of Mary Help of Christians (the Salesian Sisters). Patron saint of youth, editors, publishers, and magicians.

The Blessed Virgin Mary; Prayer; The Church and the Faith

❧ **ST. JOHN CHRYSOSTOM:** Born in Antioch, Syria, c. 347; died in Comana (now Sar), Turkey, on September 14, 407. Patriarch of Constantinople and Doctor of the Church. Patron saint of orators.

Mercy; Trials; Temptations; The End Times; The Church and the Faith

❧ **ST. JOHN CLIMACUS:** Born in Syria, c. 525; died on Mount Sinai, Egypt, c. 605. Abbot of the Monastery of Saint Catherine and mystical writer.

Prayer {2}; Imperfections; The Salvation of Souls {2}

❧ **ST. JOHN OF THE CROSS:** Born in Fontiveros, Spain, on June 24, 1542; died in Ubeda, Spain, on December 14, 1591. Carmelite priest, poet, mystic, spiritual writer, and co-founder with St. Teresa of Ávila of the reform movement of Discalced Carmelites. Patron saint of contemplatives and mystical theology.

Love; Suffering; Temptations; Hope; Holy Desires; Grace and the Divine Indwelling; Encouraging Prayers {2}

❧ **ST. JOHN EUDES:** Born in Normandy, France, on November 14, 1601; died in Caen, France, on August 19, 1680. Priest, author, and founder of the Order of Our Lady of Charity and the Congregation of Jesus and Mary (the Eudists). Patron saint of missionaries and women fallen into prostitution.

The Blessed Virgin Mary; Divine Providence; Prayer; Encouraging Prayers

❧ **ST. JOHN HENRY NEWMAN:** Born in London, United Kingdom, on February 21, 1801; died in Birmingham, UK, on August 11, 1890. Convert, cardinal, scholar, historian, and writer.

Introduction; The Blessed Virgin Mary {2}; Encouraging Poems

❧ **ST. JOHN MARIE VIANNEY:** Born in Dardilly, France, on May 8, 1786; died in Ars, France, on August 4, 1859. Parish priest, miracle worker, propagator of devotion to Saint Philomena. Patron saint of parish priests.

Prayer; Suffering; Trials; Temptations {2}; Sickness; Sanctity; The Salvation of Souls

⸙ **ST. JUAN DIEGO:** Born in Cuautitlán (near Mexico City) in 1474; died in Mexico City on May 30, 1548. Aztec Indian convert who received the apparitions of Our Lady of Guadalupe in 1531. Patron saint of indigenous people.

Sorrow

⸙ **ST. LAWRENCE JUSTINIAN:** Born in Venice, Italy, on July 1, 1381; died in Venice on January 8, 1456. Canon Regular of Saint Augustine, bishop, reformer, and first Patriarch of Venice.

The Holy Mass; Prayer

⸙ **ST. LEO THE GREAT:** Born in Italy c. 400; died in Rome on November 10, 461. Pope who saved Rome from being sacked by Attila the Hun in 452.

Temptations

⸙ **ST. LEONARD OF PORT MAURICE:** Born in Porto Maurizio, Italy, on December 20, 1676; died in Rome on November 26, 1751. Franciscan priest, missionary, and spiritual writer.

The Holy Mass {3}; Sanctity

⸙ **ST. LOUIS MARIE DE MONTFORT:** Born in Brittany, France, on January 31, 1673; died in Saint-Laurent-sur-Sevre, France, on April 28, 1716. Priest, missionary apostolic, spiritual writer, and founder of the Daughters of Wisdom and the Company of Mary (the Montfort Fathers). Popularized the devotion of Holy Slavery through Total Consecration to Jesus through Mary.

The Blessed Virgin Mary {11}; Love; The Holy Will of God; Divine Providence; The Passion; Prayer {2}; The Holy Rosary {5}; Suffering; Trials; Temptations; Sorrow; Confidence; Sanctity {4}; Salvation of Souls; Encouraging Prayers

⸙ **ST. MARIE OF THE INCARNATION:** Born in Tours, France, on October 28, 1599; died in Quebec, New France (now Canada), on April 30, 1672. Widow, mother of one son, Ursuline nun, and mystic. Founded the Ursulines in the New World.

Divine Providence; Sanctity

🕸 **ST. MARY MAGDALEN DEI PAZZI:** Born in Florence, Italy, on April 2, 1566; died in Florence on May 25, 1607. Discalced Carmelite nun and mystic. Patron saint of those afflicted with temptations against purity.

The Holy Eucharist

🕸 **ST. MAXIMILIAN MARIA KOLBE:** Born in Zduńska-Wola, Poland, on January 8, 1894; died at the concentration camp at Auschwitz in German-occupied Poland on August 14, 1941. Conventual Franciscan friar and priest who founded the now-worldwide Marian movement, the *Militia Immaculatae*. Patron saint of political prisoners, the pro-life movement, and those who struggle with drug addictions.

Introduction; The Blessed Virgin Mary {3}; Mercy; The Holy Will of God {2}; Sacrifice; Trials; Temptations {3}; Imperfections {1}; The End Times; Confidence; Sanctity {2}; The Salvation of Souls {8}; The Church and the Faith

🕸 **ST. MECHTILDE:** Born in Helfta, Germany, c. 1240; died there on November 19, 1298. Benedictine nun, visionary, and teacher of St. Gertrude the Great.

The Passion; The Holy Mass; The Holy Rosary

🕸 **ST. NILUS:** Born in the fourth century in Ireland; died on Mount Sinai on November 12, 430. Husband and father of two children; entered monastic life and became known as a scholar and ascetic writer.

Prayer

🕸 **ST. PACHOMIUS:** Born in Thebes (now Luxor), Egypt, c. 292; died in Egypt, c. 348. Desert father who wrote one of the earliest rules for communal monasticism.

Suffering

🕸 **ST. PAUL:** Born in Tarsus in Cilicia (now Turkey) c. 5 AD; died in Rome on June 29, 67. Convert, Apostle to the Gentiles, inspired author of fourteen Epistles in Holy Scripture.

Reasons for Hope; Love; The Perfecting of Hope; Saved by Hope

❧ **ST. PAUL OF THE CROSS:** Born in Ovada, Italy, on January 3, 1694; died in Rome on October 18, 1775. Priest, mystic, and founder of the Congregation of the Passion of Jesus Christ (the Passionists).

Trials; Imperfections; Sickness

❧ **ST. PETER:** Born in Bethsaida (now northern Israel) c. 1 BC; died in Rome on June 29, 67. Apostle and first Pope.

❧ **ST. PETER OF ALCANTARA:** Born in Alcantara, Spain, in 1499; died in Arenas de San Pedro, Spain, on October 18, 1562. Carmelite priest, mystical writer, and friend of St. Teresa of Ávila.

Love; Desolation; Good Will

❧ **ST. PETER CHRYSOLOGUS:** Born in Imola, Italy, in 406; died there on July 31, 450. Bishop and Doctor of the Church.

Confidence

❧ **ST. PETER DAMIAN:** Born in Ravenna, Italy, c. 988; died at Faenza, Italy, on February 22, 1072. Benedictine monk, cardinal, reformer, and Doctor of the Church.

Hope

❧ **ST. PETER JULIAN EYMARD:** Born in La Mure, France, on February 4, 1811; died in Grenoble, France, on August 1, 1868. Priest of the Oblates of Mary Immaculate (the Marists) and founder of the Congregation of the Blessed Sacrament. Called the Apostle of the Eucharist.

The Blessed Virgin Mary; Love; The Holy Eucharist; Sacrifice

❧ **ST. PIO OF PIETRELCINA:** Born in Pietrelcina, Italy, on May 25, 1887; died at San Giovanni Rotondo, Italy, on September 23, 1968. Capuchin friar, priest, stigmatist, mystic, and miracle-worker. Patron saint of adolescents.

Mercy {2}; The Passion; Prayer {2}; Suffering; Trials; Temptations {4}; Confidence; Holy Desires

🥀 **ST. PIUS X:** Born in Riese, Italy, on June 2, 1835; died in Rome on August 20, 1914. Reigned as Pope from 1903–1914. Famous for vigorous opposition to modernism and lowering the age at which children can make their First Holy Communion.

The Holy Eucharist; The End Times; Hope

🥀 **ST. ROBERT BELLARMINE:** Born in Montepulciano, Italy, on October 4, 1542; died in Rome on September 17, 1621. Jesuit priest, archbishop, cardinal, theologian, and Doctor of the Church; called the Father of Ecclesiology. Patron saint of catechists.

Temptations

🥀 **ST. ROSE PHILIPPINE DUCHESNE:** Born in Grenoble, France, on August 29, 1769; died in St. Charles, Missouri (USA) on November 18, 1852. Sister of the Society of the Sacred Heart, missionary, and foundress of the Society in the United States.

Divine Providence

🥀 **ST. TERESA OF ÁVILA, OCD:** Born in Ávila, Spain, on March 28, 1515; died at Alba de Tormes, Spain, on October 4 or 15, 1582. Carmelite nun, co-foundress with St. John of the Cross of the reform movement of Discalced Carmelites, spiritual writer, mystic, and Doctor of the Church.

Love {5}; Prayer; Suffering {4}; Sacrifice; Trials; Temptations {3}; Imperfections; Holy Desires {3}; Sanctity {3}; Grace and the Divine Indwelling; The Salvation of Souls

🥀 **ST. THEOPHANE VÉNARD:** Born at Saint-Loup, France, on November 21, 1829; died in Tonkin, Vietnam, on February 2, 1861. Priest member of the Paris Seminary for Foreign Missions, missionary, and martyr.

Introduction; Good Will

🥀 **ST. THÉRÈSE OF LISIEUX, OCD:** Born in Alençon, France, on January 2, 1873; died in Lisieux, France, on September 30, 1897. Discalced Carmelite nun. Famous for her autobiography and doctrine of the Little Way of Spiritual Childhood. Co-patroness of

France with St. Joan of Arc and co-patroness of the missions with St. Francis Xavier.

Love {6}; Suffering {5}; Sacrifice {3}; Temptations; Imperfections {5}; Sorrow; Desolation {3}; Sickness; Death; The End Times; Confidence {4}; Sanctity {6}; Grace and the Divine Indwelling; Encouraging Prayers {2}

❧ **ST. THOMAS MORE:** Born in London, England, on February 7, 1478; died there on July 6, 1535. Husband, father, lawyer, scholar, statesman, and martyr under Henry VIII. Patron saint of lawyers and politicians.

Sorrow

❧ **ST. VINCENT DE PAUL:** Born in Pouy, France, on April 24, 1581; died in Paris on August 13, 1729. Priest, founder of the Congregation of the Mission (the Vincentians), co-founder of the Daughters of Charity, and second spiritual director of St. Jane Frances de Chantal (after St. Francis de Sales). Patron saint of charitable enterprises.

Divine Providence {2}; Suffering; Desolation; Sickness; Confidence; The Salvation of Souls

❧ **ST. VINCENT PALLOTTI:** Born in Rome on April 21, 1795; died there on January 22, 1850. Priest and founder of the Society of the Catholic Apostolate (the Pallottines).

Holy Desires

BLESSEDS & VENERABLES
❖

❧ **BL. ALAN DE LA ROCHE, OP:** Born in Dinan, France, c. 1428; died at Zwolle, Holland, on September 8, 1475. Dominican preacher, theologian, and visionary who worked for the restoration of devotion to the rosary.

The Holy Rosary {5}

❧ **BL. ANNA MARIA TAIGI, OSST:** Born in Siena, Italy, on May 29, 1769; died in Rome on June 9, 1837. Trinitarian tertiary, wife, mother of seven children, mystic, and prophetess.

Sacrifice

❧ **BL. DOM COLUMBA MARMION, OSB:** Born in Dublin, Ireland, on April 1, 1858; died at Maredsous Abbey in Belgium on January 30, 1923. Benedictine monk, abbot, and spiritual writer.

Mercy {2}; *The Holy Mass*; *The Holy Eucharist*; *Temptations*; *Sickness*; *Holy Desires*; *Confidence*; *Sanctity* {3}; *Grace and the Divine Indwelling*

❧ **BL. HENRY SUSO, OP:** Born in Constance, Germany, on March 21, 1295; died in Ulm, Germany, on January 25, 1366. Dominican friar and mystic.

Mercy; *Suffering* {2}; *Temptations*

❧ **BL. JORDAN OF SAXONY, OP:** Born in Saxony, Germany, c. 1190; died on February 13, 1237, in a shipwreck near Syria. Priest, missionary, and successor to St. Dominic as Master of the Dominicans.

Desolation

❧ **BL. LOUIS DE BLOIS, OSB:** Born at Donstienne, Flanders, in October of 1506; died at Liessies, France, on January 7, 1566. Benedictine abbot and spiritual writer.

Mercy; *Temptations*; *Imperfections*; *Death*

❧ **BL. VERONICA OF BINASCO, OSA:** Born in Milan, Italy, in 1445; died there on January 13, 1497. Augustinian nun and mystic.

The Passion

❧ **VEN. ADOLPH PETIT, SJ:** Born in Ghent, Belgium, on May 22, 1822; died in Drougen, Belgium, on May 20, 1914. Jesuit priest, retreat master, and spiritual director.

Love; *Prayer*

❧ **VEN. CONSOLATA BETRONE, PC:** Born in Saluzzo, Italy, on April 6, 1903; died in Turin, Italy, on July 18, 1946. Franciscan Capuchin nun and mystic to whom was revealed the Littlest Way of Love.

Love; *Death* {3}; *The Salvation of Souls*

❧ **VEN. CORNELIA CONNELLY, SHCJ:** Born in Philadelphia, Pennsylvania (USA), on January 15, 1809; died in Sussex, England, on

April 18, 1879. Wife, mother, convert, and foundress of the Society of the Holy Child Jesus.

Sufferings; Holy Desires

❦ **VEN. LUCIA DOS SANTOS, OCD:** Born in Aljustrel, Portugal, on March 28, 1907; died in Coimbra, Portugal, on February 13, 2005. Oldest seer of the 1917 Fatima apparitions; later became a Discalced Carmelite nun.

The Holy Rosary {3}

❦ **VEN. MARIE PETYT OF ST. TERESA:** Born in Hazebrouck, present-day France, on January 1, 1623; died in Mechelen, Belgium, on November 1, 1677. Third Order Carmelite and mystic.

The Blessed Virgin Mary {2}

❦ **VEN. MARY OF AGREDA, OIC:** Born in Agreda, Spain, on April 2, 1602; died there on May 23, 1665. Franciscan abbess, mystic, and author of the four-volume work, *The Mystical City of God*.

The Blessed Virgin Mary; The Holy Rosary; Suffering; The Salvation of Souls

❦ **VEN. MOTHER MARY POTTER, LCM:** Born in London, England, on November 22, 1847; died in Rome on April 9, 1913. Foundress of the Little Company of Mary (the Blue Sisters).

The Salvation of Souls

❦ **VEN. MOTHER CATHERINE AURELIA, APB:** Born in Quebec, Canada, on July 11, 1833; died there on July 6, 1905. Foundress of the Sisters Adorers of the Precious Blood.

Trials; Sorrow; Hope; Grace and the Divine Indwelling

❦ **VEN. PATRICK PEYTON, CSC:** Born in Attymass, Ireland, on January 9, 1909; died in San Pedro, California, on June 3, 1992. Priest of the Congregation of the Holy Cross, founder of the Family Rosary Crusade, and producer of over 600 television and radio shows championing the power of the Rosary.

The Holy Rosary {2}

❦ **VEN. POPE PIUS XII:** Born in Rome on March 2, 1876; died at

Castel Gandolfo, Italy, on October 9, 1958. Reigned from 1939 to 1958 and authored forty-one papal encyclicals.

The End Times

❧ **VEN. TERESA QUEVEDO, CCV:** Born in Madrid, Spain, on April 14, 1930; died there on April 8, 1950. Sister of the Carmelite Sisters of Charity. Known for her childlike love of our Blessed Mother.

Confidence

❧ **VEN. FRANCIS LIBERMANN, CSSP:** Born in Saverne, France, on April 14, 1804; died in Paris on February 2, 1852. Jewish convert, and priest of the Congregation of the Holy Ghost Fathers (the Spiritans).

Holy Desires

CLERGY & RELIGIOUS
✣

❧ **BISHOP FORNERUS:** Bishop of Bamberg, Germany. Quoted by Fr. Martin von Cochem in *The Incredible Catholic Mass* (published in 1704).

The Holy Mass {2}

❧ **BISHOP JACQUES-BÉNIGNE BOSSUET:** Born in Dijon, France, on September 27, 1627; died in Paris, France, on April 12, 1704. Renowned orator and theologian.

Mercy; Prayer; Suffering; Death; Confidence

❧ **BR. FRANCIS MALUF, MICM:** Born in Mashrah, Lebanon, on July 19, 1913; died in Richmond, New Hampshire (USA), on September 5, 2009. Convert, philosopher, author, and founding member of the Slaves of the Immaculate Heart of Mary.

The Holy Will of God; Prayer {2}; The End Times; Confidence; Sanctity {2}; The Church and the Faith

❧ **BR. MARCEL VAN, CSSR (SERVANT OF GOD):** Born in Ngăm Giáo, Vietnam, on March 15, 1928; died in the concentration camp at Yen Bihn, North Vietnam, on July 10, 1959. Redemptorist brother and mystic.

Love; Suffering; Sanctity

❧ **CARDINAL GIOVANNI BONA:** Born in Mondovi, Italy, on October 10, 1609; died in Rome on October 28, 1674. Cistercian abbot, cardinal, liturgist, and spiritual writer.

The Holy Mass

❧ **CARDINAL HENRY EDWARD MANNING:** Born in Totteridge, England, on July 15, 1808; died in London on January 14, 1892. Influential thinker and writer.

The Church and the Faith

❧ **DOM BRUNO WEBB, OSB:** Born in London, England, on July 17, 1892; died at Pluscarden Abbey in Blackburn, Scotland, on September 30, 1976. Cistercian monk and spiritual writer.

Mercy

❧ **DOM EUGENE BOYLAN, OCSO:** Born in Wicklow, Ireland, on February 3, 1904; died in Roscrea, Ireland, on January 5, 1964. Trappist monk and spiritual writer.

Love {3}; Mercy; Prayer; Sanctity {3}

❧ **DOM FRANCESCO DE LUCIA:** Born in Mugnano del Cardinale, Italy, on September 19, 1772; died in Mugnano, Italy, on April 9, 1847. Priest and first rector of the sanctuary of St. Philomena.

Suffering

❧ **DOM JEAN-BAPTISTE CHAUTARD, OCSO:** Born in Briançon, France, on March 12, 1858; died at Diou, France, on September 29, 1935. Trappist priest, abbot, and spiritual writer.

Love {2}; The Salvation of Souls {8}

❧ **DOM JOHN CHAPMAN, OSB:** Born in Ashfield, England, on April 25, 1865; died in Somerset, England, on November 7, 1933. Convert, Benedictine priest, abbot, scholar, and spiritual writer.

Prayer

❧ DOM PROSPER GUÉRANGER, OSB (SERVANT OF GOD): Born in Sablé-sur-Sarthe, France, on April 4, 1805; died at Solesmes, France, on January 30, 1875. Benedictine priest, abbot, founder, and author of *The Liturgical Year*.

The Church and the Faith {2}

❧ DOM VITALIS LEHODEY, OCR: Born in Hambye, France, on December 17, 1857; died in Bricquebec, France, on May 6, 1948. Cistercian priest and spiritual writer.

Love; The Holy Will of God {5}; *Divine Providence* {4}; *The Holy Eucharist; Suffering; Temptations* {4}; *Imperfections; Desolation; The End Times; Good Will* {3}; *Grace and the Divine Indwelling; The Salvation of Souls* {2}

❧ DON FELIX SARDA Y SALVANY: Born in Sabadell, Spain, on May 21, 1844; died in Barcelona, Spain, on January 2, 1916. Priest and writer.

The Church and the Faith

❧ FR. AMBROSIO DE LOMBEZ, OFM CAP: Born in Lombez, France, on March 20, 1708; died in Luz-Saint-Sauveur, France, on October 25, 1778. Capuchin priest and spiritual director.

Desolation

❧ FR. BEDE JARRETT, OP: Born in Greenwich, England, on August 22, 1881; died in London on March 17, 1934. Dominican priest and spiritual writer.

Imperfections

❧ FR. CHARLES ARMINJON: Born in Chambery, France, on April 15, 1824; died in Lyon, France, on June 17, 1885. Priest, seminary professor, and retreat master.

Death; The End Times

❧ FR. CORNELIUS À LAPIDE, SJ: Born in Bocholt, Belgium, on December 17, 1567; died in Rome on March 12, 1637. Jesuit priest and scriptural exegete.

Mercy; Temptations

🕊️ **FR. DIEGO ALVAREZ, OP:** Born in Medina de Rioseco, Spain, c. 1550; died in Trani, Italy, on May 10, 1635. Dominican archbishop and theologian.

Suffering

🕊️ **FR. DOLINDO RUOTOLO (SERVANT OF GOD):** Born in Naples, Italy, on October 6, 1882; died there on November 19, 1970. Franciscan priest and mystic.

The Holy Rosary

🕊️ **FR. EMILE NEUBERT, SM:** Born in Ribeauvillé, France, on May 8, 1878; died in Art-sur-Meurthe, France, on August 29, 1967. Marianist priest, theologian, and pioneer in Mariology.

Love {3}; Prayer {3}; Trials; Temptations; Confidence {2}; The Salvation of Souls {4}

🕊️ **FR. FRANCIS XAVIER LASANCE:** Born in Cincinnati, Ohio (USA), on January 24, 1860; died there on December 11, 1946. Parish priest and spiritual writer.

Mercy; Imperfections; Good Will; Sanctity

🕊️ **FR. FREDERICK FABER, CO:** Born in Calverley, England, on June 28, 1814; died in London on September 26, 1863. Convert, Oratorian priest, theologian, and spiritual writer.

Introduction {2}; The Blessed Virgin Mary {4}; Love {4}; Mercy {6}; The Holy Will of God; The Holy Mass; The Holy Eucharist; Prayer {3}; Suffering {2}; Trials; Sorrow {6}; Death {8}; Hope; Confidence {4}; Sanctity {4}; Grace and the Divine Indwelling {9}; The Salvation of Souls; The Church and the Faith; Encouraging Poems

🕊️ **FR. GABRIEL OF ST. MARY MAGDALEN, OCD:** Born in Bevere-Audenaerse, Belgium, on January 24, 1893; died in Rome on March 15, 1953. Carmelite priest, theologian, and spiritual writer.

Mercy; The Passion {2}; Trials; Imperfections; Desolation; Good Will

🕊️ **FR. JEAN BAPTISTE SAINT-JURE, SJ:** Born in Metz, France, on February 19, 1588; died in Paris on April 30, 1657. Jesuit priest and spiritual writer.

The Holy Will of God; Suffering

🕈 **FR. JEAN C.J. D'ELBÉE, SSCC:** Born in Vendée, France, on September 7, 1892; died in Montgeron, France, on December 3, 1982. French priest, Superior General of the Congregation of the Sacred Hearts of Jesus and Mary, and author of *I Believe in Love: A Personal Retreat Based on the Teaching of St. Thérèse of Lisieux.*

Divine Providence {2}

🕈 **FR. JEAN PIERRE DE CAUSSADE, SJ:** Born in Cahors, France, on March 7, 1675; died in Toulouse, France, on December 8, 1751. Jesuit priest and spiritual writer.

Divine Providence; Suffering; Temptations; Imperfections

🕈 **FR. JEREMIAS DREXEL, SJ:** Born in Augsburg, Germany, on August 15, 1581; died in Munich, Germany, on April 19, 1638. Jesuit professor, preacher, and spiritual writer.

Divine Providence; Good Will

🕈 **FR. JOHN HARDON, SJ (SERVANT OF GOD):** Born in Midland, Pennsylvania (USA), on June 18, 1914; died in Clarkston, Michigan (USA), on December 30, 2000. Jesuit priest, theologian, teacher, author, and founder of the Institute on Religious Life.

Holy Desires

🕈 **FR. JOHANNES TAULER, OP:** Born in Strasboug, France, c. 1300; died there on June 16, 1361. Dominican priest, theologian, and mystic.

The Holy Will of God; The Passion {2}

🕈 **FR. JOSEPH VARIN, SJ:** Born in Besançon, France, on February 7, 1796; died in Paris on April 19, 1850. Jesuit priest instrumental in founding several religious communities for Sisters in post-Revolution France, including St. Madeleine Sophie Barat's Society of the Sacred Heart.

Imperfections

❧ **FR. LAWRENCE LOVASIK, SVD:** Born in Tarentum, Pennsylvania, on June 22, 1913; died in Pittsburgh, Pennsylvania, on June 9, 1986. Priest of the Society of the Divine Word, prolific writer, and founder of the Sisters of the Divine Spirit.

The Salvation of Souls

❧ **FR. LORENZO SALES, IMC:** Born in Musalacense, Italy, on January 7, 1889; died in Turin, Italy, on January 7, 1972. Italian priest, Secretary General of the Missionary Institute of Our Lady of Consolation, and spiritual director of Venerable Consolata Betrone.

Love {2}

❧ **FR. LOUIS COLIN, SS:** Born in Lignières, France, on January 14, 1835; died in Montreal, Canada, on November 27, 1902. Sulpician priest and superior.

Mercy; Confidence

❧ **FR. MARTIN VON COCHEM, OSF:** Born at Cochem, Germany, on December 13, 1625; died at Waghäusel, Germany, on September 10, 1712. Franciscan Capuchin priest, theologian, and spiritual writer.

The Holy Mass {5}; *The Holy Eucharist; Trials; Death* {2}; *Grace and the Divine Indwelling* {2}

❧ **FR. MATTHIAS J. SCHEEBEN:** Born in Meckenheim, Germany, on March 1, 1835; died in Cologne, Germany, on July 21, 1888. Writer and dogmatic theologian.

Love; Divine Providence

❧ **FR. MICHAEL MÜLLER, CSSR:** Born in Brueck, Germany, on December 18, 1825; died in Regensburg, Germany, on August 28, 1899. Redemptorist priest, superior, and spiritual writer.

Prayer; The Holy Rosary {8}

❧ **FR. PAUL OF MOLL, OSB:** Born in Antwerp, Belgium, on March 7, 1824; died in Dendermonde, Belgium, on February 24, 1896. Benedictine priest and miracle worker.

Love {2}; *The Church and the Faith*

%& **FR. PAUL O'SULLIVAN, OP:** Born in Tralee, Ireland, on February 7, 1871; died in Lisbon, Portugal, on November 21, 1958. Dominican priest and spiritual writer.

The Holy Mass; Sorrow; Encouraging Prayers

%& **FR. REGINALD GARRIGOU-LAGRANGE, OP:** Born in Auch, France, on February 21, 1877; died in Rome on February 15, 1964. Dominican priest, theologian, and spiritual writer.

Love; Prayer; The Salvation of Souls

%& **FR. THOMAS À KEMPIS, CRV:** Born in Kempen, Germany, in 1379 or 1380; died in Zwolle, Netherlands, on July 25, 1471. Canon Regular of Windesheim and author of *The Imitation of Christ*.

Love; Suffering; Temptation; Desolation

%& **FR. WALTER CISZEK, SJ (SERVANT OF GOD):** Born in Shenandoah, Pennsylvania (USA), on November 4, 1904; died in Scranton, Pennsylvania, on December 8, 1984. Jesuit priest and clandestine missionary to the Soviet Union.

Suffering; Temptations {2}; Sickness; The Salvation of Souls {2}

%& **FR. WALTER FARRELL, OP:** Born in Chicago, Illinois (USA), on July 21, 1902; died there on November 23, 1951. Dominican priest, theologian, teacher, writer, and lecturer.

The Holy Will of God

%& **FR. WILLIAM DOYLE, SJ (SERVANT OF GOD):** Born in Dalkey, Ireland, on March 3, 1873; died in Langemarck, Belgium, on August 16, 1917. Jesuit priest and military chaplain.

Love {2}; Divine Providence; The Holy Eucharist {3}; Prayer; Suffering; Sacrifice {7}; Trials {2}; Temptations {2}; Imperfections {5}; Desolation {8}; Death {2}; Holy Desires {2}; Sanctity {8}; Grace and the Divine Indwelling; The Salvation of Souls {2}

%& **MERE FRANÇOISE DE JESUS:** Born in 1877; died in 1932. Religious Sister and foundress of la Compagnie de la Vierge. Quoted by Fr. Garrigou-Lagrange in *The Three Ages of the Interior Life*.

The Church and the Faith

❧ **MOTHER AGNES OF JESUS, OCD:** Born Marie-Pauline Martin in Alençon, France, on September 7, 1861; died in Lisieux, France, on July 28, 1951. Carmelite nun, superior, and "little mother" to St. Thérèse of the Child Jesus.

Prayer; Sacrifice; Sorrow; Grace and the Divine Indwelling

❧ **MOTHER MARY LOYOLA, IBVM:** Born in London, 1845; died in York, England, in 1930. Convert, superior of the Institute of the Blessed Virgin (the Loreto Sisters), and prolific spiritual writer.

Grace and the Divine Indwelling

❧ **MSGR. JEAN-JOSEPH GUAME:** Born at Fuans, France, on May 5, 1802; died in France on November 19, 1879. Priest, theologian, and spiritual writer.

Introduction; Prayer; Grace and the Divine Indwelling

❧ **MSGR. VERNON JOHNSON:** Born in England in 1866; died in 1969. Convert, priest, and organizer of the Association of the Priests of St. Thérèse.

Love {2}; Mercy {2}; Divine Providence; Suffering {2}; Sacrifice; The End Times; Confidence

❧ **PÈRE JEAN-JACQUES OLIER, SS:** Born in Paris, France, on September 20, 1608; died there on April 2, 1657. Priest and founder of the Congregation of St. Sulpice (the Sulpicians).

Sickness

❧ **PÈRE JEAN-JOSEPH HUGUET:** Born in France on September 7, 1812; died there on February 21, 1884. Priest, prolific writer and editor, and director of the Third Order of Mary (the Marists).

Sickness {3}

❧ **PÈRE LOUIS LIAGRE, CSSP:** Born in Tourcoing, France, on December 19, 1859; died in Orly, France, on January 24, 1936. Priest and novice master of the Congregation of the Holy Spirit (the Spiritans). Author of *A Retreat with St. Thérèse*.

Love; Confidence {2}

✤ **PÈRE GUSTAVE DE RAVIGNAN, SJ:** Born at Bayonne, France, on December 1, 1795; died in Paris on February 26, 1858. Jesuit priest, preacher, and spiritual writer.

The Salvation of Souls

✤ **POPE ADRIAN VI:** Born in Utrecht (in the Netherlands) on March 2, 1459; died in Rome on September 14, 1523. Tutor to Charles V and later successor of Pope Leo X.

The Holy Rosary

✤ **POPE LEO XIII:** Born in Rome on March 2, 1810; died in Rome on July 20, 1903. Successor of Pope Pius IX. Best known for his social encyclicals and attempts to revive scholasticism in the Church.

The Holy Rosary

✤ **POPE PIUS XI:** Born in Desio, Italy, on May 31, 1857; died in Vatican City on February 10, 1939. Scholar and diplomat; established the feast of Christ the King.

✤ **REV. ALBAN GOODIER:** Born in Great Harwood, England, on April 14, 1869; died in Teignmouth, England, on March 13, 1939. Jesuit writer and archbishop of Bombay, India.

Grace and the Divine Indwelling

✤ **REV. DANIEL CONSIDINE, SJ:** Born in Old Pallas, Ireland, on January 1, 1849; died in Roehampton, Ireland, on January 10, 1922. Jesuit priest and spiritual writer.

Divine Providence; Prayer

✤ **REV. FR. ALBAN BUTLER:** Born in Northampton, England, on October 24, 1710; died in Saint-Omer, France, on May 15, 1773. Author of the four-volume work, *The Lives of the Fathers, Martyrs, and Other Principal Saints* ("Butler's Lives").

The Holy Will of God; Grace and the Divine Indwelling

℣ **REV. GABRIEL MARTIN:** Born in Vendée, France, on April 21, 1873; died there on October 4, 1949. Missionary priest and founder. Author of *The "Little Way" of Spiritual Childhood: According to the Life and Writings of Blessed Thérèse de l'Enfant Jesus.*

> *The Blessed Virgin Mary; Divine Providence* {2}; *Suffering* {2}; *Confidence; Sanctity*

℣ **RICHARD OF ST. LAWRENCE:** Died c. 1250 in France. Priest and theologian, best known for his *De laudibus beatae Mariae Virginis,* a work in praise of Our Lady.

> *The Blessed Virgin Mary*

℣ **SR. JOSEFA MENÉNDEZ, RSCJ:** Born in Madrid, Spain, on February 4, 1890; died in Poitiers, France, on December 29, 1923. Nun of the Society of the Sacred Heart and mystic.

> *Love* {2}; *Mercy* {5}; *Divine Providence; The Holy Eucharist* {5}; *Sacrifice* {2}; *The Salvation of Souls*

℣ **SR. LOUISE VANDERSCHRIEK, SND:** Born in Bergen-op-Zoom, Netherlands, on November 14, 1813; died in Cincinnati, Ohio (USA), on December 3, 1886. Religious superior and foundress of the American branch of the Sisters of Notre Dame de Namur.

> *Sacrifice; Hope*

℣ **SR. MARY ANGELITA, BVM:** Born in Vincennes, Indiana (USA), on July 16, 1878; died on April 3, 1934. Religious of the Congregation of the Sisters of Charity of the Blessed Virgin Mary. Educator and poet.

> *Encouraging Poems*

℣ **SR. MARY CHRISTINA, SHCJ:** Born in London on June 2, 1853; died in St. Leonard's-on-Sea, England, on July 13, 1882. Religious of the Society of the Holy Child Jesus.

> *Encouraging Poems* {2}

℣ **SR. MARY MARTHA CHAMBON, VHM:** Born in Croix Rouge, France, on March 6, 1841; died in Chambéry, France, on March

21, 1907. Visitandine nun, visionary, and propagator of the Rosary of the Holy Wounds.

The Passion

❧ **SR. MARY OF THE TRINITY, PC:** Born in Pretoria, South Africa, on April 26, 1901; died in Jerusalem on June 25, 1942. Poor Clare nun and mystic.

Love {3}; *Divine Providence* {3}; *Prayer*; *Confidence*

❧ **TERTULLIAN:** Born in Carthage, North Africa (now Tunisia), c. 160; died there c. 230. Priest, apologist, theologian, and Father of the Church.

Death

LAYMEN

❧ **ADELAIDE ANNE PROCTER:** Born in London on October 30, 1825; died there on February 3, 1864. Convert and poet.

Encouraging Poems

❧ **FRANCIS THOMPSON:** Born in Preston, United Kingdom, on December 16, 1859; died in London on November 13, 1907. Poet.

Encouraging Poems

❧ **GODFREY KURTH:** Born in Arlon, Belgium, on May 11, 1847; died in Asse, Belgium, on January 4, 1916. Historian.

The Church and the Faith {2}

❧ **HAMISH FRASER:** Born in Inverness, Scotland, on August 16, 1913; died in Saltcoats, Scotland, on October 17, 1986. Convert, husband, father of seven children, and anti-communist journalist.

The End Times

❧ **LOUISE IMOGEN GUINEY:** Born in Roxbury, Massachusetts (USA), on January 7, 1861; died in Chipping Campden, England, on November 2, 1920. Writer and poet.

Encouraging Poems

☙ ORESTES BROWNSON: Born in Stockbridge, Vermont (USA), on September 16, 1803; died in Detroit, Michigan (USA), on April 17, 1876. Convert, publicist, and apologist.

The Blessed Virgin Mary; Hope; The Church and the Faith {2}

ABOUT THE SLAVES OF THE
IMMACULATE HEART OF MARY

Spes Nostra: Profound Words of Encouragement and Consolation for Weary Members of the Mystical Body was compiled by the Slaves of the Immaculate Heart of Mary (*Mancipia Immaculati Cordis Mariae*), a Community based in Richmond, New Hampshire. The Brothers, Sisters, and Third Order members of the M.I.C.M. Order are dedicated to a two-fold Crusade: the propagation and defense of Catholic dogma — especially *Extra Ecclesiam Nulla Salus* — and the conversion of America to the One True Church. Founded in Cambridge, Massachusetts, in 1949, by Father Leonard Feeney and the fervent Catholics of Saint Benedict Center, the Slaves in Richmond engage in a number of apostolates geared towards education, the formation of lay apostles, and the conversion of non-Catholics.

❧ *Education.* Immaculate Heart of Mary School is a private school with an average enrollment of between thirty and sixty students.

❧ *Adult studies program.* The Saint Augustine Institute of Wisdom offers a four-year course designed to ground Catholics in the basics of the Faith so as to make them effective apostles whatever their state in life.

❧ *Conference.* The annual Saint Benedict Center Conference has featured over the years speakers such as Fr. Nicholas Gruner, John F. McManus of the John Birch Society, Charles A. Coloumbe, Dr. David Lang, Dr. Robert Hickson, and C.J. Doyle of the Catholic Action League of Massachusetts.

❧ *Radio show.* Br. André Marie, M.I.C.M., Prior, hosts a weekly radio show called *Reconquest* on Mike Church's online *Veritas Radio Network*. Since the program's inception in 2015, Brother André has interviewed such guests as E. Michael Jones, Dr. Peter Kwasniewski, Steve Cunningham of *Sensus Fidelium*, Ryan Grant of Mediatrix Press, and Timothy Flanders of OnePeterFive.

🕊 *Website.* Catholicism.org features thousands of articles on topics of Catholic interest, and the Slaves' store site offers thousands of audio files, including comprehensive courses in Sacred Scripture, history, philosophy, and apologetics.

🕊 *Print publications.* First published in 2023, their book *The Liturgical Rosary: Meditations for Each Hour, Day, and Season of the Liturgical Year* is a beautiful work intended to enhance the devotional lives of Catholics by joining more intimately the mysteries of the Rosary with the liturgical texts of the traditional Roman Rite liturgy.

🕊 *Agricultural effort.* Formalized in 2019, the Saint Isidore Project allows the Slaves to raise much of their own food, and offers, in addition, a unique venue for apostolic outreach to local community members.

🕊 *Missionary* work. As missionaries to the United States of America, the Slaves of the Immaculate Heart of Mary employ a powerful form of door-to-door missionary work, by means of which the Religious have provided Catholic literature, blessed rosaries, Miraculous Medals, and scapulars *gratis* to millions.

For more information please visit
Catholicism.org & SaintPhilomenaConvent.org

These things I have spoken to you,
that in Me, you may have peace.

In the world you shall have distress;
but have confidence,

*I have overcome
the world.*

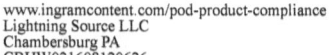